ARMC

ARMCHAIR CRICKET 1975

Edited by Brian Johnston

British Broadcasting Corporation

*Published by the
British Broadcasting Corporation,
35 Marylebone High Street,
London W1M 4AA*

ISBN 0 563 12832 1

First published 1975

© *The Contributors and the
British Broadcasting Corporation 1975*

*Printed in England by
John Blackburn Ltd, Leeds, West Yorkshire*

Contents

INTRODUCTION *Brian Johnston*	7
FORTY YEARS ON THE AIR *E. W. Swanton*	9
THE ART OF CRICKET COMMENTARY *Brian Johnston*	18
TELEVISION PRODUCTION *David Kenning*	24
RADIO PRODUCTION *Peter Baxter*	29
THE COMMENTATORS AND SCORERS *John Arlott*	32
THE SCORER *Bill Frindall*	45
ROUND THE COUNTIES *Bill Frindall*	57
CRICKET RECORDS *Bill Frindall*	92
I – FIRST-CLASS MATCH RECORDS	92
II – TEST MATCH RECORDS	103
III – ENGLAND *v* AUSTRALIA RECORDS	109
THE 1974 SEASON	112
COUNTY CHAMPIONSHIP	112
THE GILLETTE CUP	112
THE BENSON AND HEDGES CUP	112
THE JOHN PLAYER LEAGUE	113
FIRST-CLASS AVERAGES	113
THE PRUDENTIAL CUP *Christopher Martin-Jenkins*	121
COUNTY CHAMPIONSHIP	127
THE GILLETTE CUP	128

CONTENTS – *continued*

THE BENSON AND HEDGES CUP	132
THE JOHN PLAYER LEAGUE	136
THE 1975 AUSTRALIANS *Richie Benaud*	140
THE CRICKET FOLLOWER'S GUIDE *Brian Johnston*	153
TEST GROUNDS	184
LIST OF MATCHES – 1975	188
1975 GUIDE TO THE JOHN PLAYER LEAGUE *Bill Frindall*	199

ACKNOWLEDGEMENTS

The diagram on page 165 from *All about Cricket* by Brian Johnston is reproduced by courtesy of W. H. Allen, and the diagrams on pages 175–6 from *Sports on View* edited by Peter Dimmock by courtesy of Faber and Faber Ltd. The plans of the Test grounds are reproduced by kind permission of Sporting Handbooks Ltd. Other illustrations are gratefully acknowledged as follows: pages 32–42 (top), 43 Norman Hollands; 42 (bottom) Sport & General; 44 Sheffield Newspapers Ltd; 59 Raymonds, Derby; 63 *Western Mail*; 65, 71, 75 Universal Pictorial Press and Agency Ltd; 67 Central Press Photos Ltd; 69 J. D. Hunt, Tonbridge; 73 Neville Chadwick, Leicester; 77 *Northampton Chronicle and Echo*; 79 *Newark Advertiser*; 81 L. G. Charrett; 85 *Brighton Gazette*; 87, 89 Ken Kelly; 91 Photopress (Leeds) Ltd; 140–51 D. E. Benaud and Associates.

The cartoon on page 56 is by Kenneth Mahood.

Introduction
Brian Johnston

This is the fourth edition of *Armchair Cricket*. It was first published by the BBC in 1955, then followed revised editions in 1966 and 1968. Now in 1975 – an important and busy year with the Prudential Cup and a four Test series against Australia – we bring it up to date once again. All records and statistics are correct up to the end of the English 1974 season, and Test records to the start of the Australian series in England in July 1975.

As before, this book is mainly designed to help people who have started to take an interest in cricket as a result of watching TV or listening to the radio. Many of these Armchair enthusiasts have only an elementary knowledge of the game. We know from the many letters which we receive that they are often puzzled by some of the cricketing terms used by BBC commentators and also find the laws of cricket difficult to understand and interpret. They will, we hope, find all the answers in the Cricket Follower's Guide. There is also a growing band of statisticians and amateur scorers and Bill Frindall has fully catered for them.

We also get many enquiries – especially from overseas – for more details of the various BBC commentators. So John Arlott has bravely agreed to write a potted biography of each of the regular Test commentators. To save him embarrassment I have 'done' him!

With the advent of so many new competitions we have devoted more space to the laws, regulations and main records for each competition and, especially useful for those going to the match, there are career details of every county cricketer and photographs of every county side. There are also the past season's averages, the Final 1974 County Championship Table and the 1975 fixture list. An extra aid to the viewer or listener are the diagrams of the six Test Grounds.

Finally the special features include Christopher Martin-Jenkins on the Prudential Cup, Richie Benaud giving his personal assessment of the Australian Team and a fascinating 'look back' over his forty years of broadcasting cricket on TV and radio by that G.O.M. Jim Swanton.

I should just like to end by thanking all the many people who have helped me with this book and hope that it will prove to be as useful and popular as the other editions seem to have been.

Forty Years on the Air
E. W. Swanton

In looking back over something approaching forty years of broadcasting from cricket grounds it may be as well from the start to admit there is much more I have forgotten than remembered. At least I assume that to be the case, for forty years is a goodly chunk in anyone's life, and the number of days I have been 'on duty' – either on sound or on television – has run into upwards of a thousand. Not every match on which one writes or broadcasts is undeniably memorable: some are decidedly otherwise, and these naturally tend to fall quickly into oblivion. But for all that, there have been great moments in plenty; and I suppose the special responsibility – and privilege – of being one of those describing such moments, heightens the pleasure of the occasion. For myself I have never ceased to be grateful for the many and varied opportunities I have had as a broadcaster.

The beginnings of any significant venture in life usually leave a firm enough impression for all time. I remember with great clarity – perhaps embarrassing clarity might be the truer phrase – the first time I ventured a live broadcast on a game of cricket. It was in 1938 – a golden summer of Bradman and Hammond, Verity and O'Reilly, the young Compton and Hutton, and (though we didn't know it then) the last time we were to see the Australians for a decade. Of course my début before the outdoor microphone was not one of the Tests, though I was present at all but one of them as a writer. It was the comparatively humble occasion of Surrey v Lancashire at the Oval at the very end of the season, but a Surrey v Lancashire match of the 'thirties was more of an occasion than it is today.

Why the very end of the season should have marked my début had an important reason. I had made up my mind in

1938 that I would spend the following winter in South Africa with the M.C.C. touring side, the first to tour there for eight years. I had never been abroad with an M.C.C. side before, and I didn't see any immediate prospect unless I took the initiative myself. So it was as a free-lance that I decided to go – and to seek some assignments. London newspapers at that time were only lukewarm when it came to tours other than Australia. My own paper, the *Evening Standard*, showed no interest, and in good time I approached the BBC to see if they would take some commentary or summaries and at the same time recommend me to the South African Broadcasting Corporation. I should perhaps mention that while I had never attended a cricket ground as a broadcaster in my life before the tail end of 1938, I had contributed weekly since 1934 to a review of sporting affairs sent out from Broadcasting House on the Old Empire Service. That was the extent of my experience.

Nevertheless I went to the great Lobby – S. J. de Lotbinière, Head of Outside Broadcasts – with my proposals, knowing that whether or not I made the trip depended on his reply. Lobby was a sane and cautious man, brilliant at his job, and most reasonably – and I suppose I should have expected this – pointed out my total lack of experience in the art of running commentary. Yes, I had to concede, that was so. But why not, suggested Lobby, have a trial match, while reserving his judgment on South Africa?

Thus it came about that I found myself at Surrey's final match of the season, against Lancashire at the Oval. The allotted broadcasting time was half an hour before lunch and a further half an hour in the evening, both sessions to be shared with P. G. H. Fender, who was down at Hove to cover the Sussex *v* Yorkshire game.

Looking back at this Oval début of mine, I suppose 'ordeal' is just about the most apt word to describe it – though strangely at the time, possibly with the foolhardiness of youth, I recall taking it all quite comfortably in my stride. But the fact is that rain at Hove took me completely by surprise, and before I had, so to speak, settled myself in the broadcasting chair at the Oval, I heard Percy Fender in a sentence or two from Hove announce that it was raining there, that there was no play and we would therefore go straight over to the Oval. Instead of doing fifteen minutes, therefore, I had the full half-hour session to bear by myself – and there was certainly no rain at Kennington!

To make matters that bit more tense, at that very moment Surrey had nine wickets down: and only blind optimism could envisage Brooks and Gover occupying the stage for thirty more minutes. Outside broadcasts were not in 1938 as organised as they were later to become and on the subject of what to do in the interval between innings my instructions had been precisely nil. Did I keep talking and incur the possible wrath of those expecting a return to the studio? I didn't have long to decide, for Dick Pollard fairly soon settled the issue and the players were trooping from the field. I only recall now that I was entirely alone during that broadcast, and I decided to see the whole half-hour through. Just what I said is gone forever, but I suppose it must have been something about Surrey and Lancashire matches or what sort of a season the participants had had. I later learned the O.B. department called it 'associative material', and apparently what I delivered must have fitted the bill. For at the end of the broadcast (which took in the start of the second Lancashire innings) I was told that Lobby himself had got through to the ground with a message of appreciation. He was happy with the way I had handled things. I too was happy – for there followed a broadcasting contract for South Africa. Just what would have happened had there been rain in London and sunshine at Hove, I would rather choose not to consider!

South Africa 1938-9 was a challenging experience for any tyro at the microphone, especially as no commentaries from a South African ground had ever been broadcast direct to England before. I knew all the English players well enough, naturally; and most of those likely to play for South Africa had been to England with Herbie Wade's side in '35. When I stepped off the old *Balmoral Castle* in December 1938, about a week before the start of the first Test, I had exactly twenty broadcasts lined up for the tour. But so popular did cricket broadcasting prove with listeners all over South Africa that this number multiplied itself many times before the bizarre end of the tour at Durban, and the South African Broadcasting

Corporation took many additional opportunities to put out commentaries and interviews that had not been originally scheduled.

The broadcasting points in South Africa were usually small boxes, perched somewhat precariously on stilts and usually within earshot of anyone who chose to linger underneath to hear what was going on. And there were plenty, especially youngsters, who did make this choice! My girth, even at that time, was not inconsiderable, and I suppose I was never exactly suited to precarious perches. One local columnist in Cape Town summed up in two sentences what seemed to him E. W. Swanton's impending plight:

> 'He is as tall as Pieter van der Byl; he is twice as thick. The sheerlegs on which the broadcasting box stands only just hold him.'

Well, the boxes, I am relieved to say, held out for the whole of the tour: but of course what went over the air was the only thing that really mattered. Luck played its part to set the ball rolling, for in the very first match on which I broadcast in South Africa – the first Test at Johannesburg – a hat-trick occurred almost unbelievably while I was on the air. I say 'almost unbelievably' for the commentaries were very far indeed from being ball by ball throughout the day, or anything approaching it. At Johannesburg we were on the air live only twice each day, and then for only fifteen minutes a time. Moreover, only one of these shortish sessions was transmitted direct to England – so the chances of a hat-trick occurring while I was actually broadcasting 'live' to British listeners must have been very remote indeed. But happen it did, thanks to the skill of Tom Goddard, and what had been an unusually circumspect display of South African batting was turned into high drama as Goddard dismissed Nourse, Gordon and Billy Wade in three balls. I made the most of my good fortune, and Michael Standing in London was moved to wire a note of congratulation at the end of the game. Only one other English bowler – Peter Loader in 1957 – has ever done a hat-trick in a Test since that occasion, so my début effort as a running commentator on Test match cricket was quite something to write home about.

Talking of writing home, I did send some pieces back for publication in England and did a modest amount of writing in the South African press, so that I felt my trip was beginning to pay its way. More importantly, the broadcasts stepped up, for many people were voicing regret at the limited spells of live cricket on the air. Soon I was doing two hours a day on the Tests for South African consumption, getting my first batches of 'fan mail' with their inevitable offerings of advice, and thoroughly enjoying the lavish hospitality all round. As I was remunerated by the day, the ten-day marathon at Durban had some financial compensation for me, even if the pitch turned the occasion into an impossible game of cricket.

A good many people sent me lines of appreciation when the tour was over, and perhaps I may be forgiven for quoting a paragraph from a letter from Mr H. J. Crocker, who was then Director of Publicity in Johannesburg. I quote it to show the sort of reaction the novelty of cricket broadcasting produced in those pre-war days:

'It is a trite remark that your voice has become known to many thousands of listeners here, in homes and offices and motor-cars wherever a radio set is installed, but I want to say that we have both listened and admired, and I know it is voicing the general view to remark that no more able and acceptable talks have ever been heard than the ones you have given to South Africa.'

It had all been a thoroughly exhilarating experience, in which I had tried to apply the broadcasting rules and standards developed by the BBC for its sporting commentators with, I hope, a modicum of success. At all events when I returned to England for the 1939 season I was afforded the considerable privilege of joining Howard Marshall and Michael Standing in broadcasting the three Tests against the West Indies, a series sadly overshadowed by events in Europe. In that last summer of the 'thirties I also covered several county matches on the air, including my first venture into Wales, where I saw Emrys Davies score a lovely hundred against Notts at Swansea, the broadcast being shared with the young Wynford Vaughan Thomas, then with the Welsh Outside Broadcasts Section. I was to let Vaughan Thomas know in advance of the 1940 season when I would find it convenient again to broadcast on cricket in Wales, but by that time sterner matters had supervened.

It was not until August 1945 – and not before a great deal of water had flowed beneath a great many bridges – that I made my next contact with broadcast cricket, in (of all unlikely places) the town of Kanchanaburi in Thailand. This time I was a listener, and a grateful one at that, standing beside a radiogram on the floor of the local café while waiting to bid farewell to three and a half years of Japanese detention. The knobs twiddled and we were through to something called a Victory Test at Old Trafford between England and Australia. It was cricket all right, even though I had never heard of Christofani, who was about to get a hundred. The man giving the commentary naturally interested me as well – I had played a bit of cricket with him before the war but had no inkling that he had his eye on the BBC. He was Rex Alston, who had left schoolmastering at Bedford to join Outside Broadcasts.

When I returned to England, five stone lighter than when I had left it, I made gradual efforts to pick up the threads of 1939. My thoughts turned to the BBC and I remembered the voice of Rex Alston from Old Trafford. I decided to go and see S. J. de Lotbinière, still head of Outside Broadcasts, to remind him as gently as I could that I had been one of the 1939 commentary team. Lobby was well aware of it – and he was well aware too (though he was careful to say nothing) of my emaciated shape, in stark contrast to my avoirdupois of yore. Lobby frankly, so I later learned, did not think I would be fit for the job. My physical presence gave him doubts that might not have existed had I chosen to drop him a line instead. According to Lobby, a number of candidates were in the running and he wished to keep an open mind; he would, however, he said, give me the first chance.

That chance was communicated to me in a letter from the aforesaid Rex Alston – addressing me very formally as 'Dear Swanton' – a month or so before the start of the 1946 season. There was no mention of Test matches, but I was to be thrown very early into the arena with a visit to Gloucester for the first Championship match to be played by Gloucestershire after the war. I was to do commentary on parts of all three days, as well as what were then called 'eye-witness accounts', and at least I could look forward to Walter Hammond at the wicket even if I could not, in all conscience, expect another hat-trick from Tom Goddard! Well, Goddard took seven wickets (but no hat-trick!) and Hammond satisfied every expectation with 134 in his best form off the Lancashire bowlers. My contracts for the 1946 Tests followed shortly thereafter.

For twenty years after the war I alternated between sound and television when it came to Test matches in England, sharing the running commentary and doing the close-of-play summaries. Then, as new faces came on to the commentary scene, I did only the end-of-the-day summaries on sound, television having decided to drop this feature. The early postwar team on sound consisted of Rex Alston (by now calling me Jim!), John Arlott and myself; while on television I was normally with Brian Johnston and Peter West. These days in the late 'forties were still really experimental times in the art of cricket broadcasting, and producers today I have no doubt would shudder at some of the methods employed by some of their predecessors and by some of the commentators. Techniques have certainly improved all round, not least in matters of equipment and production, but the commentator's functions have basically remained unchanged – he must develop a style, understand the game, and, when doing a television commentary, know fairly accurately when *not* to talk. These things are taken for granted today, but the pattern had to be established by a certain amount of trial and error.

Up to about the middle 'sixties a good many more matches outside the Tests were afforded lengthy broadcasting periods than is the case today. There was always, for example, Gentlemen and Players at Lord's, and of course the University Match. The Roses matches – at both venues – were regularly covered, and Middlesex *v* Surrey rarely missed out. The tourists' matches also got fairly ample treatment, and during the course of any season a good sprinkling of 'ordinary' county games got their share of the limelight over the air.

So at least we always had our eye in, as it were, and always getting the chance to perfect our method, to keep it from going rusty. The amount of first-class cricket outside the Tests also meant that there were several aspiring 'reserves' awaiting their chance. I think all commentators would agree that this regular practice is of much value. At least I found it so, and feel sympathy for the Test ball-by-ball experts of the 'seventies who suddenly find themselves doing around two hours a day without the advantage of any nets beforehand, since three-day cricket is now normally over the air only by eye-witness accounts of a minute or two: a different expertise altogether. I expect the deprivation may not matter so much, say, to John Arlott, who has spilled more cricket words into BBC microphones than anyone: such younger men, for instance, as Christopher Martin-Jenkins and Henry Blofeld, both of whom I much enjoy listening to, have been very much thrown in at the deep end.

On most occasions I attended the cricket in a dual capacity as broadcaster and writer, so my reporting enthusiasm on exciting occasions had to be translated from one medium to the other. I shall not readily forget the closing minutes of the Hampshire–New Zealanders match at Southampton in 1949, when the tourists scored 109 to win in half an hour in a brilliant assault upon the clock, victory coming just before time. The commentary was extended on that day as the excitement increased, and listeners in New Zealand heard all the drama through the Overseas Service. When I was in New Zealand with Freddie Brown's side in '50–51, I was more than once referred to as the chap who had been on the air on the day of the win against Hampshire!

Another memory of F. R. Brown's tour comes back as I think of the heroic achievement by England in dismissing Australia for 228 on the first day of the series at Brisbane. It was tremendous stuff, against all expectation, and Bedser and Bailey in particular were backed by some outstanding fielding. I was warming to the task of describing the day to English listeners at the close of proceedings, and for ten minutes I enthused over the course of events. Many a morning in England will be made by this, I thought, as I stepped from the broadcasting box at the Gabba ground – only to be confronted by an indifferent engineer of the Australian Broadcasting

Commission who calmly informed me that not a word of it had got through to England. That was nearly 25 years ago, but the pity of it all remains with me to this day.

Technical hitches, though they can never be entirely eliminated, became fewer and fewer with experience. But the minor hazard is always lurking round the corner, as I well remember from an experience when I was once finishing a television summary at the close of play in a Test at Trent Bridge. Nottinghamshire had just installed their fine electric scoreboard, which gave all the facts and figures of an innings at a glance, and I was doing an 'in vision' summary before a camera away, of course, from the commentary box and my notes. I have always liked, incidentally, to do my close-of-play summaries, whether on sound or television, as nearly off the cuff as possible, as I think spontaneity at that moment is an important element that those at home look for and appreciate. On that evening at Trent Bridge, I finished with some such words as: 'There it is then. A thoroughly good day's play and the final score once again is . . .' I looked up to the wonderful scoreboard to find to my utter dismay that it was a total blank. They had turned off all the lights. I had to make a guess at the score, but after that I always scribbled down the final total as the last ball was bowled.

Cricket broadcasting has come a long way since I sat at the Oval and watched Surrey and Lancashire in 1938, and no doubt there will be fresh techniques – and certainly fresh voices – to add to the perfection of the art in the years to come. Fashions in broadcasting necessarily change, and I do not hide the pleasure I have had in helping to mould the pattern of cricket broadcasting in the comparatively early years. It has been an important part of my life and an important part of my cricket education. I can only hope that those who have heard me or seen me have derived half the satisfaction I have obtained in talking to them on radio and television.

The Art of Cricket Commentary
Brian Johnston

'Dear Mr Johnston,

I hope you don't mind me writing to you but when I grow up I want to be a cricket commentator. Can you please tell me how to set about it and what qualifications I must have?'

This is typical of many letters I have received over the years, and it's always a terribly difficult one to answer. For instance so far as cricket goes there is only ONE staff job in the BBC – that of BBC Cricket Correspondent. I was the first one appointed in 1963 and after my retirement from the staff Christopher Martin-Jenkins succeeded me. All the other cricket commentators both on TV and radio are now freelances and have jobs apart from commentating, more often than not, in journalism. There are only about a dozen of them, so the scope for a newcomer is very limited.

Again cricket commentary is an art for which there is no school except experience at the microphone at the expense of the listener or viewer. This is one reason why cricket commentators tend to be mostly in the 40–60 age bracket. It takes that long to learn! Nowadays, except for the ball-by-ball Test Match commentaries there is little opportunity to *practise* commentary. Up to the mid-'sixties there were regular broadcasts of 20- to 30-minute periods from county matches. Now it is usually only 1- to 3-minute reports, so that the budding commentator has no chance to test his ability to keep going for long periods which is what the top commentators have to do. In addition a young voice lacks the authority of an older one and because of cricket's slower tempo this is more noticeable than with other games.

So it's not easy to become a cricket commentator and more

or less impossible without a large slice of luck, such as being available at the right place at the right time when the opportunity occurs.

Now for the qualifications:

1. Good health – 'the show must go on'.
2. A gift of the gab and the ability to keep talking.
3. A clear, strong voice which must sound confident. The accent doesn't matter, though in fact a dialect comes over particularly well in cricket. But personality *is* important and can 'come through' in a voice.
4. The ability to put into words what he is seeing, which means that besides being observant he must have a varied and colourful vocabulary and a sound use of good English. The long periods of comparative inaction during a cricket match give the listeners an all too easy chance to notice imperfections in syntax or language.
5. And most important of all – for without it he can never become a cricket commentator – he must have a deep knowledge of the game, its laws and regulations, its customs, its records, its history and its players.

Acquaintance – or even better – friendship with the players is a tremendous asset and helps give an understanding of what goes on 'in the middle'. A commentator should have played the game himself, though not necessarily in the highest class. TV commentators these days are usually ex-Test cricketers whereas on the radio they are professional broadcasters supported by ex-Test players as summarisers. But then there is a great difference in the commentary techniques of TV and radio and there is no doubt in my mind that television is the more difficult.

TELEVISION COMMENTARY

The first thing for a TV cricket commentator to realise is that he can never hope to please *every*body *any* of the time. In fact he will be jolly lucky if he manages to please *any*body *all* the time. Cricket, like golf, is a game played at a much slower tempo than most of the other televised sports such as football, racing, athletics etc. There are, of course, many moments of excitement and tension but they are spread out over a whole day, and the action is anyway much slower. This means that the commentator's remarks drop like stones on a still pond. The viewer has time to listen and digest them and to weigh up their meaning and their accuracy. In the faster games a slight fluff or inaccuracy by the commentator is soon forgotten within a few seconds as a new situation develops on the screen. So the cricket commentator's comments must be concise and fit the picture exactly, and be well thought out and accurate whilst having to be made spontaneously at a moment's notice. This means that he must have a complete and expert knowledge of the game. He has to *comment* rather than give a running commentary which is basically what happens with football or racing on TV.

So the cricket commentator always has to ask himself the vital question: 'When to talk and when not to talk?' It's easy to trot out trite instructions such as: 'Only talk when you can add to the picture' but it isn't as easy as that. First of all there is the expert viewer who plays or has played the game. He knows the laws and regulations, and all the players by sight. On switching on he only wants to hear who won the toss, the score, a report on the weather and an opinion about the pitch. After that he just wants to be kept up to date with the score and to make his own judgments on the playbacks after an appeal or a wicket has fallen. I can understand this. A commentator on TV should, in my view, be like a knowledgeable friend who sits alongside you at a sporting event, and who fills in the details which you don't know. I enjoy watching cricket with a friend but if he starts to tell me what is happening, who so-and-so is or why the captain has moved a certain fieldsman, I feel like crowning him. I think I know and just don't want to be told. But sitting alongside me there may well be someone who welcomes all this sort of information, and wants help with identity of the players and explanations of the laws. And so it is on TV. A large majority of the viewers are *not* cricket experts. I should know from some of the letters I received in the past: What is a 'chinaman', 'silly mid-off', or a 'googly'? What is the LBW law and how many ways can a batsman be out off a no ball? Or once when I said that 'Ray Illingworth has two short legs, one of them square', a lady wrote and told me not to be so personal. Or when I said that Peter May was lucky to have made a century as 'he was dropped when two', back came a letter bemoaning the carelessness of mothers with their young children.

So the TV cricket commentator has to try to strike the happy medium, knowing that there is really no such thing. He will always have irate and dissatisfied viewers who will say either: 'Why on earth can't he stop talking?', or 'Why can't he tell us more?'

RADIO COMMENTARY

As he has no camera to help him the radio commentator must paint the picture himself – with words. He is the eyes of every listener and must describe in as much detail as possible everything he sees. As opportunity offers he should describe the features of the ground so that the listener who has never been there can conjure up his own idea of what it is like. It also helps if the commentator explains the exact position from which he is broadcasting in relation to the play. A brief description of the main features and characteristics of the players brings the game to life – 'he has red, curly hair, wears size 14 boots, scratches his nose before every ball . . .' etc. There is also more time on radio for details and records of players' careers.

All this information is useful to fill in the gaps which do occur during a game of cricket – when the fast bowlers are walking back to the start of their long runs, during the drinks interval or when the umpires go off to search for a new ball. But there is one cardinal rule: NEVER MISS A BALL. All this information must stop as soon as the bowler starts his run. The commentator must then describe in detail exactly what is happening until the ball becomes dead.

The art of good commentary is to get into an automatic rhythm with a description of:

The bowler running up.

His approach to the umpire and wicket.

The delivery, the type of ball and where it has pitched.

The batsman's stroke.

Where the ball has gone.

Who is fielding or chasing it.

How many runs the batsmen are taking.

And finally when the ball has been returned to the wicket keeper or bowler say how many runs have been added to the team's and batsman's score.

Only then is it permissible to leave the action and to talk about something else, until the bowler returns to his mark. Then back to the rhythm again to describe the next ball.

SOME HINTS TO BUDDING COMMENTATORS

1. Have light and shade in your voice so that during quiet periods you can talk normally and not too fast. Then when there is sudden action or excitement you can increase your tempo and raise your voice, though, of course, without shouting.

2. Always think of yourself as speaking to ONE person, not to millions. You are that person's friend and guide. Tell him or her what you yourself would like to hear if you were not at the match.

3. Try not to talk over applause, especially when a batsman is returning to the pavilion after a big score. Let his reception register. This is often easier said than done, as there are many details about his innings to give to the listener before the new batsman comes out.

4. Try not to describe in too much detail how a batsman is out. Leave that to the expert summariser.

5. Remember that you are a commentator not a critic. So don't criticise an umpire's decision. Whatever you may think about it, he is in a better position to judge than you.

6. At the end of each over, give the bowler's analysis, the total and the scores of the two batsmen. Then shut up, so that the summariser can come straight in.

There is one problem which is common to both TV and radio commentators – when to give the score. The answer is as often and as unobtrusively as possible without interrupting the action, and at the very least whenever a run is scored and at the end of each over. This may be annoying to the lucky viewers or listeners who stay switched on for the whole period. But tens of thousands are switching on every minute and there's nothing more infuriating than having to wait for five or ten minutes before hearing the score. That's why in these days of an over taking up to five minutes it's a good idea to slip in the score during an over even if a run hasn't been added. In addition of course newcomers will want to hear details of what has happened before, so the scorecard should be shown on TV or read out on radio at least every ten minutes. There remains one fundamental difference between the TV and radio commentators today. On TV with their galaxy of ex-Test players they nowadays concentrate solely on the cricket. They give an extremely expert and professional analysis of the play, with critical opinions on the captains' tactics and the skills of the batsmen and bowlers. But they are not encouraged to be humorous about the fringe aspects of cricket, which provide so much of the colour and fun – the fat member asleep in the pavilion, the bored blonde knitting in the crowd, the umpire's funny hat, etc. But, probably because they have more time to fill, radio commentators are given a freer rein, and indulge in more lighthearted descriptions and reminiscences, and a certain amount of friendly banter in the box.

But whatever the style of commentary one final word of warning to ALL commentators – NEVER MISS A BALL. If you do it's sure to be the one that takes a wicket.

Television Production
David Kenning

The relationship between commentator and producer is in many ways the key to a successful outside broadcast. The cricket television commentary team usually consists of a presenter, two commentators and sometimes one extra contributor.

The presenter must have a considerable appreciation of cricket, retain a journalistic approach under pressure and the ability to appear on the screen looking relaxed and talking sense while tuning one ear to his 'deaf aid'. On this he hears a variety of instructions from the producer referring to the next piece of recording he is to talk about, the fact that the expected interviewee isn't coming, that he has got to talk by himself for three minutes or alternatively he has got just ten seconds to give the outstanding details of the day, trail tomorrow's coverage and say goodnight! It's the presenter who bears the brunt of the pressures of television and who has to cover up the occasional hiccups of technical equipment or the people who operate it.

The Test match commentators in recent years have been Richie Benaud and Jim Laker. Although the pace of cricket is perhaps slower than many other television sports, the basic tenets of television commentary still hold good – their job is to identify, to illustrate and to illuminate for the benefit of viewers who will range from an overseas visitor who has never seen a cricket match in his life to the international cricketer. It is essential but restricting that the commentator and producer should work together, the picture and voice should be related – it is obviously undesirable that the screen should show a fielder chasing a stray dog while the commentator is giving a learned discourse on a batsman's stance at the wicket. To aid this relationship the commentator wears headphones to hear the producer's instructions and at the same time has a separate microphone that is heard only by the producer and so is able to say, 'can you give me a shot of the extra fielder on the square leg boundary?' and when the correct shot is on the screen the viewer will hear 'an extra man on the boundary looking for a catch from the short pitched ball'. You may recall Richie Benaud saying exactly those words before Kallicharran caught Geoff Boycott off the last ball of the day in the 1973 Test against West Indies at Lord's. It is, of course, exactly this sort of expertise that makes it a privilege to watch a cricket match in the company, as it were, of two of the shrewdest cricket brains in the world.

A television outside broadcast is the result of the labours of a team of over thirty people that range from drivers who deliver the vans crammed with technical equipment costing nearly half a million pounds, to highly qualified engineers who produce the technical quality of BBC broadcasts, cameramen, sound recordists and a host of other experts in their own fields.

The siting of cameras, the situation of the commentary box, the routing of several miles of cables, the booking of the ten or so communication circuits and a host of details, both technical and as mundane as where the cameramen can eat, are organised at a meeting involving the producer, the senior engineer and a representative of the ground authority several weeks in advance – and even if you have been televising from the same ground for several years you always go to check that nothing crucial to your coverage has altered: beware the new score box that blocks the camera's view of a quarter of the field!

The basic pattern of the picture coverage of cricket has not greatly changed over the years. The master camera is positioned directly in line behind the wicket, ideally at the lowest height that will enable the camera lens to see over the umpire's head; an exercise in trigonometry that results in the scaffolding being built to a height of between 25–30 feet, depending on the distance from the wicket. This camera provides the standard shot that includes both batsman and bowler, although sometimes for the sake of variety or to illustrate a particular point it will use its zoom lens and show a close-up of the batsman. But once the ball has been hit and another picture of the fielder selected this master camera zooms out again so that the producer always has a shot available of both batsmen running. The second camera is positioned near the master camera and is usually referred to as the fielding camera. It has a wider angle lens and pans away from the wicket to show the fielder chasing the ball. It is important that this camera's shot is wide enough initially so that the viewer can see the whole scene. This is particularly important when batsmen are going for quick singles in the vicinity of the wicket. These two cameras provide the basic coverage and would give an adequate picture for a news-type replay of the outstanding incidents of the day. But for long hours of transmission more is required. Nowadays the viewer has come to expect the close-up of a fielder's jubilation after making a catch, his stare of disbelief at an imaginary rough patch of ground after he has let the ball go through his legs for a boundary, the dejection of the dismissed batsman, the triumphant bowler with his hands held high as he shouts 'How's that' or indeed his frustration as yet again the batsman plays and isn't good enough to get an edge. These are the pictures that give the viewer a sense of the atmosphere and drama of the match.

A further two cameras are normally used for this purpose, positioned where possible at ground level, which has the drawback that at some grounds the shots get blocked by crowds during breaks in play. But in general they give a much more pleasing picture. It's better to have spectators and sky in the background than grass, as you get with elevated cameras. One of these cameras is situated just off the line of the wicket and follows the fielder and the ball but has a much tighter lens than the wide-angle elevated fielding camera.

The fourth camera is placed square to the wicket again with a close-up lens and provides the close shots of the action in the wicket area. To operate these four cameras it is customary to have six cameramen who work roughly on the basis of one hour on and thirty minutes off. It is essential to have this sort of relief system in order that the cameraman's reactions can remain sharp throughout the day. The strain of trying to follow a small cricket ball on a television camera's $4'' \times 3''$ viewfinder is considerable and he can never afford to relax.

A major innovation in all sports broadcasts during recent years has been slow-motion replays. The pace of cricket gives ample opportunity for its use and undoubtedly the slowing down or freezing of the action can be revealing and at times controversial. It's a tool that needs to be used with care, particularly if it tends to throw doubt on umpires' decisions. The commentator has to remember that the angle of the camera can be misleading and it would be wrong if it were used as a constant pillory against umpires who have to make an instant judgment. The equipment that provides the slow-motion replays is known as the video disc.

Television pictures are in essence a series of still frames known as 'fields' and the video disc capitalises on this by recording the electronic information needed to make up one still picture or 'field' lasting 1/50 of a second in separate concentric rings on the surface of a metal disc revolving at 3000 rpm. The equipment has the ability to replay one of these rings continuously, thus producing a 'frozen frame', and by altering the number of times each ring is 'read' before switching to the next ring variable speed slow motion is achieved. Thus if each ring was 'read' twice you would slow the action down to half speed and ten times would give you 1/10th of the original speed.

Apart from slow-motion replays which are of pictures only, the producer has available a videotape recording which plays back pictures at normal speed with sound. This recording is usually made in a mobile vehicle on site. The maximum duration of a reel of videotape is ninety minutes, which means that at the end of a day's play a continuous recording of the six hours play would be on four different reels of tape and therefore in order to have available for summaries all the outstanding incidents of the day a system of retaining only the significant play has evolved. This means that at the end of an over of no great consequence the machine winds back and records over the top of previously recorded material; in this way the whole of a day's play is on one tape and therefore that much more quickly available. The only drawback being that because of the length of time needed for the recording machine to settle down and record transmittable pictures, it's impossible to play this recording continuously because of the breaks in recording until the tape has been edited; an expensive and time-consuming business.

The other pictorial source the producer has available to select on his mixer is the caption camera that shows the scorecard details, bowler's figures etc. These are achieved by the caption artist who works in close contact with the television scorer and his never-ending stream of statistics. It's his job to keep all the required information up to date which he does with small white magnetic figures that are placed on a black metal plate and put in front of a special caption camera. They may then be superimposed over the picture of a colour camera with the result that as no light passes through the black areas of the screen, only the white sections are visible over the top of the colour picture. While many people regret the passing of the copper plate handwritten cards, there is no doubt that statistics are available nowadays in a fraction of the time previously taken.

It's the producer's task to guide and utilise the talents and equipment available to him in the best way he can and while no outside broadcast can function without a team effort it's the producer in the end who has the sole responsibility for what appears or is heard on the television screen.

Radio Production
Peter Baxter

'Keep it friendly and informal, but don't forget to keep giving the score!' A simple brief for Test match commentators, belying the great concentration required to give ball-by-ball commentary, although producers do continually nag about that score. Nothing is more infuriating for the listener than to hear, '... and that's another run to the total', and not to hear what that total is! But as for the rest of the brief, the commentary box is a very friendly and informal place anyway and the producer tries to make the exacting job of the commentator as easy as he can. And the humour of the commentary box is a great help. Everyone must be on his guard, for instance, with that doyen of practical jokers, Brian Johnston. A favourite trick of his, best practised during a stoppage for rain, is to seat himself in front of a dead microphone when he sees a colleague about to come into the box and embark upon a statistical survey of English batting for the last thirty years. He then greets the newcomer, who if the plan has worked should be under the impression that Brian is on the air, with, 'So those are the English batting averages, now how about the West Indian averages? I think you're the man for that.' It is then a question of how long everyone can keep from laughing or how long it takes for the truth to dawn on the victim.

The commentator is the eyes of the radio listener describing what he sees as he sees it, preserving a balance between technical description of the play and painting the overall picture. For analysis and opinion he has a summariser to call on who is almost invariably a former Test player. The commentary team usually comprises three commentators and two summarisers. We always include a representative of the visiting country in the team either as a commentator or as a summariser. In recent years these have included such names as Alan McGilvray from Australia, Tony Cozier from the West Indies and Alan Richards from New Zealand as commentators and in 1974 of course there were Billy Ibadulla representing Pakistan and the delightful character you may have heard referred to as 'Prince', Fatesingh Gaekwad the former Maharaja of Baroda.

Test Match Special involves two producers. If you have listened to Radio 3 at 11.25 on a Test match morning, waiting for the start of play, you will have heard one of them. 'Good morning, welcome to Test Match Special on this second day of the third Test . . .' You may have thought that the man who makes that announcement has nothing more to do until he reads the lunchtime cricket scoreboard or until the rain comes down and he has to play music. But he is the producer responsible for the overall programme. He sits in a studio in the basement of Broadcasting House, paying strict attention to what is going out on the air, putting himself in the place of the listener at home. He can give directions from the studio to the scorer or the producer at the ground, one of whom will always be wearing headphones.

The producer at the ground is usually the one who organised the outside broadcast and is now responsible for its smooth running. Some time before the match he will have discussed with the engineers his technical requirements, made arrangements with the ground authorities and drawn up plans for all the radio broadcasts from the ground. And there are a lot more broadcasts from the ground than many people realise. For instance you will probably have heard a commentator say, 'We welcome World Service listeners with the news that . . .'. All over the world countless listeners will be eagerly awaiting this short spell of commentary while in the commentary box the producer waits to hear the signal that BBC World Service have joined the broadcast so that he can let the commentator know. At the end of the day's play there will probably be a report by the visiting commentator to his own country and there are reports throughout the day on Radio 4's news bulletins, Radio 2's Sports Desks and BBC External Services' foreign language programmes. All this has to be woven into the pattern so that anyone involved, be he in studio, control room or actually commentating, knows what should be happening and when.

Of course all these plans can go very sadly astray if, for instance, rain holds up play and early lunch is taken or the extra hour which may be taken comes into force. Then the producer must be prepared to alter his programme quickly and above all keep everyone informed. During rainy sessions we like to start discussions in the box about some topical point or speculate on future Test teams. As a discussion gets under way all the broadcasting team are usually eager to chip in and make their points, although Henry Blofeld found his enthusiasm waning a little a short while ago when he was chairing one of these discussions during a mid-afternoon stoppage. He was holding forth about the relative merits of two batsmen when a card landed in front of him which read, 'Keep going until six o'clock.' His look of panic increased as he saw that everyone appeared to be leaving. The commentary box is a good place for practical jokers. Maybe this is the point to add to that original brief for commentators the cardinal rule for all broadcasters: 'Whatever you do, don't dry up!'

The Commentators and Scorers
John Arlott

JOHN ARLOTT, OBE
Born 25 February 1914. John Arlott, one-time policeman on the beat, played for Hampshire Club and Ground. Occasional 12th man for Hampshire. Poet, author, wine expert, cricket correspondent of the *Guardian*, and cricket broadcaster. First BBC commentary on radio 1946. Has commentated for radio or TV on every Test played in this country since the war. Has an immense knowledge of cricketers and their history and his vivid word pictures of a game have won large radio audiences for cricket. To many people his gravel voice and Hampshire burr *are* cricket, and his witty, picturesque phrases are unique to him. Who could better: 'Mann's inhumanity to Mann', when Tufty Mann bowled George Mann. Or of a bowler with a crab-like run with bent knees: 'He looks like Groucho Marx chasing a pretty waitress'. In recent years he has widened his scope with his commentaries and interviews on BBC-2 TV on the Sunday John Player matches. (B.J.)

TREVOR BAILEY
Born 3 December 1923. Trevor Bailey, of Cambridge University, Essex and England, a relative late-comer to the radio team, settled in as a comments man within minutes. An outstanding all-rounder – a preponderantly defensive batsman; a

fast medium bowler who increased his power by thought and control; a fine close fieldsman; and a match-winner as well as a match-saver – at Test level, shrewd county captain and tactician, he was one of the most important cricketers of the 1950s. As secretary of Essex he became a capable administrator and played a considerable part in adapting their economy to the prevailing economic climate. Moreover, although he came from a rugby school – Dulwich – he played soccer well enough to win an Amateur Cup medal.

Cricket correspondent of the *Financial Times*, he 'reads' and explains the trends, strategies and techniques of a match quickly, lucidly and interestingly. Sometimes he can seem overcritical of batsmen who score at his former speed; that, however, is but human; and he is an unfailingly good-natured colleague in the commentary box.

RICHIE BENAUD

Born 6 October 1930. Richie Benaud, of New South Wales, played in 63 Tests for Australia – 28 of them as captain – took 248 wickets (more than any other Australian in Tests) and scored 2201 runs (Garfield Sobers is the only other player to have performed the double of 2000 runs and 200 wickets in Test cricket), and he was a fine fieldsman in the gully. He had always a sharply observant eye for the game and a shrewd appreciation of tactics, and those talents are apparent in his commentaries. He has reported Test matches for newspapers in various parts of the world and has written several books. He

generally spends the English winter in Australia – or overseas with a touring Australian team – but has returned here for some years now to act as a television commentator. No weight of work – and he has often combined radio, television and newspaper reporting on the same Test match – can disturb his equilibrium or his courtesy.

His style is relaxed, his humour dry, and his reading of a game impeccable.

Henry Blofeld

Born 23 September 1939. Henry Blofeld played his main cricket for Eton, Cambridge University and Norfolk. He was a correct opening batsman, quick in reaction, sound in technique, who, if he could have devoted himself to it, might have held a worthy place in the first-class game. Certainly he played well enough once to look like taking Norfolk to the first win by a minor county over a first-class county (Hampshire) in the Gillette Cup competition. He decided, however, to become a full-time journalist.

He has reported cricket for the *Sunday Express* and the *Guardian* but is a relative late-comer to cricket broadcast commentary. He toured West Indies (in 1973–4 as broadcaster as well as reporter) and Australia with MCC sides and is the author of *Cricket in Three Moods* – 'Eighteen months of Test cricket and the ways of life behind it'.

A natural conversationalist with a taste for humour and the good life, he has a considerable reputation among his friends as a raconteur.

Denis Compton

Born 23 May 1918. Denis Compton of Middlesex played in 78 Tests for England as a brilliantly intuitive batsman, bowler of slow left-arm wrist or finger spin, and a fieldsman first in the deep and, later, close to the wicket. He was probably the most popular cricketer of his generation, not only in England but in most countries of the world. For all the apparent human fallibility which endeared him to the ordinary club players among the spectators, his technique, eye, speed of reaction, determination, balance and timing combined to make him one of the most gifted batsmen in cricket history. He scored 5807 runs in Tests, but it can well be believed that, but for the five seasons lost to war and the knee injury which eventually ended his career, he must have set an unsurpassable aggregate of Test runs. An outstanding outside left for Arsenal, only the Second World War and the claims of cricket stopped him going above 'Victory' to full international soccer selection for England.

He reports cricket for the *Sunday Express*, has published several autobiographical books, and broadcasts on television as spontaneously as he used to bat.

TED DEXTER
Born 15 May 1935. Ted Dexter of Cambridge University and Sussex played for England in 62 Tests, as captain in 30, and was one of the most exciting cricketers the game has known. Tall, strongly built and quick-witted, he could bowl usefully on the faster side of medium with natural life from the pitch, field handsomely, but, above all, on his day he batted in a style at once so elegant, commanding and powerful that few bowlers could contain him. As one of the first major powers in

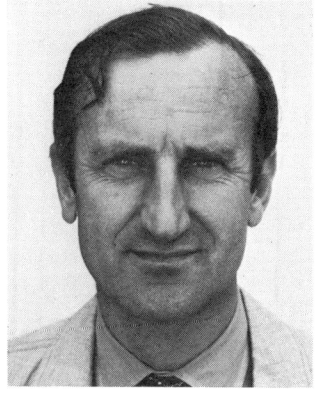

the one-day game he was responsible for much of the success of Sussex in the early days of the Gillette Cup.

It was a loss to English cricket – though a true reflection of the English social scene – when, after the 1968 season, still only 33, he gradually phased himself out of the first-class game to make a business career.

As a reporter with the *Observer* and more lately with the *Sunday Mirror* he has written with the independence and, often, the originality of his play. As a commentator he is never content with the humdrum of the cliché, but is constantly fresh and is not afraid to take a stand in a minority of one.

NEIL DURDEN-SMITH

Born 18 August 1933. Neil Durden-Smith was a serious cricketer – right-hand bat and off-spin bowler – at Aldenham School; he has played for the Royal Navy, Combined Services and Hertfordshire: and has considerable and successful experience of top-class hockey.

He was A.D.C. to the Governor-General of New Zealand – and former captain of Worcestershire – Lord Cobham, before he joined the BBC. Then he joined the Outside Broadcast Department and was closely concerned with the arrangements for the broadcasting of the 1966 World Cup. His opening Test broadcast was in 1969 when he became the first of the 'new' generation of radio cricket commentators. He has been a regular performer on the panels of Sporting Chance and Treble Chance. After managing the Anglo-American Sporting Club, he is now managing director of a public relations and promotions company.

BILL FRINDALL

Born 3 March 1939. Bill Frindall has been the official scorer for BBC sound broadcasting since the death of Arthur Wrigley in 1965. Quick-witted and quick-moving, he has played much club cricket – in France, Germany, Switzerland and Holland, as well as England – as a seam bowler and middle order batsman and, although a fervent Surrey man, once turned out for Hampshire Second XI. He brings a vast amount of documentation – often four briefcases full – to matches and anticipates and produces the appropriate records and references at high speed.

He compiled the *Kaye Book of Cricket Records* and is responsible for the statistics in *Wisden* and for a number of other publications – in many cases unpaid in aid of some benefit or charity.

In addition to his travelling library he rarely appears without a folding chair, umbrella, cushions, a three-course picnic lunch, plus coffee – and his wife – all in a car provided and constantly repossessed – for service purposes – by Ken Barrington. He still finds time to be helpful to a wide variety of people.

ALAN GIBSON

Born 28 May 1923. Alan Gibson is an accomplished all-round broadcaster with a scholarly and original mind. He was a President of the Oxford Union, more than once a Liberal Parliamentary candidate; and is a steadily successful performer on Round Britain Quiz, an authority on English hymn-writers, and a regular broadcaster, especially in the West of England where he has written some major scripts and taken

regular part in some long-running programmes.

Born in Yorkshire, brought up in East London (where his father was a Nonconformist parson), he now lives permanently in Bristol. A ruminative pipe-smoker and an enthusiast – indeed, a leading crusader – for beer from the wood, he strives thoughtfully to impose relaxation upon a quickly reacting mind.

He has a wide vocabulary and literacy, a highly individual style of commentary and an engaging but charitable sense of humour. He writes quite the most amusing of all contemporary cricket accounts – and sometimes features – for *The Times*, and also reports rugby for that paper.

BRIAN JOHNSTON
Born 24 June 1912. Brian Johnston is the cheerful chappie of cricket commentary: to him both cricket and commentary are entertainment. Characteristically he called his autobiography *It's Been a Lot of Fun*. The war saw him in the Guards Armoured Division (he won the M.C.) but when it ended he set about getting into 'show business' – joined the BBC and has been broadcasting ever since. His 'Let's Go Somewhere' was for years a most original and popular item in *In Town Tonight*; he was question master of 'Treble Chance'; has taken over from Franklin Engelmann on 'Down Your Way'; and has broadcast cricket on both television and sound in many countries.

An Etonian and an enthusiastic wicket-keeper at club level, he has an unwavering devotion to cricket. At Oxford he contrived to play four days a week and throughout the summer vacation – and still got a degree. He lives near Lord's: indeed, if he did not pass 'headquarters' on his way to work, the day would not seem right to him. In 1963 he became the first cricket correspondent ever appointed by the BBC and held that post until his retirement in 1972. Remarkably fit in his early sixties, he lives life with unimpaired gusto. His puns are all his own work.

JIM LAKER

Born 9 February 1922. Jim Laker of Surrey, Essex and England was probably the finest off-spin bowler in the history of cricket, a useful batsman and a capable catcher in the gully. In 46 Test matches he took 193 wickets and, in 1956, he harried the Australians throughout the summer and, in the Old Trafford Test, took nineteen wickets – a performance unparalleled in the first-class game.

As a player he always had a keen eye for his opponents' strengths and weaknesses and he retains it now, so that his examination and exposition of technique is as good as that of any broadcaster. He was, too, a profound tactician, as is apparent in his interpretation of any phase of a match; and he is a sound judge of the behaviour of a pitch. He has an authentic Yorkshire accent, a dry humour, a deliberately laconic delivery and a deceptively fast reaction to any movement or action on the field. Among long-distance observers of a rapid incident he is more likely than anyone else to read it accurately. He takes his work seriously.

CHRISTOPHER MARTIN-JENKINS

Born 20 January 1945. Christopher Martin-Jenkins, thirty this year, is the youngest member of the sound radio commentary team and achieved his earliest ambition when he first broadcast Test cricket in 1972. A capable batsman at Marlborough and in London club cricket, who appeared in trials at Cambridge and has played for Surrey Second XI. A devoted follower of the game, he was for three years assistant editor of *The Cricketer*. He toured West Indies with Mike Denness's

MCC side in 1973–4 (and wrote an account of the tour called *Testing Time*) and Australia in 1974–5, broadcasting commentary, reports and interviews back to England.

He succeeded Brian Johnston as the BBC's cricket correspondent when, after acting in that capacity for a year, he was officially appointed to the post in 1974. He has covered a wide range of activities and duties for BBC's Sports Department, as news-reader, reporter (his recording equipment is never far from hand), compère, interviewer and scriptwriter; he is a charitable critic and a superbly inventive mimic.

Don Mosey

Born 3 October 1924. Don Mosey, whose first Test commentary was in 1974, is an authentic northern voice, and voice of the North. As a cricket correspondent of the *Daily Mail* he spent several seasons with the Yorkshire team before he joined the Outside Broadcasts staff of the North Region of the BBC, based on Manchester. Yorkshire-born and with a deep feeling for the county, he has made some warmly evocative – and sometimes splendidly humorous – broadcasts of county matches. He is best known in the North, since his opportunities to spread himself have necessarily been few in the recent county cricket broadcasting pattern of shorter periods on more matches. He has, though, achieved some minor triumphs of one-minute vignettes of character when little more than a score-flash could have been expected of him. His first Test

broadcast – at Headingley in 1974 – was also the first for Fred Trueman – as a comments man – and they were both in true Yorkshire voice on their native soil.

Don Mosey is a capable golfer and his son Ian, an extremely promising young professional, something more than that.

IRVING ROSENWATER
Born 11 September 1932. Irving Rosenwater, the television scorer, is a dedicated cricket researcher and statistician. Patient, painstaking and determinedly unhurried, he is a purist, never happier than when he is delving into some recondite corner of cricket history. So he has written, and issued in limited editions, pamphlets on *Charles Dickens and Cricket*, *J. N. Pentelow*, *F. S. Ashley-Cooper the Herodotus of Cricket* and *The Story of a Cricket Playbill*. His scorebooks are immaculate. A complete idealist about his work, he compiled the records section of *Wisden* until he resigned on an issue of statistical principle. His contributions to the *Cricketer* include the compilation of the monthly crossword. For a period he acted as secretary to Jim Swanton.

He is probably the most profound student of the facts of cricket the game has ever known, and nothing in his life can have pleased him more than being banned at the highest level of cricket scholarship – the Cricket Society quizzes – because his virtual omniscience made any competition in which he took part 'no contest'.

E. W. SWANTON
Born 11 February 1907. E. W. (Jim) Swanton is the senior of all current BBC cricket broadcasters. He gave his first commentary in 1938 and in South Africa, in 1938–9, made the BBC's first cricket broadcasts from overseas.

A heavy-scoring batsman in club cricket, he played for

Middlesex against the Universities in 1937 and 1938; he was co-founder of the Romany club and founder of The Arabs. He has, too, managed his own sides on tours to the West Indies and the Far East.

Co-author with H. S. Altham of the later editions of *The History of Cricket*, he has written a dozen other cricket books. Until 1939 he reported sport for the Amalgamated Press and, from 1927, for the *Evening Standard*. After the Second World War, in which he served with the Bedfordshire Yeomanry and was taken prisoner of war, he became rugby and cricket correspondent of the *Daily Telegraph*. He has covered every post-war tour of Australia and a number to West Indies and South Africa. He did much to establish the Cricket Writers' Club, of which he was the first chairman. After he ceased to do running commentary he devoted his broadcasting attention to summaries.

Fred Trueman

Born 6 February 1931. One of the newest recruits to the panel – at Headingley in 1974 – was Fred Trueman of Yorkshire and England. In the course of twenty years, an unusually long career for a fast bowler, he took more wickets – 307 – in Test matches than anyone else in the history of cricket. By no means without ability as a batsman, he could hit very hard indeed, and he scored three centuries in first-class cricket matches; he was a fine all-round fieldsman, an accurate and strong ambidextrous thrower from the deep field and a brilliant catcher at

short leg.

A relishable character and quick thinker with a strong sense of humour, Fred is a natural talker and broadcaster. He has worked much on commercial television in Yorkshire where he has compèred his own programme, and for some years he has written regularly on the game. The alert cricket mind, sharp observation and technical understanding which informed his own play are apparent in his wise, pertinent and often revealingly funny comments.

Peter Walker

Born 17 February 1936. Peter Walker, Glamorgan and England, was a talented all-rounder. Born in Bristol and brought up in South Africa – his father was a literary and dramatic critic in Johannesburg – he came back to England to play cricket. Tall and long-armed he was a capable batsman with considerable hitting power. His left-arm bowling never seemed so effective as it might have been, probably through lack of confidence, and the fact that he never quite decided whether to bowl orthodox slow spin or medium pace over the wicket. In the field he must rank with the greatest close fieldsmen. Utterly fearless at short leg, his vast reach enabled him to take some amazing catches. He made more catches than any other Glamorgan fieldsman. In 1961 he performed the double – 1347 runs and 101 wickets – and also took 73 catches.

Although he is a relative newcomer he has presented Test matches and BBC-2 Sunday cricket for television, and has had considerable broadcasting experience in Wales. Currently chairman of the Cricketers' Association, where he proved a most effective negotiator at an important juncture, his knowledge of contemporary players as well as the technicalities of the game make him a perceptive commentator or interviewer.

PETER WEST
Born 12 August 1920. Peter West is a highly professional broadcaster who began cricket commentary in 1948 and is now the senior member of the television team, having moved from commentary to presentation. A considerable athlete at Cranbrook – captain of the school at five sports – his games-playing career was ended by rheumatism. After reporting for *Exchange Telegraph* he became the first editor and virtual creator of the Playfair Cricket Annual. His experience of broadcasting is wide across sport – rugby and various aspects of the Olympic Games – and in parlour games and dancing. He has reported cricket for *The Times* and is now that paper's rugby correspondent.

A faithful Kent supporter, he has lately moved to Sussex and will drive hard and late to get home from a distant match to his family. As partner in a public relations firm, he handles, among other accounts, that of the Benson & Hedges Cup. He takes much thought about – and pride in – his work and, year in, year out, is unfailingly polite, good-tempered and helpful.

The Scorer
Bill Frindall

Most cricket enthusiasts know that Hedley Verity was a left-arm spin bowler of the highest class, whose analysis of all ten wickets for only ten runs in 1932 remains the best recorded in all first-class cricket. Not many realise that it was Verity's bowling which led to a scorer being deemed an essential part of any BBC cricket commentary.

In 1934 – just nine years before he was to be fatally wounded in action with the Eighth Army in Sicily – Verity took fourteen Australian wickets on the third day of the Lord's Test. When England, who had been heavily defeated in the previous Test, enforced the follow-on, the BBC altered their scheduled programme to allow extended coverage of the match. Imagine the problems of the lone commentator, Howard Marshall, with no assistant to record scorecard details or keep bowling figures as wickets fell inevitably on a rain-affected pitch, being suddenly called upon to broadcast frequent periods of commentary instead of his usual brief reports. No wonder the experience led to his requesting a scorer for the next Test at Old Trafford. The Lancashire Secretary sent one of the ground staff to the commentary point; he was a 22-year-old leg-break bowler from Stockport, named Arthur Wrigley. Through radio Arthur became an international cricketing institution and thousands of listeners mourned his sudden death in 1965.

Arthur Wrigley was the pioneer. He evolved a system of keeping records to provide virtually instantaneous answers to any conceivable question a commentator might throw at him. Often he was able to act as a catalyst by producing a relevant fact to trigger off a discussion among the commentary team. After the war television produced its own scorer, Roy Webber, and between them they developed a special system of scoring far superior to the orthodox one still used by most scorers, because it provides a considerable amount of additional information about each ball bowled. Such extra data became necessary when ball-by-ball commentaries of the entire day's play were introduced in 1948. The basis of this system probably originated in Australia; the MCC scorebook of the 1928–9 tour of Australia, preserved at Lord's, employed a similar layout and it has been used in Australia for many years.

The scoring system which I use varies only in minor details from that described by Arthur Wrigley in earlier editions of *Armchair Cricket*. At broadcasts it involves the use of three foolscap forms which I designed before I began working for the BBC in 1966. These are reproduced on pages 49, 53 and 55 and are now used by all the BBC's network and local radio scorers, as well as by Irving Rosenwater who scores for the television commentary team at Test Matches. They have also been combined into one loose-leaf scorebook sheet for general use by cricket clubs and this sheet has been used by Surrey's official scorer, Jack Hill, since 1971.

The three sheets comprise a ball-by-ball record of play; an innings scorecard with partnership details; and a cumulative record of bowling analyses and extras.

To avoid the irritating rustle of paper being picked up by our microphones I use three hardboard-based frames, into which the sheets are slotted. At first I fastened the sheets to their boards with rubber bands but one day at Lord's someone picked up a board, accidentally released the band and scored a direct hit on Freddy Brown's right ear as he was broadcasting. Listeners must have been puzzled by his sudden change of voice!

My scoring implements consist of several black-ink fountain-pens, red, blue and green felt-tipped pens, adhesive white strips (to camouflage errors!), three stop watches (one for each batsman at the wicket and the other for the team's innings), an electronic calculator, and a flask of black coffee to facilitate alertness during dull phases of play.

Now to look at completed samples of each scoring sheet. I have taken them from my records of the Third Test against Pakistan, the last of the 1974 season and the fiftieth Test that I have scored for the BBC. It was a high-scoring draw on a very

THE SCORER 47

plumb Oval pitch and featured a double-century by Zaheer Abbas and the slowest recorded hundred in all English first-class cricket by Keith Fletcher.

BALL-BY-BALL RECORD OF PLAY *(Sheet 1)*
This sheet forms the basis of the scoring system and, unlike the other two, it is not used by the commentators as a 'script'. The example is a record of the final session of the second day's play. At tea Pakistan had scored 534 for five wickets off 152 overs. The two 'not out' batsmen were Imran Khan, who had scored 16 runs off 26 balls with one four, and Zaheer Abbas, who had faced 400 balls and whose 233 included 22 fours. To facilitate checks of the scores shown on the main scoreboard – this and not my sheet is used by the commentator when he gives the score (total and not out batsmen) after each run and at the end of each over – the batsmen are listed on my sheet in the order that they appear on the board. Hence, Imran (L Bat) appeared on the left of the scoreboard while Zaheer (R Bat) was on the right. 'M 29' means that 29 of the 152 overs have been maidens. 'NB/17' denotes that there have been 17 calls of 'no-ball' in the innings. The note '10 HR 151/530' under the heading 'NOTES' shows that Pakistan had scored 530 runs off 151 overs after 10 hours of batting and it will be used to calculate the number of runs scored and overs bowled in the next (eleventh) hour.

Play resumed at 4.36 pm (one minute late!) and Bob Willis took up the attack from the Vauxhall End, opposite to our commentary box perched high on the pavilion roof. It was his 25th over and he began it to Zaheer, who scored a single off the first ball. This gave the strike to Imran, who scored two runs off the second. The third ball of the over was a no-ball off which Imran failed to score. A single off the third 'legitimate' ball gave Zaheer the bowling and he immediately took another single. Willis's fifth ball was a bouncer and I denote this type of delivery with an arrow in the direction of up. 'Shooters' can be shown by arrows pointing downwards. Imran then scored one run off the last ball of the over to keep the strike.

Those of you familiar with the normal scoring method will notice that there is considerably less writing to do while the over is in progress. Instead of recording each run in three different areas of the normal scoresheet (batting section, bowling section and tally section), this system requires just a single entry. It is immediately possible to tell exactly what has happened to each ball: who bowled it to whom, from which end and at what time. Unless a wicket falls, the bulk of the entries is made when there is no action to record while the fielders are changing ends. It is only necessary to carry down a total if it has altered during the over just completed. Therefore there is no need to enter anything in either batsman's 'boundaries' column nor in the 'W' (wickets lost) column. At the end of the first over after tea Pakistan have scored 541 for five off 153 overs, six runs plus one no-ball coming from it. Imran has increased his score by four to 20, Zaheer has taken his to 235 with those two singles and the no-ball has moved extras on to 34. A no-ball is counted as a ball received because the batsman can score from it. Conversely a wide is not counted because the batsman cannot score runs off it. Thus Imran received five balls during that over and Zaheer faced two. The no-ball was the 18th called during the innings.

You are probably wondering about those tiny numbers above the number of runs scored in the batsman's record. This is a shorthand method of showing where the runs have been scored and it is based on the following key:

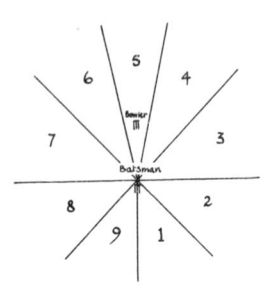

It is only approximate but it does show if a batsman has a favourite scoring area. Frequently it reveals an offside or onside strength and sometimes a front-foot or back-foot preference. In the over just recorded, both Zaheer's runs came from hits in front of the wicket on the legside, whilst all three of Imran's

THE SCORER

(Sheet 1)

were scored behind the wicket on the offside. 'IE' over the last ball single shows that Imran scored the run in area 'I' with an edged stroke.

Willis's over, no-ball and the five runs he conceded are entered on the Bowling Analysis (sheet 3) and we are then ready to record the next over.

This is bowled by Derek Underwood from the Pavilion End and started at 4.42 pm. It was his 43rd of the innings and produced singles off the second and fourth balls. At the end of it the relevant totals are changed, Underwood's analysis on sheet 3 is updated – and we are prepared for another over from Willis. His second ball produced a chance of a run out as Zaheer took a quick run to mid-wicket. Imran escaped when the throw to the wicket-keeper was either inaccurate or misfielded and the batsmen were able to take an extra run for the overthrow. All this data can be shown in the 'NOTES' column by writing '2 [the second ball of the over]: R.O. chance (Imran) (1 + 1 overthrow)'.

At 4.49 pm Underwood began his 44th over and Imran took a single backward of point from the first ball to bring up the 550 for Pakistan. The appropriate stopwatch shows that the innings has been in progress for 616 minutes and this is entered in a special table on sheet 2 and the commentator's attention drawn to it. He can then tell the listeners that Pakistan's last fifty runs have taken 49 minutes.

Underwood's third ball ends Zaheer's innings. From my note in the dismissal section on sheet 2, the commentators will be able to describe how Zaheer was out when they summarise the day's play for new listeners later in the session. 'Missed cut at "arm" ball' means that Zaheer was trying to cut a ball which he misread as a leg-break but it moved the other way – into the bat – as a result of the bowler's arm action. In effect it was a gentle inswinger, Underwood being a left-handed bowler.

The fall of a wicket produces a pressure-point in any scoring system and it is vital that with this system the scorer evolves his own order of recording the end of one innings and preparing for the start of the next. When this becomes a routine he need never be really under pressure. First, Zaheer's watch must be stopped, the length of his innings noted and the watch zero-ed ready for the incoming batsman (Intikhab Alam). A 'W' is entered to record that Underwood's third ball accounted for Zaheer's wicket and all totals are carried down. Zaheer's columns are ruled off and Intikhab's name is written on the next line. The remainder of the over is then recorded on the line below that, so that Underwood's 44th over occupies three lines. The time that the wicket fell (4.50) is noted in the 'TIME' column as well as on sheet 2. After entering all the details of Zaheer's second double-century against England, we are ready to start the watch for Intikhab and record the last three balls of the over.

And so the process continues until Intikhab declares Pakistan's innings closed at 5.44 pm with the total of 600 for seven wickets. All three watches are stopped, their respective times recorded. Sheet 2 is completed for the commentators to read the complete scorecard and discuss the various individual performances during the ten-minute interval before the start of England's innings. At this stage a number of cross-checks have to be made. The overs, maidens, runs and wickets recorded on sheet 3 have to agree in total with 165·3–30–600–7 shown on sheet 1. The total of balls received by the nine players who batted (1014) should equal the number of overs times six, plus no-balls (165·3×6+21).

Before we look briefly at England's eight overs at the wicket up to the close of play, there are four points to be explained in the final phase of the Pakistan innings. The 'x' over the fourth 'legitimate' ball of Old's 26th over means that Sarfraz played a positive stroke at a ball outside the off stump and missed; in other words, he was beaten by the ball. 'LB' over the last ball of Old's 28th over shows that one leg-bye was scored, this is added to the extras and, as the batsmen have crossed, Sarfraz will face the first ball of the next over. The last ball of Arnold's 36th over produced an all-run 'four' – the ninth such 'four' of the innings and is denoted '4 all run/9'. It is included in the boundaries. Lastly, '11 HR' on the next line shows that at the end of the 164th over Pakistan had been batting eleven hours for their 593 runs.

All three stop-watches have been zero-ed and are restarted as Asif Masood (who, in a memorable spoonerism, was referred to by Brian Johnston as 'Masif Arsood') opens the bowling from our end at 5.56. After Amiss has scored one run from his first ball, Masood bowls a no-ball which hits Lloyd on the pad. This can be recorded by putting 'P' above the dot. If there had been a leg-before-wicket appeal that was not upheld by the umpire, then 'lbw' is entered over that ball (see the first ball of Sarfraz's 4th over). No-balls are shown with a ring round either a dot or the number of runs scored, while wides are denoted by 'x', just as in the orthodox method of scoring.

When stumps are drawn the watches are stopped but not zero-ed, the time is entered on sheet 1 and all the totals are carried down.

INNINGS SCORECARD *(Sheet 2)*

This sheet is the commentator's main script. For each batsman it records the starting and finishing times of his innings, the length of his innings in minutes (recorded by a stop watch), his method of dismissal and score, the total at which his wicket fell, details of his boundaries and number of balls faced, and a note of his dismissal with any personal milestone achieved during that innings. The abbreviation 'C2' after Zaheer's scoreline denotes that it was his second century in Test matches.

As Sadiq and Majid were out on the previous day, a red line is ruled across the sheet to remind the commentator to exclude these dismissals from any summary of the second day's play. If Zaheer and not Majid had been out overnight, a line would not have worked and I would have had to use another coloured pen in writing the names of those who batted on the second day.

For limited-overs matches an extra column is ruled after 'Balls' and headed 'OVER OUT'. It is used to show the over in which each wicket fell, time being irrelevant in these matches where the length of an innings or partnership must be measured in overs.

The lower half of this sheet shows the bowling analyses (taken from sheet 3 at the completion of the innings), the hourly run and over rates, the time taken for each fifty runs scored by the team, the individual scores of not out batsmen and the total at the start of each interval of play (including stoppages for rain or bomb alerts), and full partnership details together with a note of any records.

A scorer's function is to provide the commentator with data as quickly and clearly as possible. To this end I use coloured pens to pick out the more important entries. Players' names and scores are shown in green. Highlights – wickets, boundaries, hundred partnerships and exceptionally fast scoring rates – appear in red. Blue is used for records and rain.

When I began scoring for the BBC I used a slide-rule to

THE SCORER

PAKISTAN v. ENGLAND 3RD TEST at KENNINGTON OVAL on AUGUST 22, 23, 24, 26, 27 1974. Toss: PAKISTAN
(3rd time in 3 match series)

PAKISTAN — 1ST INNINGS

IN at	OUT at	MINS. BATTED	No.	BATSMAN	HOW OUT	BOWLER	RUNS	4's	TOTAL	6's	4's	balls	NOTES
11:30	12:41	71	1	SADIQ	c't OLD	WILLIS	21	1	66	·	2	44	Hooked bouncer to deep fine leg.
11:30	3:12	182	2	MAJID	BOWLED	UNDERWOOD	98	2	166	·	12	163	Missed sweep at flighted leg-break.
12:43	4:50	545	3	ZAHEER	BOWLED	UNDERWOOD	240	6	550	·	22	410	100 off 108 balls @ Missed cut at 'arm' ball
3:15	11:58	202	4	MUSHTAQ	BOWLED	ARNOLD	76	3	338	·	9	171	Beaten by break-back — middle stump out — inside edge?
12:01	2:16	95	5	ASIF IQBAL	c & BOWLED	GREIG	29	4	431	·	5	55	Hard return drive — waist-high to left.
2:19	3:42	83	6	WASIM RAJA	c't DENNESS	GREIG	28	5	503	·	5	70	Drove to long-on — Denness fen dropped to hard catch.
3:44	4:55	50	7	IMRAN KHAN	c't KNOTT	WILLIS	24	7	550	·	1	40	Tried to run down fast short off-side ball — one-handed catch.
4:53	(5:44)	51	8	INTIKHAB	NOT OUT		32				2	26	
4:58	(5:44)	46	9	SARFRAZ	NOT OUT		14				·	35	
			10	WASIM BARI	┐ did-not-bat								
			11	ASIF MASOOD	┘		38						

EXTRAS (b.6, lb.18, nb.14, w.-)

TOTAL 600-7 dec at 5·44pm 2nd day OFF 165·3 OVERS IN 670 MINUTES (11 HOURS 10 MINS)

LUNCH 111-1 MAJID 68* ZAHEER 18*
1ST DAY OFF 30 OVERS IN 120 MINS (3·7 R/OVER)

TEA 232-2 ZAHEER 74* MUSHTAQ 29*
1ST DAY OFF 63 OVERS IN 244 MINS (3·7 R/OVER)

CLOSE 317-2 ZAHEER 115* MUSHTAQ 67*
1ST DAY OFF 94 OVERS IN 368 MINS (3·4 R/OVER)

LUNCH 430-3 ZAHEER 187* ASIF IQBAL 25*
2ND DAY OFF 122 OVERS IN 479 MINS (3·5 R/OVER)

TEA 534-5 ZAHEER 235* IMRAN 16*
2ND DAY OFF 152 OVERS IN 603 MINS (3·5 R/OVER)

PAKISTAN'S total included one 6, nine all-run 4s and 25 threes.

14 MAIDEN BALLS / HR
3·6 RUNS / OVER
59 RUNS / 100 BALLS

† FIFTH HIGHEST PAKISTAN TOTAL
HIGHEST PAKISTAN TOTAL AT THE OVAL
SEVENTH HIGHEST TOTAL AGAINST ENGLAND IN ENGLAND

Wkt	Partnership Between	Runs	Mins
1st	Sadiq / Majid	66	71
2nd	Majid / Zaheer	100	109
3rd	Zaheer / Mushtaq	172	202
4th	Zaheer / Iqbal	93	95
5th	Zaheer / Raja	72	83
6th	Zaheer / Imran	47	46
7th	Imran / Intikhab	0	2
8th	Intikhab / Sarfraz	50*	46
9th			
10th			
		600	

† PAKISTAN 3rd WKT RECORD IN ALL TESTS

BOWLING

BOWLER	O	M.	R.	W
ARNOLD	37	5	106	1
WILLIS	28	3	102	2
OLD	29.3	3	143	0
UNDERWOOD	44	14	106	2
GREIG	25	5	92	2
LLOYD	2	0	13	0
	165.3	30	600	7

New ball taken at 11·35am 2nd day PAKISTAN 320-2 (95·2 OVERS)

Hr.	Overs	Runs
1	14	64
2	16	47
3	15	55
4	17	60
5	17	56
6	15	35
7	16	40
8	13	73
9	16	45
10	13	55
11	13	63

Runs	Mins	Overs	Last 50
50	48	11·3	48
100	114	28·2	66
150	161	40	47
200	211	52·5	50
250	256	66·5	45
300	321	83·5	65
350	406	105·2	85
400	462	125·3	46
450	506	135·5	53
500	567	143·3	62
550	616	155·1	49
600	670	165·3	54

(Sheet 2)

calculate scoring and over rates, but since 1969 I have used a Toshiba electronic calculator supplied on permanent free loan by ADM Business Systems. Their managing director, David Greenhalgh, a sports enthusiast, had already given one to the BBC's motor-racing correspondent for calculation of lap speeds, and he suspected that it would be far more accurate than a slide-rule for my requirements – as indeed it is. The early model was cumbersome and needed its own power cable in the commentary box, but now I use a pocket-sized version with its own rechargeable battery.

CUMULATIVE RECORD OF BOWLING ANALYSES AND EXTRAS *(Sheet 3)*

This sheet, like sheet 2, is a commentator's script. Entries are made only at the end of each over or at the completion of a session of play.

Last season I adapted the sheet to record the number of boundaries scored off each bowler. The example shows that Arnold conceded nine fours, Willis eleven fours, Old fourteen fours and two sixes, Underwood fourteen fours and a five, Greig ten fours and Lloyd one four.

A coloured line is ruled under a bowler's figures every time he is taken off. This allows the commentator to find instantly the length of a bowler's current spell. Intervals for meals and stoppages for rain are also noted.

Extras are recorded in special columns on the right of the sheet and no-balls and wides are also recorded against each bowler. In this innings Old has been no-balled twelve times.

In an innings as long as this one – 165·3 overs – it is necessary to start a new sheet for the second day's play.

In addition to actually scoring the match a BBC scorer has to have at his fingertips a large amount of information about the 22 players taking part. I have a looseleaf filing system with sections for each current county cricketer (there are over 300 in any one season) and all overseas players who have toured this country or played in Test cricket. Every match is recorded on a special form designed to hold a season's matches for that player and the first sheet in each player's file summarises his record of batting, bowling and fielding season-by-season

Sheet 3

'Would you believe it? Wilkins is the first red-haired, left-handed slow bowler to be no-balled twice in the third over of the second day; and, incidentally, Bill tells me that is the fifty-second piece of useless information he has given this morning, and his five thousandth of the season . . .'

throughout his career. A separate section records their Test career in even more detail. Before each match I extract the records of the 22 players from large binders and put them in smaller ring-binders for use in the commentary box.

I also need to have access to the scores of all previous Test matches – 764 had been played before the start of this 1975 season – records of all best team, individual and ground performances in Test and first-class matches (these are contained in my *Book of Cricket Records* published by Kaye and Ward in 1968 and updated on blank interleaves), and notes of all team and individual milestones likely to occur in that particular match. With all the scoring equipment as well, I have to travel to every match by car and to carry three or four very large briefcases up a terrifying number of stairs at most grounds.

From that brief description it can be seen that a great deal of research and preparation has to be completed before each day's play. Then the scorer is on duty for the full six hours of play, whereas the commentator does only two hours a day in twenty-minute spells, and the summariser three hours. But please don't think that I am complaining! I realise only too well how extremely fortunate I am to be paid for my hobby and to have a reserved seat at every major match.

Round the Counties
Compiled by Bill Frindall

These career records are complete to the end of the 1974 season. They do not include the MCC tour of Australasia or any other first-class matches played in the 1974–5 overseas season (except where a player has improved his highest score or best bowling analysis before the time of going to press). Test match records are complete to 9 July 1975 and include the 1970 England *v* Rest of the World series but, as the Australian Board of Control stated that the matches between Australia and a World XI in 1971–2 were not Tests, these are excluded.

The forename by which a player is known is shown in bold type. The county in which a player is born is given only when this differs from the one he now represents. Benefit/Testimonial refers to the 1975 season.

Abbreviations used:
*	Not out
av	Average
b	Born
BB	Best innings bowling analysis
Cap	Awarded 1st XI cap by current county
Ct	Catches
Career	Career aggregates in first-class matches
Début	First appearance in first-class cricket
HS	Highest score
Ht	Height
LB	Bowls Leg-breaks
LF	Bowls left-arm fast
LFM	Bowls left-arm fast-medium
LHB	Bats left-handed
LM	Bowls left-arm medium
OB	Bowls off-breaks
occ	Occasional
RF	Bowls right-arm fast
RFM	Bowls right-arm fast-medium
RHB	Bats right-handed
RM	Bowls right-arm medium
SLA	Bowls orthodox slow left-arm
SLC	Bowls slow left-arm 'chinamen'
St	Stumpings
Tests	Number of Test caps
WK	Wicket-keeper

DERBYSHIRE

Secretary: Major D. J. Carr; *Captain:* J. B. Bolus; *Testimonial:* M. H. Page; *Honours:* County Champions (1) 1936; Gillette Cup Finalists (1) 1969.

Bolus, John Brian, b Whitkirk, Yorks, 31 Jan 34. Ht 5'10½". RHB, occ LM. Début 1956. Cap 1973. Captain since 1973. Played for Yorks 1956–62 and for Notts 1963–72 (captain 1972). Tests 7 (1963–4). HS 202*. BB 4–40.

Cartwright, Harold, b Halfway 12 May 51. Ht 5'11½". RHB. Début 1973. Uncapped. HS 63.

Harvey-Walker, Ashley John, b East Ham, Essex, 21 Jul 44. Ht 6'3½". RHB, OB. Début 1971 scoring 110* *v* Oxford University. Uncapped. HS 117. BB 2–8.

Hendrick, Michael, b Darley Dale 22 Oct 48. Ht 6'3". RHB, RFM. Début 1969. Cap 1972. Tests 8 (1974–5). HS 46. BB 8–45.

Hill, Alan, b Buxworth 29 Jun 50. Ht 6'0". RHB, occ OB. Début 1972. Uncapped. HS 140*.

Miller, Geoffrey, b Chesterfield 8 Sep 52. Ht 6'1". RHB, OB. Début 1973. Uncapped. HS 71. BB 5–88.

Morris, Alan, b Staveley 23 Aug 53. Ht 5'8½". RHB. Début 1974. Uncapped. HS 37.

Page, Michael Harry, b Blackpool, Lancs, 17 Jun 41. Ht 5'10½". RHB, occ OB. Début and Cap 1964. Testimonial 1975. HS 162. BB 1–0.

Rhodes, Harold James, b Hadfield 22 Jul 36. Son of A. E. G. Rhodes (Derbys and England). Ht 6'2". RHB, RFM. Début 1953. Cap 1958. Retired 1969. Played for Notts in limited-overs matches 1970–73. Tests 2 (1959). HS 48. BB 7–38. 1 hat-trick.

Rowe, Lawrence George, b Kingston, Jamaica, 8 Jan 49. Ht 5'9". RHB, occ RM. Début 1968–9. Uncapped. Tests (West Indies) 12 (1972–4) scoring 214 and 100* on début. HS 302. BB 1–22.

Russell, Philip Edgar, b Ilkeston 9 May 44. Ht 5'11". RHB, RM/OB. Début 1965. Uncapped. HS 72. BB 6–61.

Sharpe, Philip John, b Shipley, Yorks, 27 Dec 36. Ht 5'7". RHB, occ OB. Début 1956. Uncapped. Played for Yorks 1958–74. Tests 13 (1963–70). HS 203*. BB 1–1.

Smith, Godfrey Philip (known as **Geoffrey**), b Derby 27 May 53. RHB. Uncapped. Joined staff 1973 but has yet to play for 1st XI.

Stevenson, Keith, b Derby 6 Oct 50. Ht 5'11". RHB, RM. Début 1974. Uncapped. HS 33. BB 4–127.

Swarbrook, Frederick William, b Derby 17 Dec 50. Ht 5'7". LHB, SLA. Début 1967. Uncapped. HS 90. BB 6–48.

Taylor, Robert William, b Stoke, Staffs, 17 Jul 41. Ht 5'8". RHB, WK. Début 1960. Cap 1962. Tests 1 (1971). HS 74*. Most dismissals – Innings 7, Match 10.

Venkataraghavan, Srinivasaraghavan ('**Venkat**'), b Madras, India, 21 Apr 46. Ht 5'11½". RHB, OB. Début 1963–4. Cap 1973. Tests (India) 28 (1965–74). HS 137. BB 9–93.

Ward, Alan, b Dronfield 10 Aug 47. Ht 6'3". RHB, RF. Début 1966. Cap 1969. Tests 5 (1969–71). HS 44. BB 7–42.

Ward, John Michael, b Sandon, Staffs, 14 Sep 48. No relation to Alan Ward. Ht 5'9½". RHB. Début 1970. Uncapped. HS 85.

ROUND THE COUNTIES

DERBYSHIRE 1974

Standing: J. M. Ward, A. Morris, C. J. Tunnicliffe, A. Hill, G. P. Smith, A. J. Harvey-Walker, G. Miller, H. Cartwright, R. S. Swindell, K. Stevenson.
Seated: A. J. Borrington, P. E. Russell, A. Ward, M. H. Page, R. W. Taylor, J. B. Bolus (Capt.), E. Smith (Coach), M. Hendrick, L. G. Rowe, F. W. Swarbrook.

	Matches	Runs	Av	100s	Ct/St	Wkts	Av	5 Wkts Innings	10 Wkts Match
J. B. Bolus	449	24378	33·95	37	193	24	36·91	—	—
H. Cartwright	23	612	17·48	—	13	—	—	—	—
A. J. Harvey-Walker	47	2002	24·71	2	15	9	29·11	—	—
M. Hendrick	86	442	8·33	—	53	234	23·12	7	2
A. Hill	34	1417	23·61	2	11	—	—	—	—
G. Miller	28	759	18·51	—	16	48	24·58	1	—
A. Morris	3	113	22·60	—	1	—	—	—	—
M. H. Page	236	10501	28·30	8	234	7	72·85	—	—
H. J. Rhodes	321	2427	9·48	—	85	1072	19·69	42	4
L. G. Rowe	72	4977	44·43	12	65	1	160·00	—	—
P. E. Russell	108	1462	14·05	—	78	240	29·90	4	—
P. J. Sharpe	453	20499	30·87	25	570	2	84·00	—	—
K. Stevenson	9	83	10·37	—	2	18	36·33	—	—
F. W. Swarbrook	126	2426	18·24	—	82	248	34·41	6	—
R. W. Taylor	375	6995	16·26	—	856/102	—	—	—	—
S. Venkataraghavan	201	4486	18·69	1	196	834	23·68	48	15
A. Ward	114	695	9·14	—	40	354	21·46	13	4
J. M. Ward	40	1425	21·59	–	19	—	—	—	—

ESSEX

Secretary: S. R. Cox; *Captain:* K. W. R. Fletcher; *Benefit:* B. E. A. Edmeades; *Honours:* Third in County Championship (1) 1897; John Player League Runners-up (1) 1971.

Acfield, David Laurence, b Chelmsford 24 Jul 47. Ht 5'9½". RHB, OB. Début 1966. Cap 1970. HS 42. BB 7–36.

Boyce, Keith David, b St Peter, Barbados, 11 Oct 43. Ht 6'0". RHB, RFM. Début 1964–5. Cap 1967. Tests (West Indies) 17 (1971–5). HS 147*. BB 9–61 on Essex début. 1 hat-trick.

Cooke, Robert Michael Oliver, b Adlington, Cheshire, 30 Sep 43. Ht 5'9". LHB, occ LB. Début 1972. Uncapped. HS 139. BB 1–37.

East, Raymond Eric, b Manningtree 20 Jun 47. Ht 6'1½". RHB, SLA. Début 1965. Cap 1967. HS 89*. BB 8–63. 1 hat-trick.

Edmeades, Brian Ernest Arthur, b Matlock, Derbys, 17 Sep 41. Ht 5'11". RHB, RM. Début 1961. Cap 1965. Benefit 1975. HS 163. BB 7–37.

Fletcher, Keith William Robert, b Worcester, Worcs, 20 May 44. Ht 5'9". RHB, occ LB. Début 1962. Cap 1963. Captain since 1974. Tests 50 (1968–75). HS 228*. BB 4–50.

Gooch, Graham Alan, b Leytonstone 23 Jul 53. Ht 6'0". RHB, RM. Début 1973. Uncapped. HS 114*. BB 1–17.

Hardie, Brian Ross, b Stenhousemuir, Stirlingshire, 14 Jan 50. Ht 5'10¾". RHB. Début 1970. Cap 1974. Played for Scotland 1970–2. HS 133.

Hobbs, Robin Nicholas Stuart, b Chippenham, Wilts, 8 May 42. Ht 5'10½". RHB, LB. Début 1961. Cap 1964. Tests 7 (1967–71). HS 100. BB 8–63.

Lever, John Kenneth, b Ilford 24 Feb 49. Ht 6'0½". RHB, LFM. Début 1967. Cap 1970. HS 91. BB 7–90.

McEwan, Kenneth Scott, b Bedford, South Africa, 16 Jul 52. Ht 5'9". RHB, occ WK. Début 1972–3. Cap 1974. HS 126. BB 1–0 taking wicket with second ball in first-class cricket.

Pont, Keith Rupert, b Wanstead 16 Jan 53. Ht 6'2½". RHB, RM. Début 1970. Uncapped. HS 113. BB 3–50.

Saville, Graham John, b Leytonstone 5 Feb 44. Ht 5'10". RHB, occ LB. Début 1963. Cap 1970. Assistant Secretary since 1974. HS 126*. BB 2–30.

Smith, Neil, b Dewsbury, Yorks, 1 Apr 49. Ht 5'11". RHB, WK. Début 1970. Uncapped. Played for Yorks 1970–1. HS 77. Most dismissals – Innings 4, Match 6.

Turner, Stuart, b Chester, Cheshire, 18 Jul 43. Ht 6'0½". RHB, RM. Début 1965. Cap 1970. HS 121. BB 6–87. 1 hat-trick.

ESSEX 1974

Standing: R. M. O. Cooke, D. L. Acfield, N. Smith, S. Turner, K. R. Pont, B. R. Lock, G. A. Gooch, J. K. Lever, B. R. Hardie, K. S. McEwan.
Seated: R. E. East, R. N. S. Hobbs, K. W. R. Fletcher (Capt.), B. E. A. Edmeades, K. D. Boyce.

	Matches	Runs	Av	100s	Ct/St	Wkts	Av	5 Wkts Innings	10 Wkts Match
D. L. Acfield	173	1030	9.19	—	58	378	28.39	14	—
K. D. Boyce	227	7185	22.10	3	179	668	25.18	27	5
R. M. O. Cooke	37	1331	23.76	2	19	1	108.00	—	—
R. E. East	218	3354	16.44	—	148	525	25.60	24	4
B. E. A. Edmeades	302	10729	24.95	13	96	362	25.37	10	1
K. W. R. Fletcher	386	21269	37.77	37	359	26	47.00	—	—
G. A. Gooch	16	655	28.47	1	5	3	51.00	—	—
B. R. Hardie	36	1809	30.15	2	23	—	—	—	—
R. N. S. Hobbs	383	4374	11.91	1	255	991	26.21	47	8
J. K. Lever	178	1144	11.32	—	85	429	27.23	12	—
K. S. McEwan	42	1821	27.59	2	47/2	1	0.00	—	—
K. R. Pont	40	1228	21.92	1	24	12	38.25	—	—
G. J. Saville	126	4474	23.67	3	103	3	25.33	—	—
N. Smith	42	729	15.18	—	70/15	—	—	—	—
S. Turner	149	3644	20.24	3	104	326	24.43	7	—

GLAMORGAN

Secretary: W. Wooller; *Captain:* Majid J. Khan; *Benefit:* E. W. Jones; *Honours:* County Champions (2) 1948, 1969.

Armstrong, Gregory Delisle, b Bank Hall, Barbados, 11 May 50. Ht 5'11". RHB, RF. Début 1973-4. Uncapped. HS 15*. BB 4-45.
Cordle, Anthony Elton, b St Michael, Barbados, 21 Sep 40. Ht 5'11". RHB, RFM. Début 1963. Cap 1967. HS 81. BB 9-49.
Davis, Roger Clive, b Cardiff 15 Jan 46. Brother of F.J. (Glamorgan). Ht 5'11". RHB, OB. Début 1964. Cap 1969. HS 134. BB 6-82.
Dudley-Jones, Robert David Louis, b Bridgend 26 May 52. Ht 6'2". RHB, RM. Début 1972. Uncapped. HS 5. BB 4-31.
Ellis, Geoffrey Phillip, b Llandudno, Caernarvons, 24 May 50. Ht 5'10". RHB, RM. Début 1970. Uncapped. HS 116. BB 2-35.
Francis, David **Arthur**, b Clydach 29 Nov 53. Ht 5'7". RHB. Début 1973. Uncapped. HS 52*.
Harrison, Stuart Charles, b Cwmbran, Monmouths, 21 Sep 51. Ht 6'2½". RHB, RM. Début 1971. Uncapped. HS 15. BB 3-55.
Hill, Leonard Winston, b Caerleon, Monmouths, 14 Apr 42. Ht 5'7". RHB, occ WK. Début 1964. Cap 1974. HS 96*.
Hopkins, John Anthony, b Maesteg 16 Jun 53. Brother of J.D. (Middlesex). Ht 5'10". RHB, occ WK. Début 1970. Uncapped. HS 88.
Jones, Alan, b Swansea 4 Nov 38. Ht 5'7½". LHB, occ OB. Début 1957. Cap 1962. Tests 1 (1970). HS 187*. BB 1-24.
Jones, Alan Lewis, b Alltwen 1 Jun 57. No relation to Alan or Eifion. Ht 5'9". LHB. Début 1973 when aged 16 and at school. Uncapped. HS 54.
Jones, Eifion Wyn, b Velindre 25 Jun 42. Brother of Alan Jones. Ht 5'6". RHB, WK. Début 1961. Cap 1967. Benefit 1975. HS 146*. Most dismissals – Innings 7, Match 8.
Khan, Majid Jahangir, b Jullundur, India, 28 Sep 46. Son of Dr Jahangir Khan (Cambridge University and India). Ht 5'10". RHB, RM/OB. Début 1961-2 scoring 111* and taking 6-67. Cap 1968. Captain since 1973. Tests (Pakistan) 26, 3 as captain (1964-75). HS 241. BB 6-67 on début. 1 hat-trick.
Llewellyn, Michael John, b Clydach 27 Nov 53. Ht 6'1". LHB, OB. Début 1970. Uncapped. HS 112*. BB 4-35.
Lloyd, Barry John, b Neath 6 Sep 53. Ht 6'0". RHB, OB. Début 1972. Uncapped. HS 45*. BB 4-49.
Lyons, Kevin James, b Cardiff 18 Dec 46. Ht 5'8½". RHB, RM. Début 1967. Uncapped. HS 92. BB 1-36.
Nash, Malcolm Andrew, b Abergavenny, Monmouths, 9 May 45. Ht 6'1½". LHB, LM/SLA. Début 1966. Cap 1969. HS 89. BB 7-15.
Norkett, Kim Thomas, b Malta 24 Dec 55. Ht 5'9". RHB, RFM. Uncapped. Played in one John Player League match 1974 but has yet to appear in first-class cricket.
Richards, Gwyn, b Maesteg 29 Nov 51. Ht 5'6". RHB, occ OB. Début 1971. Uncapped. HS 61.
Solanky, John William, b Dar-es-Salaam, Tanganyika, 30 Jun 42. Ht 5'10". RHB, RM/OB. Début 1963-4. Cap 1973. HS 71. BB 5-37.
Thomas, Richard James, b Griffithstown, Monmouths, 18 Jun 44. Ht 5'9½". RHB, RM. Début 1974. Uncapped. HS 8*. BB 1-40.
Williams, David **Lawrence**, b Tonna 20 Nov 46. Ht 5'11". LHB, RM. Début 1969. Cap 1971. HS 37*. BB 7-60.

GLAMORGAN 1974

Standing: Standing: A. L. Jones, J. W. Solanky, M. J. Llewellyn, R. D. L. Dudley-Jones, S. C. Harrison, G. P. Ellis, K. J. Lyons, P. Clift (Coach).
Seated: E. W. Jones, D. L. Williams, Majid J. Khan (Capt.), A. Jones, M. A. Nash, R. C. Davis. *On ground:* D. A. Francis, G. Richards.

	Matches	Runs	Av	100s	Ct/St	Wkts	Av	5 Wkts Innings	10 Wkts Match
G. D. Armstrong	6	46	9·20	—	3	13	41·53	—	—
A. E. Cordle	211	3855	14·60	—	91	460	25·24	12	2
R. C. Davis	185	5849	20·30	3	186	212	30·99	4	—
R. D. L. Dudley-Jones	5	15	3·00	—	1	13	27·00	—	—
G. P. Ellis	37	1279	22·05	1	9	7	61·00	—	—
D. A. Francis	16	306	13·90	—	10	—	—	—	—
S. C. Harrison	4	28	7·00	—	1	6	42·50	—	—
L. W. Hill	58	1993	24·30	—	30/1	—	—	—	—
J. A. Hopkins	28	589	13·69	—	18/1	—	—	—	—
A. Jones	431	23274	31·75	33	230	2	112·00	—	—
A. L. Jones	5	110	12·22	—	—	—	—	—	—
E. W. Jones	221	5006	19·25	2	484/51	—	—	—	—
Majid J. Khan	264	18251	43·97	51	292	188	32·03	3	—
M. J. Llewellyn	40	1151	18·86	1	31	22	27·18	—	—
B. J. Lloyd	21	162	6·48	—	12	23	41·21	—	—
K. J. Lyons	54	1513	19·90	—	26	1	205·00	—	—
M. A. Nash	177	3539	16·85	—	87	513	23·89	23	1
G. Richards	30	858	17·16	—	15	—	—	—	—
J. W. Solanky	50	1484	21·50	—	13	87	27·35	4	—
R. J. Thomas	1	8	—	—	—	1	40·00	—	—
D. L. Williams	140	369	5·42	—	36	341	26·83	12	1

GLOUCESTERSHIRE

Secretary: G. W. Parker; *Captain:* A. S. Brown; *Benefit:* none; *Honours:* County Champions (3) 1874, 1876, 1877; Joint Champions (1) 1873; Gillette Cup Winners (1) 1973.

Brassington, Andrew James, b Bagnall, Staffs, 9 Aug 54. Ht 5'11". RHB, WK. Début 1974. Uncapped. HS 8*.

Brown, Anthony Stephen, b Bristol 24 June 36. Ht 6'2". RHB, RM. Début 1953. Cap 1957. Captain since 1969. HS 116. BB 8–80. 1 hat-trick. Shares world record for most catches in an innings by a non-wicket-keeper (7).

Davey, Jack, b Tavistock, Devon, 4 Sep 44. Ht 6'2". LHB, LFM. Début 1966. Cap 1971. HS 37*. BB 6–95.

Dixon, John Henry, b Bournemouth, Hants, 3 Mar 54. Ht 6'5". RHB, RM. Début 1973. Uncapped. HS 7. BB 5–51.

Dunstan, Malcolm Stephen Thomas, b Redruth, Cornwall, 14 Oct 50. Ht 5'11". RHB. Début 1971. Uncapped. HS 52.

Foat, James Clive, b Salford Priors, Warwicks, 21 Nov 52. Ht 5'11". RHB, occ RM. Début 1972. Uncapped. HS 62*.

Graveney, David Anthony, b Bristol 2 Jan 53. Son of J.K.R. (Glos.) and nephew of T.W. (Glos., Worcs. and England). Ht 6'3". RHB, SLA. Début 1972. Uncapped. HS 50*. BB 8–85.

Hignell, Alastair James, b Cambridge, Cambs, 4 Sep 55. Ht 5'9". RHB. Début 1974. Uncapped. HS 27.

Knight, Roger David Verdon, b Streatham, Surrey, 6 Sep 46. Ht 6'3". LHB, RM. Début 1967. Cap 1971. Played for Surrey 1968–70. HS 164*. BB 6–44.

Nicholls, Ronald Bernard, b Sharpness 4 Dec 33. Ht 6'0". RHB, occ OB, occ WK. Début 1951. Cap 1957. HS 217. BB 2–19.

Page, Julian Thomas, b Bristol 1 May 54. Ht 6'0". LHB, LM. Début 1974 for Cambridge University but has represented Gloucestershire in just one JPL match. Uncapped. HS 11. BB 1–14.

Procter, Michael John, b Durban, South Africa, 15 Sep 46. Ht 5'11". RHB, RF/OB. Début 1965. Cap 1968. Tests (South Africa 7, Rest of the World 5) 12 (1967–70). Scored six hundreds in successive innings 1970–1 to equal world record. HS 254. BB 9–71. 1 hat-trick – scoring 51 and 102 in same match.

Sadiq Mohammad, b Junagadh, India, 3 May 45. Youngest brother of Wazir, Raees, Hanif, and Mushtaq. Ht 5'7". LHB, LB. Début 1959–60. Cap 1973. Tests (Pakistan) 19 (1969–75). HS 184*. BB 5–29.

Shackleton, Julian Howard, b Todmorden, Yorks, 29 Jan 52. Son of Derek (Hampshire and England). Ht 6'3". RHB, RM. Début 1971. Uncapped. HS 18. BB 4–38.

Shepherd, David Robert, b Bideford, Devon, 27 Dec 40. Ht 5'10". RHB, occ RM. Début 1965 scoring 108. Cap 1969. HS 153. BB 1–1.

Stovold, Andrew Willis-, b Bristol 19 Mar 53. Ht 5'8". RHB, WK. Début 1973. Uncapped. HS 102.

Thorn, Philip Leslie, b Bristol 17 Nov 51. Ht 5'7". RHB, SLA. Début 1974. Uncapped. HS 25. BB 2–53.

Zaheer Abbas, Syed, b Sialkot, Pakistan, 24 Jul 47. Ht 5'11½". RHB, occ OB. Début 1965–6. Uncapped. Tests (Pakistan) 17 (1969–75). Scored two double-centuries *v* England: 274 in 1971 and 240 in 1974. HS 274. BB 4–54.

GLOUCESTERSHIRE 1974

Standing: D. R. Shepherd, Zaheer Abbas, J. H. Shackleton, J. Davey, D. A. Graveney, R. D. V. Knight, J. C. Foat, A. Brassington, G. Wiltshire (Coach), R. B. Nicholls.
Seated: R. Swetman, J. B. Mortimore, A. S. Brown (Capt.), G. W. Parker (Secretary/Manager), M. J. Procter, C. A. Milton, Sadiq Mohammad.

	Matches	Runs	Av	100s	Ct/St	Wkts	Av	5 Wkts Innings	10 Wkts Match
A. J. Brassington	4	17	4·25	—	4/1	—	—	—	—
A. S. Brown	455	11765	17·98	3	458	1144	25·52	52	8
J. Davey	123	442	6·59	—	22	290	28·02	3	—
J. H. Dixon	6	13	2·60	—	1	9	44·00	1	—
M. S. T. Dunstan	12	283	16·64	—	4	—	—	—	—
J. C. Foat	25	527	14·63	—	15	—	—	—	—
D. A. Graveney	45	587	12·48	—	16	94	28·19	5	1
A. J. Hignell	8	161	12·38	—	9	—	—	—	—
R. D. V. Knight	163	8230	29·49	10	127	169	34·65	2	—
R. B. Nicholls	531	23474	26·19	18	283/1	8	74·00	—	—
J. T. Page	2	31	7·75	—	—	1	95·00	—	—
M. J. Procter	230	13122	38·14	35	201	802	18·15	32	7
Sadiq Mohammad	144	8701	38·33	17	117	135	26·31	5	—
J. H. Shackleton	9	74	12·33	—	4	19	29·21	—	—
D. R. Shepherd	199	7728	24·07	11	69	2	34·00	—	—
A. W. Stovold	22	915	24·07	1	20/4	—	—	—	—
P. L. Thorn	4	45	11·25	—	4	4	56·75	—	—
Zaheer Abbas	143	10021	50·35	32	109	8	32·62	—	—

HAMPSHIRE

Secretary: E. D. R. Eagar; *Captain:* R. M. C. Gilliat; *Testimonial:* E. Knights (Head Groundsman at Southampton); *Honours:* County Champions (2) 1961, 1973; John Player League Runners-up (1) 1969.

Barrett, Peter, b Winchester 3 Jun 55. Ht 5'8". LHB. Uncapped. Joined staff 1973 but has yet to play for 1st XI.

Baldry, David Andrew James, b Cardiff, Glamorgan, 13 Jun 55. Ht 5'9½". RHB. Uncapped. Joined staff 1974 but has yet to play for 1st XI.

Cowley, Nigel Geoffrey, b Shaftesbury, Dorset, 1 Mar 53. Ht 5'7". RHB, OB. Début 1974. Uncapped. HS 43. BB 3–31.

Gilliat, Richard Michael Charles, b Ware, Herts, 20 May 44. Ht 6'0". LHB, occ LB. Début 1964. Cap 1969. Captain since 1971. HS 223*. BB 1–3.

Greenidge, Cuthbert **Gordon**, b St Peter, Barbados, 1 May 51. Ht 5'9". RHB, RM. Début 1970. Cap 1972. Tests (West Indies) 5 (1974–5) scoring 93 and 107 on début. HS 273* including 13 sixes. BB 5–49.

Herman, Robert Stephen, b Southampton 30 Nov 46. Son of O.W. (Hampshire). Ht 6'1½". RHB, RFM. Début 1965. Cap 1972. Played for Middlesex 1965–71. HS 56. BB 8–42.

Hill, Michael John, b Harwell, Berks, 1 Jul 51. Ht 6'0". LHB, WK. Début 1973. Uncapped. HS 17*.

Jesty, Trevor Edward, b Gosport 2 Jun 48. Ht 5'8½". RHB, RM. Début 1966. Cap 1971. HS 133. BB 5–24.

Lewis, Richard Victor, b Winchester 6 Aug 47. Ht 5'10". RHB, occ LB. Début 1967. Uncapped. HS 136. BB 1–59.

Mottram, Thomas James, b Liverpool, Lancs, 7 Sep 45. Ht 6'4". RHB, RM. Début 1972. Uncapped. HS 15*. BB 6–63.

Murtagh, Andrew Joseph, b Dublin, Eire, 6 May 49. Ht 5'10". RHB, occ RM. Début 1973. Uncapped. HS 47.

Rice, John Michael, b Chandler's Ford 23 Oct 49. Ht 6'3". RHB, RM. Début 1971. Uncapped. HS 29. BB 4–64.

Richards, Barry Anderson, b Durban, South Africa, 21 Jul 45. Ht 6'0". RHB, OB. Début 1964–5. Cap 1968. Tests (South Africa, Rest of the World 5) 9 (1970). Played one match for Gloucestershire 1965. HS 356 – scoring 325 on the first day for South Australia *v* Western Australia (Perth) 1970–1. BB 7–63.

Roberts, Anderson Montgomery Everton, b Urlings Village, Antigua, 29 Jan 51. Ht 6'0". RHB, RF. Début 1969–70. Cap 1974. Tests (West Indies) 8 (1974–5). HS 48*. BB 8–47 including four wickets in five balls.

Sainsbury, Peter James, b Southampton 13 June 34. Ht 5'8½". RHB, SLA. Début 1954. Cap 1955. The only player to appear in both Hampshire's Championship-winning teams. HS 163. BB 8–76.

Stephenson, George **Robert**, b Derby, Derbys, 19 Nov 42. Ht 5'8". RHB, WK. Début 1967. Cap 1969. Played for Derbyshire 1967–8. HS 82. Most dismissals – Innings 5, Match 8.

Taylor, Michael Norman Somerset, b Amersham, Bucks, 12 Nov 42. Identical twin brother of D.J.S. (Somerset). Ht 5'11". RHB, RM. Début 1964. Cap 1973. Played for Nottinghamshire 1964–72. HS 105. BB 7–53. 1 hat-trick.

Turner, David Roy, b Chippenham, Wilts, 5 Feb 49. Ht 5'6". LHB, occ RM. Début 1966. Cap 1970. HS 181*. BB 1–4.

ROUND THE COUNTIES 69

KENT 1974

Standing: L. E. G. Ames (Retiring Manager), D. Nicholls, D. A. Laycock, G. W. Johnson, R. A. Woolmer, R. B. Elms, A. G. E. Ealham, J. C. T. Page (Manager).
Seated: A. P. E. Knott, D. L. Underwood, B. W. Luckhurst, M. H. Denness (Capt.), Asif Iqbal, J. N. Shepherd, B. D. Julien.
Absent: M. C. Cowdrey.

	Matches	Runs	Av	100s	Ct/St	Wkts	Av	5 Wkts Innings	10 Wkts Match
Asif Iqbal	276	13808	35.77	22	212	241	30.07	5	—
G. S. Clinton	1	23	11.50	—	—	—	—	—	—
M. C. Cowdrey	666	41618	43.44	105	618	62	52.22	—	—
M. H. Denness	361	18378	32.87	23	318	1	47.00	—	—
A. G. E. Ealham	176	5834	26.04	3	114	2	47.00	—	—
R. B. Elms	44	229	7.89	—	8	74	38.55	3	—
J. N. Graham	169	372	3.91	—	33	561	21.97	26	3
J. M. H. Graham-Brown	7	99	24.75	—	2	1	77.00	—	—
R. W. Hills	4	72	24.00	—	—	5	34.60	—	—
G. W. Johnson	155	5607	23.96	6	125	176	32.40	3	1
B. D. Julien	99	2822	24.75	2	65	256	28.02	7	—
A. P. E. Knott	304	10206	28.11	—	729/92	1	77.00	—	—
B. W. Luckhurst	351	20465	39.20	44	352	63	43.04	—	—
D. Nicholls	169	5966	21.53	2	261/10	2	11.50	—	—
C. J. C. Rowe	14	237	29.62	—	2	5	49.20	—	—
J. N. Shepherd	210	6190	23.71	4	166	567	26.06	33	1
C. J. Tavaré	9	152	15.20	—	2	—	—	—	—
P. A. Topley	12	110	12.22	—	8	9	48.66	—	—
D. L. Underwood	344	2457	9.00	—	149	1333	19.44	90	29
R. A. Woolmer	136	3376	24.82	3	89	254	23.86	11	1

LANCASHIRE
Secretary: A. K. James; *Captain:* D. Lloyd; *Joint Testimonial:* K. Shuttleworth and J. Sullivan; *Honours:* County Champions (8) 1881, 1897, 1904, 1926, 1927, 1928, 1930, 1934; Joint Champions (4) 1879, 1882, 1889, 1950; Gillette Cup Winners (3) 1970, 1971, 1972; John Player League Champions (2) 1969, 1970.

Abrahams, John, b Cape Town, South Africa, 21 Jul 52. Ht 5'8". LHB, occ OB. Début 1973. Uncapped. HS 78.

Dodds, Geoffrey John, b Newcastle upon Tyne, Northumberland, 6 Apr 56. Ht 5'10". RHB, LM. Uncapped. Joined staff 1974 but has yet to play for 1st XI.

Edmonds, James William, b Smethwick, Staffs, 4 Jun 51. Ht 6'5". RHB, LFM. Uncapped. Joined staff 1974 but has yet to play for 1st XI.

Engineer, Farokh Maneksha, b Bombay, India, 25 Feb 38. Ht 5'11½". RHB, WK, occ LB. Début 1958–9. Cap 1968. Tests (India 46, Rest of the World 2) 48 (1961–75). HS 192. BB 1–40. Most dismissals – Innings 6, Match 8.

Good, Antony John, b Kumasi, Gold Coast, 10 Nov 52. Ht 6'0". RHB, RFM. Début 1973. Uncapped. HS 6. BB 1–63.

Goodwin, Keith, b Oldham 21 Jun 38. Ht 5'6". RHB, WK. Début 1960. Cap 1965. HS 23. Most dismissals – Innings 5, Match 7.

Hayes, Frank Charles, b Preston 6 Dec 46. Ht 5'11". RHB. Début 1970. Cap 1972. Tests 7 (1973–4) scoring 106* on début. HS 187.

Hughes, David Paul, b Newton-le-Willows 13 May 47. Ht 5'11". RHB, SLA. Début 1967. Cap 1970. HS 88*. BB 7–24.

Kennedy, Andrew, b Blackburn 4 Nov 49. Ht 5'10". LHB. Début 1970. Uncapped. HS 81.

Lee, Peter, b Arthingworth, Northants, 27 Aug 45. Ht 5'10½". RHB, RFM. Début 1967. Cap 1972. Played for Northants 1967–71. HS 26. BB 8–53.

Lever, Peter, b Todmorden, Yorks, 17 Sep 40. Ht 6'0". RHB, RFM. Début 1960. Cap 1965. Tests 17 (1970–5). HS 88*. BB 7–70. 1 hat-trick.

Lloyd, Clive Hubert, b Georgetown, British Guiana, 31 Aug 44. Ht 6'3½". LHB, RM. Début 1963–4. Cap 1969. Tests (West Indies 43, Rest of the World 5) 48, 7 as captain (1966–75). Captained West Indies on 1974–5 tour of India and Pakistan. HS 242*. BB 4–48.

Lloyd, David, b Accrington 18 Mar 47. Ht 6'0". LHB, SLA. Début 1965. Cap 1968. Captain since 1973. Tests 9 (1974–5). HS 214*. BB 7–38.

Lyon, John, b St Helens 17 May 51. Ht 5'7½". RHB, WK. Début 1973. Uncapped. HS 48. Most dismissals – Innings 3, Match 4.

Pilling, Harry, b Ashton-under-Lyne 23 Feb 43. Ht 5'3" (shortest English current first-class cricketer). RHB, occ OB. Début 1962. Cap 1965. HS 144. BB 1–42.

Ratcliffe, Robert Malcolm, b Accrington 29 Nov 51. Ht 6'1". RHB, RM. Début 1972. Uncapped. HS 12*. BB 5–44.

Reidy, Bernard Wilfrid, b Whalley 18 Sep 53. Ht 5'11". LHB, SLA. Début 1973. Uncapped. HS 60. BB 1–58.

Shuttleworth, Kenneth, b St Helens 13 Nov 44. Ht 6'3". RHB, RFM. Début 1964. Cap 1968. Joint Testimonial 1975. Tests 6 (1970–1). HS 71. BB 7–41.

Simmons, Jack, b Clayton-le-Moors 28 Mar 41. Ht 6'1½". RHB, OB. Début 1968. Cap 1971. HS 112. BB 7–64.

Snellgrove, Kenneth Leslie, b Shepton Mallet, Somerset, 12 Nov 41. Ht 5'9½". RHB. Début 1965. Cap 1971. HS 138. BB 2–23.

Sullivan, John, b Ashton-under-Lyne 5 Feb 45. Ht 5'11". RHB, RM. Début 1963. Cap 1969. Joint Testimonial 1975. HS 81*. BB 4–19.

Trim, Geoffrey Edward, b Manchester 6 Apr 56. Ht 5'6". RHB. Uncapped. Joined staff 1974 but has yet to play for 1st XI.

Wood, Barry, b Ossett, Yorks, 26 Dec 42. Ht 5'6½". RHB, RM. Début 1964. Cap 1968. Tests 7 (1972–5). Played 5 matches for Yorks 1964. HS 186. BB 7–52.

LANCASHIRE 1974

Standing: F. M. Engineer, R. H. Tattersall, F. C. Hayes, B. W. Reidy, A. Kennedy, R. M. Ratcliffe, P. Lee, J. Lyon, J. Abrahams, J. Simmons, D. P. Hughes.
Seated: P. Lever, K. Shuttleworth, D. Lloyd (Capt.), K. Goodwin, J. Sullivan, H. Pilling, K. L. Snellgrove.
Absent: C. H. Lloyd, B. Wood.

	Matches	Runs	Av	100s	Ct/St	Wkts	Av	5 Wkts Innings	10 Wkts Match
J. Abrahams	16	355	15.43	—	13	—	—	—	—
F. M. Engineer	287	11487	29.45	12	578/113	1	117.00	—	—
A. J. Good	1	6	6.00	—	—	1	63.00	—	—
K. Goodwin	124	636	5.78	—	229/27	—	—	—	—
F. C. Hayes	107	4817	34.65	8	88	—	—	—	—
D. P. Hughes	167	2756	17.78	—	93	381	29.95	15	2
A. Kennedy	24	919	27.02	—	13	—	—	—	—
P. Lee	97	369	8.02	—	16	273	27.27	13	1
P. Lever	260	3287	14.87	—	86	669	25.72	24	2
C. H. Lloyd	220	14216	47.38	35	135	106	36.07	—	—
D. Lloyd	212	9567	31.99	17	175	140	28.48	2	1
J. Lyon	19	187	12.46	—	33/1	—	—	—	—
H. Pilling	268	12367	32.03	20	63	1	195.00	—	—
R. M. Ratcliffe	10	50	7.14	—	1	9	51.88	1	—
B. W. Reidy	5	164	41.00	—	7	1	82.00	—	—
K. Shuttleworth	185	1900	15.70	—	82	487	24.39	17	1
J. Simmons	140	2196	20.91	1	87	306	28.37	9	2
K. L. Snellgrove	106	3948	25.30	2	36	3	9.00	—	—
J. Sullivan	153	4261	20.58	—	84	76	29.15	—	—
B. Wood	209	9636	31.28	15	173	198	28.13	7	—

LEICESTERSHIRE

Secretary: F. M. Turner; *Captain:* R. Illingworth; *Benefit:* M. E. J. C. Norman; *Honours:* Third in County Championship (2) 1953, 1967; Benson and Hedges Cup Winners (1) 1972; John Player League Champions (1) 1974.

Balderstone, John **Christopher**, b Huddersfield, Yorks, 16 Nov 40. Ht 6'0½". RHB, SLA. Début 1961. Cap 1973. Played for Yorks 1961–9. HS 140. BB 6–84.

Birkenshaw, **Jack**, b Rothwell, Yorks, 13 Nov 40. Ht 5'9". LHB, OB. Début 1958. Cap 1965. Tests 5 (1973–4). Played for Yorks 1958–60. HS 131. BB 8–94. 2 hat-tricks.

Booth, **Peter**, b Shipley, Yorks, 2 Nov 52. Ht 6'0". RHB, RFM. Début 1972. Uncapped. HS 57. BB 4–18.

Davison, **Brian** Fettes, b Bulawayo, S. Rhodesia, 21 Dec 46. Ht 6'1". RHB, RM. Début 1967–8. Cap 1971. HS 142. BB 5–52.

Dudleston, **Barry**, b Bebington, Cheshire, 16 Jul 45. Ht 5'11". RHB, OCC SLA, OCC WK. Début 1966. Cap 1969. HS 171*. BB 4–6.

Higgs, **Kenneth**, b Sandyford, Staffs, 14 Jan 37. Ht 6'0". LHB, RFM. Début 1958. Cap 1972. Tests 15 (1965–8). Played for Lancs 1958–69. HS 63. BB 7–19. 2 hat-tricks.

Humphries, **David** John, b Alveley, Shropshire, 6 Aug 53. Ht 5'8". LHB, WK. Début 1974. Uncapped. HS 60.

Illingworth, **Raymond**, b Pudsey, Yorks, 8 Jun 32. Ht 5'11½". RHB, OB. Début 1951. Cap 1969. Captain since 1969. Tests 66, 36 as captain (1958–73). Played for Yorks 1951–68. HS 162. BB 9–42.

Knew, **George** Alan, b Leicester 5 Mar 54. Ht 5'10". RHB. Début 1972. Uncapped. HS 25.

McKenzie, **Graham** Douglas, b Cottesloe, Australia, 24 Jun 41. Ht 6'1". RHB, RFM. Début 1959–60. Cap 1969. Tests (Australia 60, Rest of the World 3) 63 (1961–71). HS 76. BB 8–71.

McVicker, **Norman** Michael, b Radcliffe, Lancs, 4 Nov 40. Ht 5'10½". RHB, RFM. Début 1965. Cap 1974. Played for Warwicks 1969–73. HS 85*. BB 7–29.

Norman, **Michael** Eric John Charles, b Northampton, Northants, 19 Jan 33. Ht 5'10". RHB, OCC RM. Début 1952. Cap 1966. Benefit 1975. Played for Northants 1952–65. HS 221*. BB 2–0. Schoolmaster.

Schepens, **Martin**, b Barrow upon Soar 12 Aug 55. Ht 5'8". RHB, LB. Début 1973. Uncapped. HS 11.

Spencer, Charles **Terry**, b Leicester 18 Aug 31. Ht 6'2½". RHB, RFM. Début and cap 1952. HS 90. BB 9–63.

Steele, **John** Frederick, b Stafford, Staffs, 23 Jul 46. Brother of D.S. (Northants). Ht 5'10½". RHB, SLA. Début 1970. Cap 1971. HS 195. BB 7–29.

Stretton, **Terry** Kevin, b Cosby 23 May 53. Ht 6'0". RHB, RM. Début 1972. Uncapped. HS 6*. BB 2–71.

Tolchard, **Jeffrey** Graham, b Torquay, Devon, 17 Mar 44. Ht 5'6". RHB. Début 1970. Uncapped. HS 66.

Tolchard, **Roger** William, b Torquay, Devon, 15 Jun 46. Brother of J.G. Ht 5'9". RHB, WK, OCC RM. Début 1965. Cap 1966. HS 126*. BB 1–4. Most dismissals – Innings 6, Match 7.

LEICESTERSHIRE 1974

Standing: J. G. Tolchard, M. Schepens, D. Humphries, G. A. Knew, J. F. Steele, N. Briers, P. Booth, T. K. Stretton, B. Dudleston, M. E. J. C. Norman, N. M. McVicker.
Seated: C. T. Spencer, J. Birkenshaw, C. H. Palmer (Chairman), R. Illingworth (Capt.), W. Bentley (President), K. Higgs, M. Turner (Secretary), R. W. Tolchard, G. D. McKenzie.
Absent: J. C. Balderstone, B. F. Davison.

	Matches	Runs	Av	100s	Ct/St	Wkts	Av	5 Wkts Innings	10 Wkts Match
J. C. Balderstone	116	3941	27·75	2	52	96	23·98	2	—
J. Birkenshaw	368	9652	22·39	3	218	876	26·64	42	4
P. Booth	12	134	10·30	—	3	23	22·60	—	—
B. F. Davison	148	7513	34·15	11	124	78	29·73	1	—
B. Dudleston	177	8479	31·87	20	145/1	22	32·59	—	—
K. Higgs	406	3209	11·02	—	227	1293	23·57	41	5
D. J. Humphries	3	74	14·80	—	3/1	—	—	—	—
R. Illingworth	667	21386	28·10	20	379	1882	19·78	98	11
G. A. Knew	4	59	11·80	—	—	—	—	—	—
G. D. McKenzie	365	5474	15·41	—	193	1172	27·00	48	5
N. M. McVicker	130	2182	18·18	—	37	367	25·42	16	—
M. E. J. C. Norman	361	17423	29·43	24	161	2	82·00	—	—
M. Schepens	2	19	6·33	—	1	—	—	—	—
C. T. Spencer	506	5871	10·77	—	380	1367	26·69	47	6
J. F. Steele	124	5026	28·55	6	154	191	26·86	4	—
T. K. Stretton	5	15	3·75	—	2	4	73·25	—	—
J. G. Tolchard	62	1408	19·02	—	17	—	—	—	—
R. W. Tolchard	259	7279	28·88	6	498/68	1	4·00	—	—

MIDDLESEX

Secretary: A. W. Flower; *Captain:* J. M. Brearley; *Benefit:* J. T. Murray; *Honours:* County Champions (5) 1866, 1903, 1920, 1921, 1947; Joint Champions (1) 1949.

Barlow, Graham Derek, b Folkestone, Kent, 26 Mar 50. Ht 5'9¼". LHB. Début 1969. Uncapped. HS 70.

Brearley, John Michael, b Harrow 28 Apr 42. Ht 5'11". RHB, occ RM, occ WK. Début 1961. Cap 1964. Captain since 1971. HS 312*. BB 1–21.

Butcher, Roland Orlando, b East Point, Barbados, 14 Oct 53. Ht 5'8". RHB. Début 1974. Uncapped. HS 53*.

Edmonds, Phillippe Henri, b Lusaka, N. Rhodesia, 8 Mar 51. Ht 6'1½". RHB, SLA. Début 1971. Cap 1974. Cricket Writers' Club 'Young Cricketer of 1974'. HS 76. BB 7–38.

Emburey, John Ernest, b Peckham, Surrey, 20 Aug 52. Ht 6'2". RHB, OB. Début 1973. Uncapped. HS 4*. BB 3–50.

Featherstone, Norman George, b Que Que, S. Rhodesia, 20 Aug 49. Ht 5'11". RHB, OB. Début 1967–8. Cap 1971. HS 125. BB 3–32.

Gomes, Hilary Angelo, b Arima, Trinidad, 13 Jul 53. Ht 5'10½". LHB, RM. Début 1971–2. Uncapped. HS 123. BB 4–22.

Lamb, Timothy Michael, b Hartford, Cheshire, 24 Mar 53. Ht 6'0". RHB, RM. Début 1973. Uncapped. HS 40*. BB 5–57.

Marriott, Dennis Alston, b Annotto Bay, Jamaica, 29 Nov 39. Ht 5'9". RHB, LM. Début 1965. Cap 1973. Played for Surrey 1965–7. HS 24*. BB 5–71.

Murray, John Thomas, b Kensington 1 Apr 35. Ht 5'9". RHB, WK, occ RM. Début 1952. Cap 1956. Benefit 1975. Tests 21 (1961–7). Needs 12 dismissals to overtake H. Strudwick's world record of 1493. Retires after 1975 season. HS 142. BB 2–10. Most dismissals – Innings 6, Match 9.

Price, John Sidney Ernest, b Harrow 22 Jul 37. Ht 6'1". LHB, RF. Début 1961. Cap 1963. Tests 15 (1964–72). HS 53*. BB 8–48.

Radley, Clive Thornton, b Hertford, Herts, 13 May 44. Ht 5'8". RHB, occ LB. Début 1964. Cap 1967. HS 139. BB 1–7.

Ross, Nigel Patrick Dorai, b Chelsea 5 Apr 53. Ht 6'1". RHB, WK. Début 1973. Uncapped. HS 30.

Selvey, Michael Walter William, b Chiswick 25 Apr 48. Ht 6'2". RHB, RM. Début 1968. Cap 1973. Played for Surrey 1968–71. HS 42. BB 6–43.

Smith, Michael John, b Enfield 4 Jan 42. Ht 6'2½". RHB, occ SLA. Début 1959. Cap 1967. HS 181. BB 4–13.

Titmus, Frederick John, b St Pancras 24 Nov 32. Ht 5'9". RHB, OB. Début 1949. Cap 1953. Captain 1965–8. Tests 53 (1955–75). HS 137*. BB 9–52. 1 hat-trick. Last player to complete 'double' (1967). Recalled to England team *v* Australia 1974–5.

Vernon, Martin Jeffrey, b St Marylebone 4 Jul 51. Ht 6'2". RHB, RFM. Début 1974. Uncapped. HS 27. BB 6–58.

MIDDLESEX 1974

Standing: R. Nicholas (Physiotherapist), G. D. Barlow, J. E. Emburey, M. J. Vernon, P. H. Edmonds, M. W. W. Selvey, N. P. D. Ross, R. O. Butcher.
Seated: K. V. Jones, C. T. Radley, M. J. Smith, J. M. Brearley (Capt.), F. J. Titmus, J. T. Murray, N. G. Featherstone.

	Matches	Runs	Av	100s	Ct/St	Wkts	Av	5 Wkts Innings	10 Wkts Match
G. D. Barlow	18	651	22.44	—	4	—	—	—	—
J. M. Brearley	255	13477	34.73	17	248/12	1	99.00	—	—
R. O. Butcher	5	150	21.42	—	3	—	—	—	—
P. H. Edmonds	67	1345	16.20	—	61	217	26.45	9	3
J. E. Emburey	6	5	—	—	6	8	59.12	—	—
N. G. Featherstone	150	6222	28.41	3	138	39	29.61	—	—
H. A. Gomes	38	1201	24.02	1	14	12	44.33	—	—
T. M. Lamb	21	134	11.16	—	2	63	26.01	2	—
D. A. Marriott	30	139	10.69	—	5	67	29.70	1	—
J. T. Murray	617	18307	23.56	16	1230/252	6	40.50	—	—
J. S. E. Price	275	1090	8.44	—	104	807	23.53	26	4
C. T. Radley	256	11673	33.63	18	251	2	12.00	—	—
N. P. D. Ross	7	137	12.45	—	1	—	—	—	—
M. W. W. Selvey	69	307	8.52	—	16	174	29.78	8	—
M. J. Smith	306	13958	31.86	26	182	57	31.92	—	—
F. J. Titmus	727	20477	23.67	5	451	2615	22.13	159	25
M. J. Vernon	10	99	12.37	—	1	20	29.30	2	1

NORTHAMPTONSHIRE

Secretary: K. C. Turner; *Captain:* R. T. Virgin; *Benefit:* D. S. Steele; *Honours:* County Championship Runners-up (3) 1912, 1957, 1965.

Bedi, Bishan Singh, b Amritsar, India, 25 Sep 46. Ht 5'10". RHB, SLA. Début 1961–2. Cap 1972. Tests (India) 39 (1966–75). HS 61. BB 7–19. 1 hat-trick.

Cook, Geoffrey, b Middlesbrough, Yorks, 9 Oct 51. Ht 6'0". RHB, occ SLA. Début 1971. Uncapped. HS 122*.

Cottam, Robert Michael Henry, b Cleethorpes, Lincs, 16 Oct 44. Ht 6'3". RHB, RFM. Début 1963. Cap 1972. Tests 4 (1969–73). Played for Hampshire 1963–71. HS 62*. BB 9–25.

Dye, John Cooper James, b Gillingham, Kent, 24 July 42. Ht 6'0". RHB, LFM. Début 1962. Cap 1972. Played for Kent 1962–71. HS 29*. BB 7–45.

Griffiths, Brian James, b Wellingborough 13 Jun 49. Ht 6'3". RHB, RM. Début 1974. Uncapped. HS 6. BB 3–54.

Hodgson, Alan, b Consett, Co. Durham, 27 Oct 51. Ht 6'4½". LHB, RFM. Début 1970. Uncapped. HS 41. BB 5–36.

Larkins, Wayne, b Roxton, Beds, 22 Nov 53. Ht 5'11". RHB, occ RM. Début 1972. Uncapped. HS 109.

Mushtaq Mohammad, b Junagadh, India, 22 Nov 43. Brother of Wazir, Raees, Hanif and Sadiq. Ht 5'7". RHB, LB. Début 1956–7. Cap 1967. Tests (Pakistan 38, Rest of the World 2) 40 (1959–75). HS 303*. BB 7–18.

Romaines, Paul William, b Bishop Auckland, Co. Durham, 25 Dec 55. Ht 6'0". RHB. Uncapped. Joined staff 1973 but has yet to play for 1st XI.

Sarfraz Nawaz, b Lahore, Pakistan, 1 Dec 48. Ht 6'3". RHB, RFM. Début 1967–8. Uncapped. Tests (Pakistan) 13 (1969–75). HS 59. BB 8–27 – before lunch on first day.

Sharp, George, b West Hartlepool, Co. Durham, 12 Mar 50. Ht 5'11". RHB, WK. Début 1968. Cap 1973. HS 76*. Most dismissals – Innings 5, Match 7.

Steele, David Stanley, b Bradeley, Staffs, 29 Sep 41. Brother of J.F. (Leics). Ht 5'11½". RHB, SLA. Début 1963. Cap 1965. Benefit 1975. HS 140*. BB 8–29.

Tait, Alan, b Washington, Co. Durham, 27 Dec 53. Ht 5'10". LHB. Début 1971. Uncapped. HS 99.

Virgin, Roy Thomas, b Taunton, Somerset, 26 Aug 39. Ht 5'10". RHB, occ LB, occ WK. Début 1957. Cap 1974. Appointed captain for 1975. Played for Somerset 1957–72. HS 197*. BB 1–6.

Watts, Patrick James, b Henlow, Beds, 16 Jun 40. Brother of P.D. (Northants and Notts). Ht 6'2½". LHB, RM. Début 1959. Cap 1962. Captain 1971–4. HS 145. BB 6–18.

Willey, Peter, b Sedgefield, Co. Durham, 6 Dec 49. Ht 6'1". RHB, RM. Début 1966. Cap 1971. HS 158*. BB 5–14.

Williams, Richard Grenville, b Bangor, Caernarvonshire, 10 Aug 57. Ht 5'6¼". RHB, OB. Début 1974 when aged 16 years 10 months. Uncapped. HS 64. BB 1–36.

NORTHAMPTONSHIRE 1974

Standing: A. Tait, W. Larkins, R. T. Virgin (Capt. 1975), G. Cook, Sarfraz Nawaz, A. Hodgson, N. Maltby, P. Willey, C. Milburn, B. Griffiths, G. Sharp, R. M. H. Cottam.
Seated: R. Williams, J. C. J. Dye, D. S. Steele, P. J. Watts, Mushtaq Mohammad, P. Romaines.
Absent: B. S. Bedi.

	Matches	Runs	Av	100s	Ct/St	Wkts	Av	5 Wkts Innings	10 Wkts Match
B. S. Bedi	210	2103	11.42	—	107	910	21.39	61	8
G. Cook	77	2766	23.44	1	76	—	—	—	—
R. M. H. Cottam	263	1018	6.48	—	136	944	20.71	55	5
J. C. J. Dye	217	510	5.48	—	46	588	23.53	20	1
B. J. Griffiths	5	6	1.20	—	2	10	38.50	—	—
A. Hodgson	42	362	8.82	—	13	86	25.51	1	—
W. Larkins	25	312	9.75	1	10	—	—	—	—
Mushtaq Mohammad	392	23900	41.85	53	268	755	23.04	31	2
Sarfraz Nawaz	88	1337	18.56	—	52	285	26.09	11	2
G. Sharp	85	1617	18.37	—	152/34	—	—	—	—
D. S. Steele	275	12151	30.84	16	314	216	23.00	3	—
A. Tait	45	1421	19.20	—	9	—	—	—	—
R. T. Virgin	371	18703	30.11	31	355	4	80.25	—	—
P. J. Watts	323	13569	29.18	10	252	318	25.59	7	—
P. Willey	158	4939	23.51	5	72	156	29.65	4	—
R. G. Williams	1	79	39.50	—	—	2	38.00	—	—

NOTTINGHAMSHIRE

Secretary: Gp Capt. R. G. Wilson; *Captain:* M. J. Smedley; *Benefit:* M. J. Smedley; *Honours:* County Champions (12) 1865, 1868, 1871, 1872, 1875, 1880, 1883, 1884, 1885, 1886, 1907, 1929; Joint Champions (5) 1869, 1873, 1879, 1882, 1889.

Birch, John Dennis, b Nottingham 18 Jun 55. Ht 5'10". RHB, RM. Début 1973. Uncapped. HS 26. BB 3–45.

Cook, Charles John, b Retford 5 Jun 46. Ht 6'2". RHB, OB. Début 1974. Uncapped. HS 1. BB 1–50. Police dog-handler.

Hacker, Peter John, b Nottingham 16 Jul 52. Ht 5'10". RHB, LM. Début 1974. Uncapped. HS 0.

Harris, Michael John, b St Just-in-Roseland, Cornwall, 25 May 44. Ht 6'0". RHB, LB, WK. Début 1964. Cap 1970. Played for Middlesex 1964–8. HS 201*. BB 4–16. Most dismissals – Innings 5, Match 5.

Hassan, Basharat, b Nairobi, Kenya, 24 Mar 44. Ht 5'10½". RHB, OCC WK. Début 1963–4. Cap 1970. HS 125*.

Johnson, Peter David, b Nottingham 12 Nov 49. Ht 6'0". RHB, LB. Début 1969. Uncapped. HS 82. BB 3–34.

Latchman, Harry Chand (real name: Harichand), b Kingston, Jamaica, 26 Jul 43. Ht 5'5½". RHB, LB. Début 1965. Uncapped. Played for Middlesex 1965–73. HS 96. BB 7–91.

Nanan, Nirmal, b Preysal Village, Trinidad, 19 Aug 51. Ht 5'9". RHB, LB. Début 1969–70. Uncapped. HS 72. BB 3–12.

Randall, Derek William, b Retford 24 Feb 51. Ht 5'9". RHB. Début 1972. Cap 1973. HS 107.

Rice, Clive Edward Butler, b Johannesburg, South Africa, 23 Jul 49. Ht 5'10". RHB, RFM. Début 1969–70. Uncapped. HS 81. BB 5–65.

Smedley, Michael John, b Maltby, Yorks, 28 Oct 41. Ht 5'9½". RHB. Début 1964. Cap 1966. Appointed captain for 1975. Benefit 1975. HS 149.

Stead, Barry, b Leeds, Yorks, 21 Jun 39. Ht 5'8". LHB, LFM. Début 1959. Cap 1969. Played 2 matches for Yorks 1959. HS 58. BB 8–44. 1 hat-trick.

Taylor, William, b Manchester, Lancs, 24 Jan 47. Ht 5'10½". RHB, RFM. Début 1971. Uncapped. HS 26*. BB 6–42.

Todd, Paul Adrian, b Morton 12 Mar 53. Ht 6'1". RHB. Début 1972. Uncapped. HS 66*.

Tunnicliffe, Howard **Trevor**, b Derby, Derbys, 4 Mar 50. Ht 5'11½". RHB, RM. Début 1973. Uncapped. HS 87. BB 3–55.

White, Robert Arthur, b Fulham, Middx, 6 Oct 36. Ht 5'9". LHB, OB. Début 1958. Cap 1966. Played for Middlesex 1958–65. HS 116*. BB 7–41.

Wilkinson, Philip Alan, b Hucknall 23 Aug 51. Ht 6'3". RHB, RM. Début 1971. Cap 1974. HS 28*. BB 4–46.

NOTTINGHAMSHIRE 1974

Standing: W. H. Hare, N. Nanan, W. Taylor, H. T. Tunnicliffe, P. A. Wilkinson, P. A. Todd, J. D. Birch, P. J. Hacker, H. C. Latchman, D. W. Randall.
Seated: F. G. Woodhead (Coach), M. J. Harris, D. A. Pullan, J. D. Bond, M. J. Smedley (Capt. 1975), R. A. White, B. Hassan.
Absent: G. St A. Sobers.

	Matches	Runs	Av	100s	Ct/St	Wkts	Av	5 Wkts Innings	10 Wkts Match
J. D. Birch	7	102	9·27	—	7	5	52·20	—	—
C. J. Cook	1	1	1·00	—	1	1	105·00	—	—
P. J. Hacker	1	0	0·00	—	1	—	—	—	—
M. J. Harris	215	13092	38·05	31	143/5	74	42·77	—	—
B. Hassan	164	6882	28·08	7	134/1	—	—	—	—
P. D. Johnson	31	988	21·95	—	14	9	81·11	—	—
H. C. Latchman	193	1984	12·55	—	93	453	27·38	21	1
N. Nanan	19	433	13·53	—	12	7	22·28	—	—
D. W. Randall	58	2367	23·90	2	32	—	—	—	—
C. E. B. Rice	35	1021	24·90	—	14	103	22·65	1	—
M. J. Smedley	261	12324	31·35	24	191	—	—	—	—
B. Stead	199	1806	11·80	—	55	551	27·45	19	2
W. Taylor	68	205	5·25	—	14	175	26·92	5	1
P. A. Todd	18	453	15·10	—	14	—	—	—	—
H. T. Tunnicliffe	12	365	22·81	—	2	7	39·14	—	—
R. A. White	329	10481	23·55	5	150	490	28·29	19	3
P. A. Wilkinson	42	289	8·02	—	14	70	36·57	—	—

SOMERSET

Secretary: R. G. Stevens; *Captain:* D. B. Close; *Testimonial:* T. W. Cartwright; *Honours:* Third in County Championship (4) 1892, 1958, 1963, 1966; Gillette Cup Finalists (1) 1967; John Player League Runners-up (1) 1974.

Botham, Ian Terrence, b Heswall, Cheshire, 24 Nov 55. Ht 6'1". RHB, RM. Début 1974. Uncapped. HS 59. BB 5–59.

Breakwell, Dennis, b Brierley Hill, Staffs, 2 Jul 48. Ht 5'9". LHB, SLA. Début 1969. Uncapped. Played for Northants 1969–72. HS 97. BB 8–39.

Burgess, Graham Iefvion, b Glastonbury 5 May 43. Ht 6'2". RHB, RM. Début 1966. Cap 1968. HS 129. BB 6–51.

Cartwright, Thomas William, b Coventry, Warwicks, 22 Jul 35. Ht 6'0". RHB, RM. Début 1952. Cap 1970. Testimonial 1975. Tests 5 (1964–5). Played for Warwicks 1952–69. HS 2:0. BB 8–39. 1 hat-trick.

Clapp, Robert John, b Weston-super-Mare 12 Dec 48. Ht 6'4". RHB, RM. Début 1972. Uncapped. Only bowler to take 50 wickets in a season of limited-overs matches (51 in 1974) and holds JPL record for most wickets in a season (34 in 1974). HS 3. BB 2–48. Schoolmaster.

Close, Dennis Brian, b Leeds, Yorks, 24 Feb 31. Ht 6'1". LHB, OB. Début 1949 achieving 'double' in his first season. Cap 1971. Captain since 1972. Tests 19, 7 as captain (1949–67). Played for Yorks 1949–70, captain 1963–70. HS 198. BB 8–41.

Denning, Peter William, b Chewton Mendip 16 Dec 49. Ht 5'9". LHB, occ OB. Début 1969. Cap 1973. HS 85*. BB 1–4.

Jennings, Keith Francis, b Wellington 5 Oct 53. Ht 6'0". RHB, RM. Uncapped. Joined staff 1975 and has yet to play for 1st XI.

Jones, Allan Arthur, b Horley, Surrey, 9 Dec 47. Ht 6'4". RHB, RFM. Début 1966. Cap 1972. Played for Sussex 1966–9. HS 27. BB 9–51.

Langford, Brian Anthony, b Birmingham, Warwicks, 17 Dec 35. Ht 5'11". RHB, OB. Début 1953 taking 26 wickets in his first three matches. Cap 1957. Captain 1969–71. HS 68*. BB 9–26.

Moseley, Hallam Reynold, b Christchurch, Barbados, 28 May 48. Ht 5'11½". RHB, RFM. Début 1969. Cap 1972. HS 67. BB 5–24.

Parks, James Michael, b Haywards Heath, Sussex, 21 Oct 31. Son of J.H. (Sussex). Ht 5'10½". RHB, WK, occ LB. Début 1949. Cap 1973. Tests 46 (1954–68). Played for Sussex 1949–72, captain 1967–8. HS 205*. BB 3–23.

Richards, Isaac Vivian Alexander, b St John's, Antigua, 7 Mar 52. Ht 5'11". RHB, OB. Début 1971–2. Cap 1974. Tests (West Indies) 7 (1974–5) scoring 192* in his second match. HS 192*. BB 3–49.

Robinson, Peter James, b Worcester, Worcs, 9 Feb 43. Nephew of R. O. Jenkins (Worcs and England). Ht 5'8½". LHB, SLA. Début 1963. Cap 1966. Played 5 matches for Worcs 1963–4. Assistant head groundsman since 1974. HS 140. BB 7–10.

Roebuck, Peter Michael, b Oxford, Oxon, 6 Mar 56. Ht 6'0". RHB. Début 1974. Uncapped. HS 46 on début.

Rose, Brian Charles, b Dartford, Kent, 4 Jun 50. Ht 6'1½". LHB, occ LM. Début 1969. Uncapped. HS 125. BB 1–5.

Taylor, Derek John Somerset, b Amersham, Bucks, 12 Nov 42. Identical twin brother of M.N.S. (Hampshire). Ht 5'10½". RHB, WK. Début 1966. Cap 1971. Played 10 matches for Surrey 1966–9. HS 179. Most dismissals – Innings 5, Match 7.

SOMERSET 1974

Standing: D. Breakwell, P. W. Denning, B. C. Rose, R. J. Clapp, A. A. Jones, H. R. Moseley, S. G. Wilkinson, I. V. A. Richards, J. S. Hook.
Seated: D. J. S. Taylor, P. J. Robinson, T. W. Cartwright, D. B. Close (Capt.), J. M. Parks, G. I. Burgess.
On ground: I. T. Botham, P. A. Slocombe, V. J. Marks, P. M. Roebuck.

	Matches	Runs	Av	100s	Ct/St	Wkts	Av	5 Wkts Innings	10 Wkts Match
I. T. Botham	18	441	16·96	—	15	30	25·96	1	—
D. Breakwell	106	1905	18·31	—	42	188	28·90	6	1
G. I. Burgess	188	5580	18·91	2	81	327	28·13	13	1
T. W. Cartwright	468	13630	21·60	7	327	1517	19·03	94	18
R. J. Clapp	4	4	1·33	—	—	6	41·50	—	—
D. B. Close	715	31633	33·19	50	751/1	1119	26·03	43	3
P. W. Denning	80	2363	20·19	—	37	1	33·00	—	—
A. A. Jones	121	485	5·98	—	25	297	27·75	15	3
B. A. Langford	510	7588	13·59	—	231	1410	24·79	83	16
H. R. Moseley	84	748	13·60	—	36	209	24·02	5	—
J. M. Parks	735	36483	34·77	51	1086/93	51	43·72	—	—
I. V. A. Richards	42	2146	30·65	2	26	19	39·47	—	—
P. J. Robinson	183	4923	21·31	3	169	293	27·40	10	1
P. M. Roebuck	2	54	13·50	—	—	—	—	—	—
B. C. Rose	37	943	16·83	1	16	1	5·00	—	—
D. J. S. Taylor	133	2751	19·79	1	254/32	—	—	—	—

SURREY

Secretary: Lt Col W. H. Sillitoe; *Captain:* J. H. Edrich; *Testimonial:* J. H. Edrich; *Honours:* County Champions (18) 1864, 1887, 1888, 1890, 1891, 1892, 1894, 1895, 1899, 1914, 1952, 1953, 1954, 1955, 1956, 1957, 1958, 1971; Joint Champions (2) 1889, 1950; Benson and Hedges Cup Winners (1) 1974.

Arnold, Geoffrey Graham, b Earlsfield 3 Sep 44. Ht 6'1". RHB, RFM. Début 1963. Cap 1967. Tests 33 (1967–75). HS 73. BB 8–41. 1 hat-trick.

Aworth, Christopher John, b Wimbledon 19 Feb 53. Ht 5'10". LHB, OCC SLA. Début 1973. Uncapped. Elected Cambridge University captain 1975. HS 97.

Baker, Raymond Paul, b Carshalton 9 Apr 54. Ht 6'3". RHB, RM. Début 1973. Uncapped. HS 5. BB 6–29.

Butcher, Alan Raymond, b Croydon 7 Jan 54. Ht 5'8½". LHB, LM. Début 1972. Uncapped. HS 57. BB 6–48.

Edrich, John Hugh, b Blofield, Norfolk, 21 Jun 37. Ht 5'8". LHB, OCC RM. Début 1956. Cap 1959. Captain since 1973. Testimonial 1975. Tests 73 (1963–75). HS 310*.

Howarth, Geoffrey Philip, b Auckland, New Zealand, 29 Mar 51. Ht 5'11". RHB, OB. Début 1968–9. Cap 1974. Tests (New Zealand) 2 (1975). HS 159. BB 5–32.

Intikhab Alam Khan, b Hoshiarpur, India, 28 Dec 41. Ht 5'10". RHB, LB. Début 1957–8. Cap 1969. Tests (Pakistan 43, 17 as captain; Rest of the World 5) 48 (1959–75). Took wicket with first ball in Test cricket. HS 182. BB 8–54. 1 hat-trick.

Jackman, Robin David, b Simla, India, 13 Aug 45. Ht 5'9½". RHB, RFM. Début 1966. Cap 1970. HS 92*. BB 8–40. 3 hat-tricks.

Long, Arnold, b Cheam 18 Dec 40. Ht 5'8". LHB, WK. Début 1960. Cap 1962. Holds world record for most catches in a match (11). HS 92. Most dismissals – Innings 7, Match 11.

Owen-Thomas, Dudley Richard, b Mombasa, Kenya, 20 Sep 48. Ht 5'8". RHB, OCC OB. Début 1969. Uncapped. HS 182*. BB 3–20.

Pocock, Patrick Ian, b Bangor, Caernarvonshire, 24 Sep 46. Ht 6'1". RHB, OB. Début 1964. Cap 1967. Tests 15 (1968–74). HS 75*. BB 7–57. 2 hat-tricks. Took 7 wickets in 11 balls *v* Sussex (Eastbourne) 1972 – world record (wow2owwwwiw).

Roope, Graham Richard James, b Fareham, Hampshire, 12 Jul 46. Ht 6'1". RHB, RM, OCC WK. Début 1964. Cap 1969. Tests 8 (1973). HS 171. BB 5–14.

Skinner, Lonsdale Ernest, b Plaisance, British Guiana, 7 Sep 50. Ht 5'9". RHB, WK. Début 1971. Uncapped. HS 84.

Smith, David Mark, b Balham, 9 Jan 56. Ht 6'3½". LHB, RM. Début 1973. Uncapped. HS 8*. BB 1–19.

Verrinder, Alan Otto Charles, b Henley-on-Thames, Oxon, 28 Jul 55. Ht 6'0". RHB, RFM. Début 1974. Uncapped. HS 0. BB 1–18.

Younis Ahmed, Mohammad, b Jullundur, India, 20 Oct 47. Brother of Saeed Ahmed (Pakistan). Ht 5'10½". LHB, OCC SLA/LM. Début 1961–2. Cap 1969. Tests (Pakistan) 2 (1969). HS 155*. BB 3–12.

SURREY 1974

Standing: D. R. Owen-Thomas, R. D. Jackman, G. G. Arnold, P. I. Pocock, G. R. J. Roope, Younis Ahmed, L. E. Skinner.
Seated: G. P. Howarth, S. J. Storey, A. J. W. McIntyre (Manager), J. H. Edrich (Capt.), A. Long, M. J. Edwards, A. R. Butcher.
Absent: Intikhab Alam.

	Matches	Runs	Av	100s	Ct/St	Wkts	Av	5 Wkts Innings	10 Wkts Match
G. G. Arnold	226	2445	13·58	—	83	748	21·24	31	2
C. J. Aworth	28	1146	24·38	—	12	—	—	—	—
R. P. Baker	16	14	2·80	—	6	37	22·81	1	—
A. R. Butcher	26	271	14·26	—	9	39	25·53	1	—
J. H. Edrich	479	34342	45·91	90	257	—	—	—	—
G. P. Howarth	51	2174	27·87	2	41	32	26·65	1	—
Intikhab Alam	328	10231	23·57	8	174	1146	26·19	69	12
R. D. Jackman	205	2380	16·52	—	80	679	23·37	31	3
A. Long	352	5064	15·72	—	701/101	—	—	—	—
D. R. Owen-Thomas	96	4292	29·60	7	41	20	39·90	—	—
P. I. Pocock	304	3249	11·98	—	100	949	25·03	35	5
G. R. J. Roope	223	9900	34·49	12	306/1	170	35·13	4	—
L. E. Skinner	18	583	21·59	—	12/1	—	—	—	—
D. M. Smith	4	8	—	—	3	5	51·60	—	—
A. O. C. Verrinder	1	0	0·00	—	1	1	18·00	—	—
Younis Ahmed	225	11784	36·25	19	121	20	44·75	—	—

SUSSEX

Secretary: Lt Cdr I. M. Stoop; *Captain:* A. W. Greig; *Benefit:* None; *Honours:* County Championship Runners-up (6) 1902, 1903, 1932, 1933, 1934, 1953; Gillette Cup Winners (2) 1963, 1964.

Barclay, John Robert Troutbeck, b Bonn, W. Germany, 22 Jan 54. Ht 5'11". RHB, OB. Début 1970. Uncapped. HS 52. BB 5–28.
Buss, Antony, b Brightling 1 Sep 39. Ht 6'2". RHB, RFM. Début 1958. Cap 1963. HS 83. BB 8–23. 2 hat-tricks.
Buss, Michael Alan, b Brightling 24 Jan 44. Brother of Antony. Ht 6'1½". LHB, LM. Début 1961. Cap 1967. HS 159. BB 7–58.
Cheatle, Robert Giles Lenthall, b Paddington, Middlesex, 31 Jul 53. Ht 5'11". LHB, SLA. Début 1974. Uncapped. HS 0*.
Faber, Mark James Julian, b Horsted Keynes 15 Aug 50. Ht 5'10½". RHB, occ RM. Début 1970. Uncapped. HS 112*. BB 1–11.
Graves, Peter John, b Hove 19 May 46. Ht 5'10½". LHB, occ SLA. Début 1965. Cap 1969. HS 145*. BB 3–69.
Greenidge, Geoffrey Alan, b Bridgetown, Barbados, 26 May 48. Ht 6'0". RHB, occ LB. Début 1966–7. Cap 1970. Tests (West Indies) 5 (1972–3). HS 205. BB 7–124.
Greig, Anthony William, b Queenstown, South Africa, 6 Oct 46. Ht 6'7". RHB, RM/OB. Début 1965–6. Cap 1967. Captain since 1973. Tests 41 (1970–5). HS 167*. BB 8–25. 1 hat-trick.
Groome, Jeremy Jonathan, b Bognor Regis 7 Apr 55. Ht 6'0". RHB. Début 1974. Uncapped. HS 59.
Mansell, Alan William, b Redhill, Surrey, 19 May 51. Ht 5'8". RHB, WK. Début 1969. Uncapped. HS 72*. Most dismissals – Innings 4, Match 5.
Marshall, Roger Philip Twells, b Horsham 28 Feb 52. Ht 6'3". RHB, LFM. Début 1973. Uncapped. HS 26. BB 4–37.
Mendis, Gehan Dixon, b Colombo, Ceylon, 24 Apr 55. Ht 5'9". RHB. Début 1974. Uncapped. HS 1.
Morley, Jeremy Dennis, b Newmarket, Suffolk, 20 Oct 50. Ht 5'10". LHB. Début 1971. Cap 1973. HS 127.
Parsons, Austin Edward Werring, b Glasgow, Lanarkshire, 9 Jan 49. Ht 5'9". RHB, occ LB. Début 1971–2. Uncapped. HS 57. BB 1–41.
Phillipson, Christopher **Paul,** b Brindaban, India, 10 Feb 52. Ht 6'1". RHB, RM. Début 1970. Uncapped. HS 11*. BB 6–56.
Prideaux, Roger Malcolm, b Chelsea, Middlesex, 31 Jul 39. Ht 6'2". RHB, occ RM. Début 1958. Cap 1971. Tests 3 (1968–9). Played for Kent 1960–1 and Northants 1962–70 (captain 1967–70). HS 202*. BB 2–13.
Snow, John Augustine, b Peopleton, Worcs, 13 Oct 41. Ht 6'1". RHB, RF. Début 1961. Cap 1964. Tests 47 (1965–73). HS 73. BB 7–29.
Spencer, John, b Brighton 6 Oct 49. Ht 6'2". RHB, RM. Début 1969. Cap 1973. HS 55. BB 6–19.
Waller, Christopher Edward, b Guildford, Surrey, 3 Oct 48. Ht 5'11". RHB, SLA. Début 1967. Uncapped. Played for Surrey 1967–73. HS 47. BB 7–64.
Wisdom, Nicholas, b Barnet, Herts, 18 Mar 53. Son of Norman Wisdom. Ht 5'5". RHB, RM. Début 1974. Uncapped. HS 31*. BB 1–0.

SUSSEX 1974

Standing: M. J. J. Faber, J. Denman, C. E. Waller, J. J. Groome, R. P. T. Marshall, R. G. L. Cheatle, J. R. T. Barclay, J. D. Morley, A. W. Mansell.
Seated: U. C. Joshi, G. A. Greenidge, M. A. Buss, J. A. Snow, A. W. Greig (Capt.), A. Buss, P. J. Graves, M. G. Griffith, J. Spencer.
On ground: A. Wadey, S. Hoadley, N. Wisdom.

	Matches	Runs	Av	100s	Ct/St	Wkts	Av	5 Wkts Innings	10 Wkts Match
J. R. T. Barclay	26	391	9.77	—	17	24	35.54	1	—
A. Buss	310	4415	13.13	—	131	958	25.04	44	3
M. A. Buss	248	9689	24.04	10	182	437	28.02	16	—
R. G. L. Cheatle	1	0	0.00	—	—	—	—	—	—
M. J. J. Faber	49	1655	19.70	1	29	1	33.00	—	—
P. J. Graves	198	7915	25.69	6	157	15	52.60	—	—
G. A. Greenidge	164	8535	30.48	16	80	13	69.76	1	—
A. W. Greig	259	11557	29.18	16	247	643	27.97	25	7
J. J. Groome	9	181	11.31	—	3	—	—	—	—
A. W. Mansell	38	650	14.77	—	68/7	—	—	—	—
R. P. T. Marshall	7	124	41.33	—	1	13	36.38	—	—
G. G. Mendis	1	1	1.00	—	—	—	—	—	—
J. D. Morley	54	2085	23.16	2	22/1	—	—	—	—
A. E. W. Parsons	8	257	19.76	—	2	1	84.00	—	—
C. P. Phillipson	34	91	5.68	—	8	57	33.57	2	—
R. M. Prideaux	444	25090	34.36	41	301	3	58.66	—	—
J. A. Snow	289	3409	12.39	—	101	1003	22.19	50	7
J. Spencer	107	1029	9.18	—	41	275	26.39	10	1
C. E. Waller	60	355	8.25	—	24	143	26.39	6	—
N. Wisdom	2	35	35.00	—	—	2	16.50	—	—

WARWICKSHIRE
Secretary: L. T. Deakins; *Captain:* D. J. Brown; *Benefit:* D. L. Amiss; *Honours:* County Champions (3) 1911, 1951, 1972; Gillette Cup Winners (2) 1966, 1968.

Abberley, Robert **Neal**, b Birmingham 22 Apr 44. Ht 5'8½". RHB, occ RM. Début 1964. Cap 1966. HS 117*. BB 2–19.

Amiss, Dennis Leslie, b Birmingham 7 Apr 43. Ht 5'11". RHB, occ SLA/LM. Début 1960. Cap 1965. Benefit 1975. Tests 40 (1966–75). HS 262*. BB 3–21.

Bourne, William Anderson, b Clapham, Barbados, 15 Nov 52. Ht 6'1". RHB, RFM. Début 1970–1. Uncapped. HS 84. BB 3–31.

Brown, David John, b Walsall, Staffs, 30 Jan 42. Ht 6'4". RHB, RFM. Début 1961. Cap 1964. Appointed captain for 1975. Tests 28 (1965–70). HS 79. BB 8–64.

Field, Maxwell Nicholas, b Coventry 23 Mar 50. Ht 5'10½". RHB, RM. Début 1974. Uncapped. HS 39*. BB 4–76.

Gardom, Barrie **Keith**, b Birmingham 31 Dec 52. Ht 5'10". RHB, LB. Début 1973. Uncapped. HS 79*. BB 6–139.

Hemmings, Edward Ernest, b Leamington Spa 20 Feb 49. Ht 5'10". RHB, OB. Début 1966. Cap 1974. HS 80. BB 7–57.

Humpage, Geoffrey William, b Birmingham 24 Apr 54. Ht 5'9". RHB, WK. Début 1974. Uncapped. HS 13. Most dismissals – Innings 4, Match 5.

Jameson, John Alexander, b Bombay, India, 30 Jun 41. Ht 6'0". RHB, OB, occ WK. Début 1960. Cap 1964. Tests 4 (1971–4). HS 240* sharing 2nd wicket world record partnership of 465* with R. B. Kanhai. BB 4–22. 1 hat-trick.

Kallicharran, Alvin Isaac, b Port Mourant, British Guiana, 21 Mar 49. Ht 5'4". LHB, occ LB. Début 1966–7. Cap 1972. Tests (West Indies) 22 (1972–5) scoring 100* on début. HS 197. BB 2–22.

Kanhai, Rohan Babulal, b Port Mourant, British Guiana, 26 Dec 35. Ht 5'7". RHB, occ LB, occ WK. Début 1954–5. Cap 1968. Tests (West Indies 79, 13 as captain; Rest of the World 5) 84 (1957–74). HS 256. BB 2–5.

Lewington, Peter John, b Finchampstead, Berks, 30 Jan 50. Ht 6'2". RHB, OB. Début 1970. Uncapped. HS 34. BB 6–37.

Murray, Deryck Lance, b Port-of-Spain, Trinidad, 20 May 43. Ht 5'9". RHB, WK, occ LB. Début 1960–1. Cap 1972. Tests (West Indies 29, Rest of the World 3) 32 (1963–75). Played for Notts 1966–9. HS 166*. BB 2–50. Most dismissals – Innings 5, Match 8.

Perryman, Stephen Peter, b Birmingham 22 Oct 55. Ht 5'8". RHB, RM. Début 1974. Uncapped. Played one match without going on to the field of play.

Rouse, Stephen John, b Merthyr Tydfil, Glamorgan, 20 Jan 49. Ht 6'1". LHB, LM. Début 1970. Cap 1974. HS 55. BB 5–47.

Smith, Kenneth **David**, b Newcastle upon Tyne, Northumberland, 9 Jul 56. Ht 6'0". RHB. Début 1973. Uncapped. HS 49.

Smith, Michael John Knight, b Leicester, Leics, 30 Jun 33. Ht 6'1". RHB, occ RM. Début 1951. Cap 1957. Captain 1957–67. Tests 50, 25 as captain (1958–72). Played for Leics 1951–5. HS 204. BB 1–0.

Whitehouse, John, b Nuneaton 8 Apr 49. Ht 5'9½". RHB, occ OB. Début 1971 scoring 173. Cap 1973. HS 173. BB 1–39.

Willis, Robert George Dylan, b Sunderland, Co. Durham, 30 May 49. Ht 6'6". RHB, RF. Début 1969. Cap 1972. Tests 16 (1971–5). Played for Surrey 1969–71. HS 34. BB 8–44. 1 hat-trick.

WARWICKSHIRE 1974

Standing: A. I. Kallicharran, E. E. Hemmings, S. J. Rouse, R. G. D. Willis, B. K. Gardom, D. L. Murray.
Seated: D. L. Amiss, R. B. Kanhai, M. J. K. Smith, A. C. Smith, D. J. Brown (Capt. 1975), J. A. Jameson, R. N. Abberley.

	Matches	Runs	Av	100s	Ct/St	Wkts	Av	5 Wkts Innings	10 Wkts Match
R. N. Abberley	192	7360	23.89	2	131	4	57.75	—	—
D. L. Amiss	328	19298	40.03	38	225	15	40.20	—	—
W. A. Bourne	14	322	20.12	—	13	20	36.60	—	—
D. J. Brown	305	3209	11.97	—	110	904	24.41	33	4
M. N. Field	10	122	12.20	—	1	24	34.45	—	—
B. K. Gardom	17	427	18.56	—	6	17	41.17	1	—
E. E. Hemmings	95	2572	23.17	—	44	207	30.33	8	1
G. W. Humpage	2	13	6.50	—	5	—	—	—	—
J. A. Jameson	318	16269	33.20	25	220/1	82	37.59	—	—
A. I. Kallicharran	115	6981	42.30	18	72	10	73.60	—	—
R. B. Kanhai	365	25964	49.64	77	270/7	14	64.07	—	—
P. J. Lewington	44	216	8.00	—	19	103	29.96	2	—
D. L. Murray	252	9332	28.45	9	475/76	4	58.75	—	—
S. P. Perryman	1	—	—	—	—	—	—	—	—
S. J. Rouse	55	651	13.02	—	32	121	27.94	1	—
K. D. Smith	3	66	16.50	—	—	—	—	—	—
M. J. K. Smith	624	39129	42.11	68	587	5	61.00	—	—
J. Whitehouse	60	2724	29.29	2	28	3	63.33	—	—
R. G. D. Willis	106	833	17.35	—	54	297	25.74	5	—

WORCESTERSHIRE

Secretary: M. D. Vockins; *Captain:* N. Gifford; *Benefit:* B. L. D'Oliveira; *Honours:* County Champions (3) 1964, 1965, 1974; John Player League Champions (1) 1971; Gillette Cup Finalists (2) 1963, 1966; Benson and Hedges Cup Finalists (1) 1973.

Brain, Brian Maurice, b Worcester 13 Sep 40. Ht 6'2". RHB, RFM. Début 1959. Cap 1966. HS 38. BB 6-32.

Cass, George **Rodney,** b Overton, Yorks, 23 Apr 40. Ht 6'0". LHB, WK. Début 1964. Cap 1970. Played for Essex 1964-7. HS 104*. Most dismissals – Innings 6, Match 7.

Cumbes, James, b East Didsbury, Lancs, 4 May 44. Ht 6'2". RHB, RFM. Début 1963. Uncapped. Played for Lancs 1963-7 and 1971, and for Surrey 1968-9. HS 25*. BB 6-35.

D'Oliveira, Basil Lewis, b Cape Town, South Africa, 4 Oct 31. Ht 5'11". RHB, RM/OB. Début 1961-2. Cap 1965. Benefit 1975. Tests 48 (1966-72). HS 227. BB 6-29.

Gifford, Norman, b Ulverston, Lancs, 30 Mar 40. Ht 5'10½". LHB, SLA. Début 1960. Cap 1961. Captain since 1971. Tests 15 (1964-73). HS 89. BB 8-28. 1 hat-trick.

Headley, Ronald George Alphonso, b Kingston, Jamaica, 29 Jun 39. Son of G. A. Headley (Jamaica and West Indies). Ht 5'10½". LHB, occ LB. Début 1958. Cap 1961. Tests (West Indies) 2 (1973). HS 187. BB 4-40.

Hemsley, Edward John Orton, b Norton, Staffs, 1 Sep 43. Ht 5'9". RHB, RM. Début 1963. Cap 1969. HS 138*. BB 3-5.

Holder, Vanburn Alonza, b Bridgetown, Barbados, 8 Oct 45. Ht 6'3". RHB, RFM. Début 1966-7. Cap 1970. Tests (West Indies) 22 (1969-75). HS 122. BB 7-40.

Imran Khan Niazi, b Lahore, Pakistan, 25 Nov 52. Cousin of Majid J. Khan (Glamorgan and Pakistan). Ht 6'0". RHB, RFM. Début 1969-70. Uncapped. Tests (Pakistan) 4 (1971-4). HS 170. BB 6-54.

Inchmore, John Darling, b Ashington, Northumberland, 22 Feb 49. Ht 6'2½". RHB, RFM. Début 1973. Uncapped. HS 113. BB 5-50.

Johnson, Ivan Nicholas, b Nassau, Bahamas, 27 Jun 53. Ht 5'9". LHB, SLA. Début 1972. Uncapped. HS 55. BB 4-61.

Ormrod, Joseph **Alan,** Ramsbottom, Lancs, 22 Dec 42. Ht 5'11". RHB, occ OB. Début 1962. Cap 1966. HS 204*. BB 5-27.

Parker, John Morton, b Dannevirke, New Zealand, 21 Feb 51. Ht 6'0". RHB, occ LB, occ WK. Début 1971. Cap 1974. Tests (New Zealand) 12 (1973-5). HS 195. BB 1-14.

Pridgeon, Alan **Paul,** b Wall Heath, Staffs, 22 Feb 54. Ht 6'3". RHB, RM. Début 1972. Uncapped. HS 18*. BB 3-50.

Roberts, Christopher **Paul,** b Cleethorpes, Lincs, 12 Oct 51. Ht 6'5". RHB, RM. Début 1974. Uncapped. HS 0*. BB 1-34.

Senghera, Ravinder, b Delhi, India, 25 Jan 47. Ht 5'10". RHB, OB. Début 1974. Uncapped. HS – has not batted. BB 5-81.

Turner, Glenn Maitland, b Dunedin, New Zealand, 26 May 47. Ht 5'9½". RHB, occ RM/OB. Début 1964-5 (on Christmas Day whilst at Otago High School). Cap 1968. Tests (New Zealand) 29 (1969-75). HS 259. BB 3-18.

Wilcock, Howard **Gordon,** b New Malden, Surrey, 26 Feb 50. Ht 5'9½". RHB, WK. Début 1971. Uncapped. HS 44. Most dismissals – Innings 6, Match 6.

Wilkinson, Keith William, b Fenton, Staffs, 15 Jan 50. Ht 5'10". LHB, LM. Début 1969. Uncapped. HS 141. BB 5-60.

Yardley, Thomas **James,** b Chaddesley Corbett, 27 Oct 46. Ht 6'0". LHB, occ WK. Début 1967. Cap 1972. HS 135.

WORCESTERSHIRE 1974

Standing: K. W. Wilkinson, I. N. Johnson, A. Shutt, J. Cumbes, J. D. Inchmore,
A. P. Pridgeon, C. P. Roberts, J. M. Parker, R. Senghera, C. Boyns, H. G. Wilcock.
Seated: G. R. Cass, B. M. Brain, B. L. D'Oliveira, R. G. A. Headley, N. Gifford
(Capt.), J. A. Ormrod, G. M. Turner, V. A. Holder, T. J. Yardley.
Absent: E. J. O. Hemsley, Imran Khan.

	Matches	*Runs*	*Av*	*100s*	*Ct/St*	*Wkts*	*Av*	5 *Wkts* Innings	10 *Wkts* Match
B. M. Brain	134	774	7·44	—	31	456	23·86	18	4
G. R. Cass	139	3573	20·41	1	187/25	—	—	—	—
J. Cumbes	61	145	6·90	—	18	171	24·32	6	—
B. L. D'Oliveira	280	14575	38·97	36	180	449	26·36	14	2
N. Gifford	406	4549	13·18	—	203	1264	20·24	65	11
R. G. A. Headley	423	21695	31·12	32	357	12	49·00	—	—
E. J. O. Hemsley	102	4224	29·53	2	75	52	32·40	—	—
V. A. Holder	190	1862	11·71	1	67	613	22·68	26	3
Imran Khan	62	2528	29·05	4	23	171	28·31	7	1
J. D. Inchmore	28	274	14·42	1	12	65	27·69	1	—
I. N. Johnson	29	578	19·93	—	11	27	43·51	—	—
J. A. Ormrod	299	11948	27·40	9	263	25	40·60	1	—
J. M. Parker	76	4138	34·77	8	59/3	3	32·66	—	—
A. P. Pridgeon	15	32	5·33	—	6	19	52·94	—	—
C. P. Roberts	1	0	0·00	—	—	1	40·00	—	—
R. Senghera	3	—	—	—	—	15	18·40	1	—
G. M. Turner	251	17313	46·66	46	228	5	37·60	—	—
H. G. Wilcock	57	877	15·38	—	113/10	—	—	—	—
K. W. Wilkinson	33	960	24·61	1	22	46	32·43	1	—
T. J. Yardley	134	4239	25·69	3	110/2	—	—	—	—

YORKSHIRE

Secretary: J. Lister; *Captain:* G. Boycott; *Benefit:* None; *Honours:* County Champions (31) 1867, 1870, 1893, 1896, 1898, 1900, 1901, 1902, 1905, 1908, 1912, 1919, 1922, 1923, 1924, 1925, 1931, 1932, 1933, 1935, 1937, 1938, 1939, 1946, 1959, 1960, 1962, 1963, 1966, 1967, 1968; Joint Champions (2) 1869, 1949; Gillette Cup Winners (2) 1965, 1969; Benson and Hedges Cup Finalists (1) 1972; John Player League Runners-up (1) 1973.

Bairstow, David Leslie, b Bradford 1 Sep 51. Ht 5'9½". RHB, WK. Début 1970. Cap 1973. HS 79. Most dismissals – Innings 6, Match 9.

Bore, Michael Kenneth, b Hull 2 Jun 47. Ht 5'11". RHB, LM/SLA. Début 1969. Uncapped. HS 37*. BB 6–63.

Boycott, Geoffrey, b Fitzwilliam 21 Oct 40. Ht 5'10". RHB, occ RM. Début 1962. Cap 1963. Captain since 1971. Tests 65 (1964–74). HS 261*. BB 3–47.

Carrick, Phillip, b Leeds 16 Jul 52. Ht 5'11½". RHB, SLA. Début 1970. Uncapped. HS 46. BB 8–33.

Cooper, Howard Pennett, b Bradford 17 Apr 49. Ht 6'0". LHB, RM. Début 1971. Uncapped. HS 47. BB 4–37.

Cope, Geoffrey Alan, b Leeds 23 Feb 47. Ht 5'11½". RHB, OB. Début 1966. Cap 1970. HS 66. BB 7–36. 1 hat-trick.

Hampshire, John Harry, b Thurnscoe 10 Feb 41. Ht 6'0". RHB, occ LB. Début 1961. Cap 1963. Tests 7 (1969–72) scoring 107 on début. HS 183*. BB 7–52.

Johnson, Colin, b Pocklington 5 Sep 47. Ht 5'10". RHB, occ OB. Début 1969. Uncapped. HS 107. BB 2–22.

Leadbeater, Barrie, b Leeds 14 Aug 43. Ht 6'0". RHB, occ RM. Début 1966. Cap 1969. HS 99*. BB 1–1.

Lumb, Richard Graham, b Doncaster 27 Feb 50. Ht 6'3". RHB. Début 1970. Cap 1974. HS 123*.

Nicholson, Anthony George, b Dewsbury 25 Jun 38. Ht 6'2". RHB, RM. Début 1962. Cap 1963. HS 50. BB 9–62.

Old, Christopher Middleton, b Middlesbrough 22 Dec 48. Ht 6'3". LHB, RFM. Début 1966. Cap 1969. Tests 23 (1970–5). HS 116. BB 7–20.

Oldham, Stephen, b Sheffield 26 Jul 48. Ht 6'0½". RHB, RM. Début 1974. Uncapped. HS 5*. BB 3–7.

Robinson, Arthur Leslie, b Brompton 17 Aug 46. Ht 6'3". LHB, LFM. Début 1971. Uncapped. HS 28*. BB 6–61. 1 hat-trick.

Sidebottom, Arnold, b Barnsley 1 Apr 54. Ht 6'1". RHB, RM. Début 1973. Uncapped. HS 1. BB 3–61.

Squires, Peter John, b Ripon 4 Aug 51. Ht 5'8½". RHB. Début 1972. Uncapped. HS 67. England rugby union football international.

Stevenson, Graham Barry, b Ackworth 16 Dec 55. Ht 5'11". RHB, RM. Début 1973. Uncapped. HS 18. BB 2–23.

Townsley, Richard **Andrew** John, b Castleford 24 Jun 52. Ht 5'11½". LHB, occ RM. Début 1974. Uncapped. HS 2.

YORKSHIRE 1974

Back row: M. K. Bore, C. Johnson, J. D. Love, R. P. Hodson, P. J. Squires, G. B. Stevenson.
Middle row: C. Kaye (physiotherapist), P. Carrick, B. Leadbeater, A. L. Robinson, R. A. Hutton, R. G. Lumb, G. A. Cope, E. I. Lester (scorer).
Front row: C. M. Old, D. Wilson, P. J. Sharpe, G. Boycott (Capt.), A. G. Nicholson, J. H. Hampshire.

	Matches	Runs	Av	100s	Ct/St	Wkts	Av	5 Wkts Innings	10 Wkts Match
D. L. Bairstow	111	2194	17.69	—	257/36	—	—	—	—
M. K. Bore	62	406	8.45	—	20	131	29.93	3	—
G. Boycott	342	26686	55.36	82	136	22	44.40	—	—
P. Carrick	33	514	15.57	—	21	91	24.32	6	1
H. P. Cooper	33	274	9.78	—	20	78	25.17	—	—
G. A. Cope	121	968	10.63	—	41	331	23.53	16	3
J. H. Hampshire	364	16164	31.32	22	278	27	53.62	2	—
C. Johnson	58	1585	20.58	1	31	4	65.00	—	—
B. Leadbeater	112	3936	24.44	—	52	1	5.00	—	—
R. G. Lumb	59	2562	27.54	5	45	—	—	—	—
A. G. Nicholson	277	1594	11.55	—	84	866	19.76	39	3
C. M. Old	152	2761	18.16	1	85	419	22.00	13	1
S. Oldham	2	5	—	—	1	4	17.25	—	—
A. L. Robinson	31	116	11.60	—	12	73	24.31	3	—
A. Sidebottom	2	1	0.50	—	—	5	28.00	—	—
P. J. Squires	28	677	16.51	—	12	—	—	—	—
G. B. Stevenson	5	33	5.50	—	5	5	27.60	—	—
R. A. J. Townsley	1	2	1.00	—	—	—	—	—	—

Cricket Records
Compiled by Bill Frindall

PART I – FIRST-CLASS MATCH RECORDS
Complete to 11 September 1974

TEAM RECORDS

Highest innings total
  1107   Victoria *v* New South Wales at Melbourne   1926–7
There have been seven totals of over 900, the most recent being 951–7 dec. by Sind v Baluchistan at Karachi, 1973–4. The highest total in England is 903–7 dec. by England v Australia at The Oval in 1938.

Highest second innings total
  770   New South Wales *v* South Australia at Adelaide
1920–1

The highest in England is 703–9 dec. by Cambridge University v Sussex at Hove in 1890.

Lowest innings total
  12   Oxford University *v* MCC at Oxford   1877
  12   Northamptonshire *v* Gloucestershire at Gloucester
1907

Highest match aggregate
  2376 for 38 wkts   Bombay *v* Maharashtra at Poona   1948–9
The highest in England is 1723 for 31 wkts in the 1948 Leeds Test between England (496 and 365–8 dec.) and Australia (458 and 404–3).

Lowest match aggregate (completed match)
  105 for 31 wkts   MCC *v* Australians at Lord's   1878

Largest margin of victory
  Innings and 851 runs   Railways (910–6 dec.) *v* Dera Ismail Khan at Lahore   1964–5
The largest in England is an innings and 579 runs by England (903–7 dec.) v Australia at The Oval in 1938.

92

Victory without losing a wicket
Lancashire beat Leicestershire by 10 wickets at Manchester 1956
Karachi 'A' beat Sind 'A' by an innings and 77 runs at Karachi 1957–8
Railways beat Jammu and Kashmir by 10 wickets at Srinagar 1960–1

Largest variation in innings totals
551 Barbados (175 and 726–7 dec.) v Trinidad at Bridgetown 1926–7
551 Pakistan (106 and 657–8 dec.) v West Indies at Bridgetown 1957–8

The largest in England is 543 by Somerset (87 and 630) v Yorkshire at Leeds in 1901.

Tie matches
Before 1948 a match was considered to be tied if the scores were level after the fourth innings, even if the side batting last had wickets in hand when stumps were drawn on the final day. Law 22 was amended in 1948 by Note 4 which states: 'A "Draw" is regarded as a "Tie" when the scores are equal at the conclusion of play but only if the match has been played out.' The most recent instances have been:—

Yorkshire (106–9 dec. and 207) v Middlesex (102 and 211) at Bradford 1973
Sussex (245 and 173–5 dec.) v Essex (200–8 dec. and 218) at Hove 1974

Most runs in a day
721 Australians v Essex at Southend 1948

Fewest runs in a day
95 Australia (80) v Pakistan (15–2) at Karachi 1956–7

Team scoring most hundreds in an innings
6 Holkar (912–8 dec.) v Mysore at Indore 1945–6

The most in England is four, with the most recent instance occurring in 1961 when W. M. Lawry, C. C. McDonald, B. C. Booth and K. D. Mackay – the first four batsmen in the order – scored hundreds v Cambridge University at Cambridge.

Unusual dismissals
Although there are nine ways in which a batsman can lose his wicket, three of them occur very rarely: handled the ball,

hit the ball twice and obstructed the field.

The most recent instances in England have been:

Handled the Ball: A. Rees – Glamorgan v Middlesex at Lord's 1965

Hit the Ball Twice: J. H. King – Leicestershire v Surrey at The Oval 1906

Obstructed the Field: K. Ibadulla – Warwickshire v Hampshire at Coventry 1963

INDIVIDUAL RECORDS–BATTING

Highest innings (and most runs in a match)
499 Hanif Mohammad – Karachi v Bahawalpur at Karachi 1958–9

The highest in England is 424 by A. C. MacLaren for Lancashire v Somerset at Taunton in 1895.

Highest Maiden hundred
337* Pervez Akhtar – Railways v Dera Ismail Khan at Lahore 1964–5

The highest in England is 274 by G. Davidson for Derbyshire v Lancashire at Manchester in 1896.

Highest score on début
240 W. F. E. Marx – Transvaal v Griqualand West at Johannesburg 1920–1

The highest – and the only double-century – in England is 215* by G. H. G. Doggart for Cambridge University v Lancashire at Cambridge in 1948.

Hundreds in first three innings
J. S. Solomon (114*, 108, 121) for British Guiana in 1956–7 and 1957–8.

Most runs in a career
61,237 (av. 50·65) J. B. Hobbs (Surrey) 1905–34

Most runs in a season
3816 (av. 90·85) D. C. S. Compton (Middlesex) 1947

Most hundreds in a career
197 J. B. Hobbs (Surrey) 1905–34

Most hundreds in a season
18 D. C. S. Compton (Middlesex) 1947

Most hundreds in successive innings
6 C. B. Fry for Sussex and Rest of England 1901

6   D. G. Bradman for South Australia and D. G. Bradman's XI 1938–9
   6   M. J. Procter for Rhodesia   1970–1
Two double-centuries in a match (and most runs in a match in England)
   A. E. Fagg (244 and 202*) – Kent v Essex at Colchester 1938
Two separate hundreds in a match most times
   7   W. R. Hammond (Gloucestershire)
Highest percentage of hundreds in a career
   39·66%   D. G. Bradman – 117 hundreds in 295 completed innings   1927–49
Thousand runs in a season most times
   28   W. G. Grace (Gloucestershire) and F. E. Woolley (Kent)
Earliest dates for scoring 1000, 2000 and 3000 runs in a season
   1000 Runs: 27 May (1938) – D. G. Bradman (Australians)
   2000 Runs: 5 July (1906) – T. W. Hayward (Surrey)
   3000 Runs: 20 August (1906) – T. W. Hayward (Surrey)
   20 August (1937) – W. R. Hammond (Gloucestershire)
Highest batting averages in an English season
   D. G. Bradman achieved the unique distinction of averaging over 80 on each of his four tours of England, each time exceeding the average of the leading home batsman of that season: 98·66 in 1930, 84·16 in 1934, 115·66 in 1938, and 89·92 in 1948.

	Season	Innings	Not Outs	Runs	Average
D. G. Bradman Australians	1938	26	5	2429	115·66
W. A. Johnston Australians	1953	17	16	102	102·00
G. Boycott Yorkshire	1971	30	5	2503	100·12

Carrying bat through *both* innings of a match
H. Jupp	43*	109*	Surrey v Yorkshire at The Oval 1874
S. P. Kinneir	70*	69*	Warwickshire v Leicestershire at Leicester 1907
C. J. B. Wood	107*	117*	Leicestershire v Yorkshire at Bradford 1911
V. M. Merchant	135*	77*	Indians v Lancashire at Liverpool 1936

Fast scoring
Fastest 50: 8 min. C. Inman – Leicestershire v Nottinghamshire at Nottingham 1965
Fastest 100: 35 min. P. G. H. Fender – Surrey v Northamptonshire at Northampton 1920
Fastest 200: 120 min. G. L. Jessop – Gloucestershire v Sussex at Hove 1903
Fastest 300: 181 min. D. C. S. Compton – MCC v North-eastern Transvaal at Benoni 1948-9

Most runs in a day
345 C. G. Macartney – Australians v Nottinghamshire at Nottingham 1921

Most runs off one over
36 (666666) G. St A. Sobers off M. A. Nash – Notts v Glamorgan at Swansea 1968

Most sixes in an innings
15 J. R. Reid – Wellington v Northern Districts at Wellington 1962-3

The most in Britain is 13 by Majid J. Khan (Pakistanis v Glamorgan at Swansea in 1967) and by C. G. Greenidge (D. H. Robins' XI v Pakistanis at Eastbourne in 1974).

Most sixes in a match
17 W. J. Stewart – Warwickshire v Lancashire at Blackpool 1959

Most sixes in a season
72 A. W. Wellard – Somerset 1935

Most boundaries in an innings
68 (all fours) P. A. Perrin (343*) – Essex v Derbyshire at Chesterfield 1904

Slow scoring
Slowest 50: 361 min. T. E. Bailey – England v Australia at Brisbane 1958-9
Slowest 100: 545 min. D. J. McGlew – South Africa v Australia at Durban 1957-8
Slowest 200: 570 min. S. G. Barnes – Australia v England at Sydney 1946-7

Longest time before scoring first run
95 min. T. G. Evans (10*) – England v Australia at Adelaide 1946-7

Longest individual innings
999 min. Hanif Mohammad (337) – Pakistan v West Indies at Bridgetown   1957–8

The longest in England is 800 minutes by L. Hutton (364) for England v *Australia at The Oval in 1938.*

Highest partnership for each wicket
- **1st** 555 P. Holmes (224*), H. Sutcliffe (313): Yorkshire v Essex, Leyton   1932
- **2nd** 465* J. A. Jameson (240*), R. B. Kanhai (213*): Warwickshire v Gloucs., Birmingham   1974
- **3rd** 445 P. E. Whitelaw (195), W. N. Carson (290): Auckland v Otago, Dunedin   1936–7
- **4th** 577 V. S. Hazare (288), Gul Mahomed (319): Baroda v Holkar, Baroda   1946–7
- **5th** 405 S. G. Barnes (234), D. G. Bradman (234): Australia v England, Sydney   1946–7
- **6th** 487* G. A. Headley (344*), C. C. Passailaigue (261*): Jamaica v Tennyson's XI, Kingston   1931–2
- **7th** 347 D. St E. Atkinson (219), C. C. Depeiza (122): West Indies v Australia, Bridgetown   1954–5
- **8th** 433 A. Sims (184*), V. T. Trumper (293): Australian XI v Canterbury, Christchurch   1913–4
- **9th** 283 J. Chapman (165), A. Warren (123): Derbyshire v Warwickshire, Blackwell   1910
- **10th** 307 A. F. Kippax (260*), J. E. H. Hooker (62): New South Wales v Victoria, Melbourne   1928–9

INDIVIDUAL RECORDS—BOWLING

All ten wickets in an innings at least cost
10 for 10 H. Verity – Yorkshire v Nottinghamshire at Leeds   1932

All ten wickets in an innings on most occasions
3 A. P. Freeman:
- 10 for 131 Kent v Lancashire at Maidstone   1929
- 10 for 53 Kent v Essex at Southend   1930
- 10 for 79 Kent v Lancashire at Manchester   1931

Most wickets in a match
19 J. C. Laker (9–37, 10–53) – England v Australia at Manchester   1956

Most wickets in a day
  17 C. Blythe   Kent *v* Northamptonshire at Northampton   1907
  17 H. Verity   Yorkshire *v* Essex at Leyton   1933
  17 T. W. Goddard   Gloucestershire *v* Kent at Bristol 1939

Most wickets in début match
  14 J. Bevan (6–23, 8–36)   South Australia *v* Tasmania at Adelaide   1877–8

Most wickets in a career
  4187 (average 16·71)   W. Rhodes (Yorkshire)   1898–1930

Most wickets in a season
  304 (average 18·05)   A. P. Freeman (Kent)   1928

A. P. Freeman also holds the records for the most balls bowled in a season (12,234 in 1933) and the most runs conceded in a season (5489 in 1928).

Hundred wickets in a season most times
  23 W. Rhodes (Yorkshire)

Earliest dates for taking 100, 200 and 300 wickets in a season
  100 wickets: 12 June (1896) – J. T. Hearne (Middlesex)
                   12 June (1931) – C. W. L. Parker (Gloucestershire)
  200 wickets: 27 July (1928) – A. P. Freeman (Kent)
  300 wickets: 15 Sept (1928) – A. P. Freeman (Kent)

Four wickets with consecutive balls (Since 1946)
  F. Ridgeway   Kent *v* Derbyshire at Folkestone   1951
  A. K. Walker   Nottinghamshire *v* Leicester at Leicester   1956
  S. N. Mohol   Combined XI *v* President's XI at Poona   1965–6
  P. I. Pocock   Surrey *v* Sussex at Eastbourne   1972

A. K. Walker took a wicket with the last ball of the first innings and then a hat-trick with his first three balls in the second innings.

P. I. Pocock established a world record by taking seven wickets in eleven balls: W0W20WWWW1W.

Most hat-tricks in a career
  7 D. V. P. Wright (Kent)   1932–57

Hat-trick twice in same innings
  A. E. Trott   Middlesex *v* Somerset at Lord's   1907

J. S. Rao   Services v Northern Punjab at Amritsar   1963–4

Hat-trick in both innings of a match

A. Shaw   Nottinghamshire v Gloucestershire at Nottingham   1884
T. J. Matthews   Australia v South Africa at Manchester   1912
C. W. L. Parker   Gloucestershire v Middlesex at Bristol   1924
R. O. Jenkins   Worcestershire v Surrey at Worcester   1949

Hat-trick – all stumped

C. L. Townsend   Gloucestershire v Somerset at Cheltenham *(all stumped by W. H. Brain)*   1893

Hat-trick – all lbw

H. Fisher   Yorkshire v Somerset at Sheffield   1932
J. A. Flavell   Worcestershire v Lancashire at Manchester   1963
M. J. Procter   Gloucestershire v Essex at Westcliff   1972
B. J. Ikin   Griqualand West v Orange Free State at Kimberley   1973–4

Most runs conceded in an innings

362   A. A. Mailey   New South Wales v Victoria at Melbourne   1926–7

The most in England is 298 by L. O. Fleetwood-Smith for Australia v England at The Oval in 1938.

Most runs conceded in a match

428   C. S. Nayudu   Holkar v Bombay at Bombay   1944–5

The most in England is 331 by A. P. Freeman for Kent v MCC at Folkestone in 1934.

Most balls bowled in an innings

588   S. Ramadhin   West Indies v England at Birmingham   1957

Most balls bowled in a match

917   C. S. Nayudu   Holkar v Bombay at Bombay   1944–5

The most in England is 774 by S. Ramadhin for West Indies v England at Birmingham in 1957.

Bowlers unchanged through both completed innings of a match (Since 1945)

D. Shackleton and V. H. D. Cannings: Hampshire v Kent at Southampton   1952

D. Shackleton and M. Heath: Hampshire *v* Derbyshire at
Burton upon Trent 1958
Rajinder Pal and P. Sitaram: Delhi *v* Jammu and Kashmir
at Srinagar 1960–1
B. S. Crump and R. R. Bailey: Northamptonshire *v* Glamorgan at Cardiff 1967

Most maiden overs in succession
6-ball overs: 21 R. G. Nadkarni – India *v* England at
Madras 1963–4
The most in England is 17 by H. L. Hazell for Somerset v
Gloucestershire at Taunton in 1949.
8-ball overs: 16 H. J. Tayfield – South Africa *v* England at
Durban 1956–7

Wicket with first ball in first-class cricket
There have been seven instances in Britain since 1945, the most recent being:

| F. C. Brailsford | Derbyshire *v* Sussex at Derby | 1958 |
| W. G. Davies | Glamorgan *v* Surrey at The Oval | 1958 |

INDIVIDUAL RECORDS – ALL-ROUND CRICKET

In 1873 W. G. Grace became the first player to achieve the 'double' of 1000 runs and 100 wickets in a season. D. B. Close of Yorkshire, the youngest player (18) to do the 'double', is the only one to achieve it in the season of his début (1949). The reduction of first-class cricket in Britain has made it virtually impossible for a player to score 1000 runs and take 100 wickets in a season. In 1974 no player managed even a combination of 750 runs and 75 wickets. The last 'double' was achieved in 1967 by F. J. Titmus for Middlesex and England.

Most 'doubles'
16 W. Rhodes (Yorkshire)

Fastest 'double'
28 June (1906) – G. H. Hirst (Yorkshire) in only 16 matches

Outstanding 'doubles'
  1000 runs and 200 wickets: A. E. Trott (Middlesex) in
1899 and 1900
A. S. Kennedy (Hampshire)
in 1922
M. W. Tate (Sussex) in

1923, 1924 and 1925
2000 runs and 200 wickets: G. H. Hirst (Yorkshire) in 1906
3000 runs and 100 wickets: J. H. Parks (Sussex) in 1937
Outstanding match doubles
CENTURY AND TEN WICKETS IN ONE INNINGS

V. E. Walker	England XI v Surrey at The Oval	1859
E. M. Grace	MCC v Gentlemen of Kent at Canterbury	1862
W. G. Grace	MCC v Oxford University at Oxford	1886
F. A. Tarrant	Maharaja of Cooch Behar's XI v Lord Willingdon's XI at Poona	1918–19

CENTURY IN EACH INNINGS AND FIVE WICKETS TWICE

G. H. Hirst Yorkshire v Somerset at Bath 1906

CENTURY AND HAT-TRICK (Since 1945)

V. M. Merchant	Dr C. R. Pereira's XI v Sir Homi Mehta's XI at Bombay	1946–7
M. J. Procter	Gloucestershire v Essex at Westcliff	1972

INDIVIDUAL RECORDS – WICKET-KEEPING

Most dismissals (and catches) in an innings
8 (8 ct) A. T. W. Grout Queensland v Western Australia at Brisbane 1959–60

The most in Britain is seven, achieved on nine occasions – the most recent being by E. W. Jones (6ct, 1st) for Glamorgan v Cambridge University at Cambridge in 1970.

Most stumpings in an innings
6 H. Yarnold Worcestershire v Scotland at Broughty Ferry 1951

Most dismissals in a match
12 (8ct, 4st) E. Pooley Surrey v Sussex at The Oval 1868
12 (9ct, 3st) D. Tallon Queensland v New South Wales at Sydney 1938–9
12 (9ct, 3st) H. B. Taber New South Wales v S. Australia at Adelaide 1968–9

Most catches in a match
11 A. Long Surrey v Sussex at Hove 1964

Most stumpings in a match
9 F. H. Huish Kent v Surrey at The Oval 1911

Most dismissals (and catches) in a career
1493 (1235ct, 258st) H. Strudwick (Surrey)   1902–27
1482 (1230ct, 252st) J. T. Murray (Middlesex)   1952–74

J. T. Murray, who has announced his intention to retire from first-class cricket after the 1975 season, needs only six catches and twelve dismissals to claim both of H. Strudwick's world records.

Most stumpings in a career
415 L. E. G. Ames (Kent)   1926–51

Most dismissals in a season
127 L. E. G. Ames (Kent) – 79ct, 48st   1929

Most catches in a season
96 J. G. Binks (Yorkshire)   1960

Most stumpings in a season
64 L. E. G. Ames (Kent)   1932

Wicket-keepers' double of 1000 runs and 100 dismissals in a season
L. E. G. Ames (Kent) in 1928, 1929 and 1932
J. T. Murray (Middlesex) in 1957

Largest innings without byes
672–7 dec. A. P. Wickham Somerset *v* Hampshire at Taunton 1899

INDIVIDUAL RECORDS – FIELDING

Most catches in an innings
7 M. J. Stewart Surrey *v* Northamptonshire at Northampton 1957
7 A. S. Brown   Gloucestershire *v* Nottinghamshire at Nottingham 1966

Most catches in a match
10 W. R. Hammond Gloucestershire *v* Surrey at Cheltenham 1928

Most catches in a season
78 W. R. Hammond (Gloucestershire)   1928

Most catches in a career
1011 F. E. Woolley (Kent)   1906–38

PART II – TEST MATCH RECORDS
Complete to 9 July 1975

Abbreviations

A	Australia	RW	Rest of the World
E	England	SA	South Africa
I	India	WI	West Indies
NZ	New Zealand	T	Tie
P	Pakistan	D	Draw

Results summary
Test matches 1876-7 to 1974-5

		Tests	E	A	SA	WI	NZ	I	P	RW	T	D
England	v Australia	220	71	86	—	—	—	—	—	—	—	63
	v South Africa	102	46	—	18	—	—	—	—	—	—	38
	v West Indies	66	21	—	—	19	—	—	—	—	—	26
	v New Zealand	47	23	—	—	—	0	—	—	—	—	24
	v India	48	22	—	—	—	—	6	—	—	—	20
	v Pakistan	27	9	—	—	—	—	—	1	—	—	17
	v Rest of the World	5	1	—	—	—	—	—	—	4	—	0
Australia	v South Africa	53	—	29	11	—	—	—	—	—	—	13
	v West Indies	35	—	19	—	6	—	—	—	—	1	9
	v New Zealand	7	—	4	—	—	1	—	—	—	—	2
	v India	25	—	16	—	—	—	3	—	—	—	6
	v Pakistan	9	—	5	—	—	—	—	1	—	—	3
South Africa	v New Zealand	17	—	—	9	—	2	—	—	—	—	6
West Indies	v New Zealand	14	—	—	—	5	2	—	—	—	—	7
	v India	33	—	—	—	15	—	3	—	—	—	15
	v Pakistan	10	—	—	—	4	—	—	3	—	—	3
New Zealand	v India	16	—	—	—	—	2	7	—	—	—	7
	v Pakistan	15	—	—	—	—	1	—	5	—	—	9
India	v Pakistan	15	—	—	—	—	—	2	1	—	—	12
		764	193	159	38	49	8	21	11	4	1	280

	Tests	Won	Lost	Drawn	Tied	Toss Won
England	515	193	134	188	—	256
Australia	349	159	93	96	1	170
South Africa	172	38	77	57	—	80
West Indies	158	49	48	60	1	87
New Zealand	116	8	53	55	—	58
India	137	21	56	60	—	68
Pakistan	76	11	21	44	—	43
Rest of the World	5	4	1	0	—	2

TEAM RECORDS

Highest innings total
903–7 dec.   England v Australia at The Oval   1938

Highest fourth innings totals
To Win: 404–3   Australia v England at Leeds   1948
To Draw: 654–5   England v South Africa at Durban
   1938–9
To Lose: 440   New Zealand v England at Nottingham
   1973

Highest match aggregate
1981 for 35 wkts South Africa v England at Durban 1938–9
The highest in England is 1723 for 31 wkts in the 1948 Leeds Test between England (496 and 365–8 dec.) and Australia (458 and 404–3).

Lowest innings total
26   New Zealand v England at Auckland   1954–5
The lowest in England is 30 by South Africa v England at Birmingham in 1924.

Lowest match aggregate (completed match)
234 for 29 wkts   Australia v South Africa at Melbourne
   1931–2
The lowest in England is 291 for 40 wkts in the 1888 Lord's Test between England (53 and 62) and Australia (116 and 60).

Largest margin of victory
Innings and 579 runs   England beat Australia at The Oval
   1938

The only Test tie
Australia (505 and 232) v West Indies (453 and 284) at Brisbane   1960–1

Longest match
10 days   South Africa v England at Durban   1938–9

Side dismissed twice in a day
England (65 and 72) v Australia at Sydney (3rd day)
   1894–5
India (58 and 82) v England at Manchester (3rd day) 1952

Most runs in one day
One Team: 503–2   England v South Africa at Lord's 1924
Both Teams: 588–6   England (398–6) v India (190–0) at Manchester   1936

Fewest runs in a day's play
 95   Australia (80) v Pakistan (15-2) at Karachi   1956-7
In England: 159 Pakistan (142-6) v England (17-1) at Leeds in 1971.

Most hundreds in an innings
 5   Australia v West Indies at Kingston   1954-5

INDIVIDUAL RECORDS - BATTING

Highest individual innings
 365*   G. St A. Sobers   West Indies v Pakistan at Kingston
      1957-8
In England: 364 L. Hutton - England v Australia at The Oval in 1938.

Most runs in a match
 380   G. S. Chappell (247* and 133) - Australia v New Zealand at Wellington   1973-4

Most hundreds in successive innings
 5   E. de C. Weekes (West Indies)   1947-8 and 1948-9

Most runs in Tests
 8620 (av 58.63)   G. St A. Sobers (West Indies 8032; Rest of the World 588)

Most runs in a series
 974 (av 139.14)   D. G. Bradman - Australia v England
      1930

Highest career average
 99.94   D. G. Bradman (Australia) - 6996 runs in 52 Tests

Most hundreds in Tests
 29   D. G. Bradman: 19 v E, 4 v SA, 2 v WI, 4 v I.

Most innings of fifty and over
 63   M. C. Cowdrey (England): 16 v A, 10 v SA, 16 v WI, 10 v NZ, 5 v I, 3 v P, 3 v RW.

Most runs in a day
 309   D. G. Bradman (334) - Australia v England at Leeds
      1930

Most runs off one over
  6-ball: 22   M. W. Tate and W. Voce off A. E. Hall - E v SA at Johannesburg   1930-1
         22   R. C. Motz off D. A. Allen - NZ v E at Dunedin   1965-6

8-ball: 25   B. Sutcliffe and R. W. Blair off H. J. Tayfield –
NZ v SA at Johannesburg   1953–4

Most boundaries in an innings
57 (5 sixes, 52 fours)   J. H. Edrich (310*) – E v NZ at
Leeds   1965

Most sixes in an innings
10   ˙W. R. Hammond (336*) – E v NZ at Auckland 1932–3

Highest partnerships for each wicket

1st	413	V. Mankad, P. Roy	I v NZ	Madras	1955–6
2nd	451	W. H. Ponsford, D. G. Bradman	A v E	The Oval	1934
3rd	370	W. J. Edrich, D. C. S. Compton	E v SA	Lord's	1947
4th	411	P. B. H. May, M. C. Cowdrey	E v WI	Birmingham	1957
5th	405	S. G. Barnes, D. G. Bradman	A v E	Sydney	1946–7
6th	346	J. H. W. Fingleton, D. G. Bradman	A v E	Melbourne	1936–7
7th	347	D. St E. Atkinson, C. C. Depeiza	WI v A	Bridgetown	1954–5
8th	246	L. E. G. Ames, G. O. B. Allen	E v NZ	Lord's	1931
9th	190	Asif Iqbal, Intikhab Alam	P v E	The Oval	1967
10th	151	B. F. Hastings, R. O. Collinge	NZ v P	Auckland	1972–3

Batsman sharing in most hundred partnerships
G. St A. Sobers (46) – West Indies 42, Rest of the World 4 –
in 169 innings

INDIVIDUAL RECORDS – BOWLING

All ten wickets in an innings
J. C. Laker (10 for 53) – England v Australia at Manchester
1956

Most wickets in a match
19   J. C. Laker (9–37, 10–53) – England v Australia at
Manchester   1956

Most wickets in Tests
 307 (av 21·57)   F. S. Trueman (England) in 67 Tests
Most wickets in a series
 49 (av 10·93)   S. F. Barnes – England v South Africa (4 Tests)   1913–4
 In England: 46 (av 9·60) J. C. Laker – England v Australia (5 Tests) 1956.
Most wickets in début match
 16   R. A. L. Massie (8–84, 8–53) – Australia v England at Lord's   1972
Wicket with first ball in Tests (Since 1945)
 R. Howorth   England v South Africa at The Oval   1947
 Intikhab Alam   Pakistan v Australia at Karachi   1959–60
Hat-tricks (Since 1945)
 P. J. Loader   England v West Indies at Leeds   1957
 L. F. Kline   Australia v South Africa at Cape Town 1957–8
 W. W. Hall   West Indies v Pakistan at Lahore   1958–9
 G. M. Griffin   South Africa v England at Lord's   1960
 L. R. Gibbs   West Indies v Australia at Adelaide   1960–1
 E. J. Barlow   Rest of the World v England at Leeds   1970
Most runs conceded in an innings
 298   L. O. Fleetwood-Smith (87–11–298–1) – A v E at The Oval   1938
Most runs conceded in a match
 374   O. C. Scott (105·2–13–374–9) – WI v E at Kingston   1929–30
Most balls bowled in an innings
 588   S. Ramadhin (98–35–179–2) – WI v E at Birmingham   1957
Most balls bowled in a match
 774   S. Ramadhin (129–51–228–9) – WI v E at Birmingham   1957

INDIVIDUAL RECORDS – ALL-ROUND CRICKET
Hundred runs and ten wickets in a match
 A. K. Davidson (44 and 80; 5–135 and 6–87) – A v WI at Brisbane   1960–1
Century and seven wickets in first innings of a match
 J. M. Gregory (100 and 7–69) – A v E at Melbourne   1920–1

Century and five wickets on début
B. R. Taylor (105 and 5–86) – NZ *v* I at Calcutta   1964–5

2000 runs and 200 wickets in Tests

	Tests	Runs	Wkts
G. St A. Sobers (WI and RW)	98	8620	256
R. Benaud (A)	63	2201	248

INDIVIDUAL RECORDS – WICKET-KEEPING

Most dismissals in an innings
6 (all ct) A. T. W. Grout   A *v* SA at Johannesburg   1957–8
6 (all ct) D. Lindsay   SA *v* A at Johannesburg   1966–7
6 (all ct) J. T. Murray   E *v* I at Lord's   1967

Most dismissals in a match
9 (8ct, 1st) G. R. A. Langley   A *v* E at Lord's   1956

Most dismissals and catches in Tests
225 (209ct, 16st) A. P. E. Knott (England) in 74 Tests
                                                         1967–75

Most stumpings in Tests
52   W. A. S. Oldfield (Australia) in 54 Tests   1920–36

Most dismissals in a series
26 (23ct, 3st) J. H. B. Waite SA *v* NZ (5 Tests)   1961–2
In England: 24 (22ct, 2st) D. L. Murray – WI v E in 1963.

Most catches in a series
24   D. Lindsay   SA *v* A (5 Tests)   1966–7

Largest innings without byes
659–8 dec.   T. G. Evans   E *v* A at Sydney   1946–7
In England: 551–9 dec. A. P. E. Knott – E v NZ at Lord's in 1973.

INDIVIDUAL RECORDS – FIELDING

Most catches in an innings
5   V. Y. Richardson   A *v* SA at Durban   1935–6

Most catches in a match
7   G. S. Chappell   A *v* E at Perth   1974–5

Most catches in Tests
124   M. C. Cowdrey (England) in 118 Tests   1954–75

Most catches in a series
15   J. M. Gregory   A *v* E (5 Tests)   1920–1

MISCELLANEOUS RECORDS
Most Test appearances
  118   M. C. Cowdrey (England)   1954-75
Most Tests as captain
  44   G. St A. Sobers (WI 39, RW 5)   1965-72
Youngest Test player
  15 years 124 days   Mushtaq Mohammad – P v WI (Lahore)   1958-9
Oldest Test player
  52 years 165 days   W. Rhodes – E v WI (Kingston)   1929-30
Most Tests as umpire
  48   F. Chester (officiated in England)   1924-55

PART III – ENGLAND v AUSTRALIA RECORDS
RESULTS

Season	England	Australia	Tests	Won by England	Won by Australia	Drawn
1876-7	James Lillywhite	D. W. Gregory	2	1	1	0
1878-9	Lord Harris	D. W. Gregory	1	0	1	0
1880	Lord Harris	W. L. Murdoch	1	1	0	0
1881-2	A. Shaw	W. L. Murdoch	4	0	2	2
1882	A. N. Hornby	W. L. Murdoch	1	0	1	0
1882-3	Hon. Ivo Bligh	W. L. Murdoch	4	2	2	0
1884	Lord Harris[1]	W. L. Murdoch	3	1	0	2
1884-5	A. Shrewsbury	T. Horan[2]	5	3	2	0
1886	A. G. Steel	H. J. H. Scott	3	3	0	0
1886-7	A. Shrewsbury	P. S. McDonnell	2	2	0	0
1887-8	W. W. Read	P. S. McDonnell	1	1	0	0
1888	W. G. Grace[3]	P. S. McDonnell	3	2	1	0
1890†	W. G. Grace	W. L. Murdoch	2	2	0	0
1891-2	W. G. Grace	J. M. Blackham	3	1	2	0
1893	W. G. Grace[4]	J. M. Blackham	3	1	0	2
1894-5	A. E. Stoddart	G. Giffen	5	3	2	0
1896	W. G. Grace	G. H. S. Trott	3	2	1	0
1897-8	A. E. Stoddart[6]	G. H. S. Trott	5	1	4	0
1899	A. C. MacLaren[7]	J. Darling	5	0	1	4
1901-2	A. C. MacLaren	J. Darling[8]	5	1	4	0
1902	A. C. MacLaren	J. Darling	5	1	2	2
1903-4	P. F. Warner	M. A. Noble	5	3	2	0
1905	Hon. F. S. Jackson	J. Darling	5	2	0	3
1907-8	A. O. Jones[9]	M. A. Noble	5	1	4	0
1909	A. C. MacLaren	M. A. Noble	5	1	2	2
1911-12	J. W. H. T. Douglas	C. Hill	5	4	1	0
1912	C. B. Fry	S. E. Gregory	3	1	0	2
1920-1	J. W. H. T. Douglas	W. W. Armstrong	5	0	5	0
1921	Hon. L. H. Tennyson[10]	W. W. Armstrong	5	0	3	2

1924–5	A. E. R. Gilligan	H. L. Collins	5	1	4	0
1926	A. W. Carr[11]	H. L. Collins[12]	5	1	0	4
1928–9	A. P. F. Chapman[13]	J. Ryder	5	4	1	0
1930	A. P. F. Chapman[14]	W. M. Woodfull	5	1	2	2
1932–3	D. R. Jardine	W. M. Woodfull	5	4	1	0
1934	R. E. S. Wyatt[15]	W. M. Woodfull	5	1	2	2
1936–7	G. O. B. Allen	D. G. Bradman	5	2	3	0
1938†	W. R. Hammond	D. G. Bradman	4	1	1	2
1946–7	W. R. Hammond[16]	D. G. Bradman	5	0	3	2
1948	N. W. D. Yardley	D. G. Bradman	5	0	4	1
1950–1	F. R. Brown	A. L. Hassett	5	1	4	0
1953	L. Hutton	A. L. Hassett	5	1	0	4
1954–5	L. Hutton	I. W. Johnson[17]	5	3	1	1
1956	P. B. H. May	I. W. Johnson	5	2	1	2
1958–9	P. B. H. May	R. Benaud	5	0	4	1
1961	P. B. H. May[18]	R. Benaud[19]	5	1	2	2
1962–3	E. R. Dexter	R. Benaud	5	1	1	3
1964	E. R. Dexter	R. B. Simpson	5	0	1	4
1965–6	M. J. K. Smith	R. B. Simpson[20]	5	1	1	3
1968	M. C. Cowdrey[21]	W. M. Lawry[22]	5	1	1	3
1970–1†	R. Illingworth	W. M. Lawry[23]	6	2	0	4
1972	R. Illingworth	I. M. Chappell	5	2	2	1
1974–5	M. H. Denness[24]	I. M. Chappell	6	1	4	1

In Australia	119	43	59	17
In England	101	28	27	46
Totals	220	71	86	63

†The matches at Manchester in 1890 and 1938 and at Melbourne (Third Test) in 1970–1 were abandoned without a ball being bowled and are excluded.

The following deputised for the official touring captain or were appointed by the home authority for only a minor proportion of the series:
[1]A. N. Hornby (First). [2]W. L. Murdoch (First), H. H. Massie (Third), J. M. Blackham (Fourth). [3]A. G. Steel (First). [4]A. E. Stoddart (First). [5]J. M. Blackham (First). [6]A. C. MacLaren (First, Second and Fifth). [7]W. G. Grace (First). [8]H. Trumble (Fourth and Fifth). [9]F. L. Fane (First, Second and Third). [10]J. W. H. T. Douglas (First and Second). [11]A. P. F. Chapman (Fifth). [12]W. Bardsley (Third and Fourth). [13]J. C. White (Fifth). [14]R. E. S. Wyatt (Fifth). [15] C. F. Walters (First). [16]N. W. D. Yardley (Fifth). [17]A. R. Morris (Second). [18]M. C. Cowdrey (First and Second). [19]R. N. Harvey (Second). [20]B. C. Booth (First and Third). [21]T. W. Graveney (Fourth). [22]B. N. Jarman (Fourth). [23]I. M. Chappell (Seventh). [24]J. H. Edrich (Fourth).

Highest innings totals
England in England	903–7d	The Oval	1938
England in Australia	636	Sydney	1928–9
Australia in England	729–6d	Lord's	1930
Australia in Australia	659–8d	Sydney	1946–7

Lowest innings totals
England in England	52	The Oval	1948
England in Australia	45	Sydney	1886–7
Australia in England	36	Birmingham	1902
Australia in Australia	42	Sydney	1887–8

Highest match aggregate
1753–40 wkts	Adelaide	1920–1

Lowest match aggregate

| | 291–40 wkts | Lord's | 1888 |

Highest individual innings

England in England	364 L. Hutton	The Oval	1938
England in Australia	287 R. E. Foster	Sydney	1903–4
Australia in England	334 D. G. Bradman	Leeds	1930
Australia in Australia	307 R. M. Cowper	Melbourne	1965–6

Best innings bowling analyses

England in England	10–53 J. C. Laker	Manchester	1956
England in Australia	8–35 G. A. Lohmann	Sydney	1886–7
Australia in England	8–31 F. Laver	Manchester	1909
Australia in Australia	9–121 A. A. Mailey	Melbourne	1920–1

Best match bowling analyses

England in England	19–90 J. C. Laker	Manchester	1956
England in Australia	15–124 W. Rhodes	Melbourne	1903–4
Australia in England	16–137 R. A. L. Massie	Lord's	1972
Australia in Australia	13–77 M. A. Noble	Melbourne	1901–2

Highest batting aggregate in a series

England in England	562 (av 62·44)	D. C. S. Compton	1948
England in Australia	905 (av 113·12)	W. R. Hammond	1928–9
Australia in England	974 (av 139·14)	D. G. Bradman	1930
Australia in Australia	810 (av 90·00)	D. G. Bradman	1936–7

Highest wicket aggregate in a series

England in England	46 (av 9·60)	J. C. Laker	1956
England in Australia	38 (av 23·18)	M. W. Tate	1924–5
Australia in England	31 (av 17·67)	D. K. Lillee	1972
Australia in Australia	36 (av 26·27)	A. A. Mailey	1920–1

Highest wicket partnerships – England

1st	323	J. B. Hobbs and W. Rhodes	Melbourne	1911–12
2nd	382	L. Hutton and M. Leyland	The Oval	1938
3rd	262	W. R. Hammond and D. R. Jardine	Adelaide	1928–9
4th	222	W. R. Hammond and E. Paynter	Lord's	1938
5th	206	E. Paynter and D. C. S. Compton	Nottingham	1938
6th	215	L. Hutton and J. Hardstaff jr	The Oval	1938
7th	143	F. E. Woolley and J. Vine	Sydney	1911–12
8th	124	E. H. Hendren and H. Larwood	Brisbane	1928–9
9th	151	W. H. Scotton and W. W. Read	The Oval	1884
10th	130	R. E. Foster and W. Rhodes	Sydney	1903–4

Highest wicket partnerships – Australia

1st	244	R. B. Simpson and W. M. Lawry	Adelaide	1965–6
2nd	451	W. H. Ponsford and D. G. Bradman	The Oval	1934
3rd	276	D. G. Bradman and A. L. Hassett	Brisbane	1946–7
4th	388	W. H. Ponsford and D. G. Bradman	Leeds	1934
5th	405	S. G. Barnes and D. G. Bradman	Sydney	1946–7
6th	346	J. H. W. Fingleton and D. G. Bradman	Melbourne	1936–7
7th	165	C. Hill and H. Trumble	Melbourne	1897–8
8th	243	R. J. Hartigan and C. Hill	Adelaide	1907–8
9th	154	S. E. Gregory and J. M. Blackham	Sydney	1894–5
10th	127	J. M. Taylor and A. A. Mailey	Sydney	1924–5

The 1974 Season

COUNTY CHAMPIONSHIP
FINAL TABLE

		P	W	D	L	T	Bonus Points Batting	Bowling	Total Points
1	WORCESTERSHIRE (6)	20	11	3	6	–	45	72	227
2	Hampshire (1)	19	10	3	6	–	55	70	225
3	Northamptonshire (3)	20	9	2	9	–	46	67	203
4	Leicestershire (9)	20	7	7	6	–	47	69	186
5	Somerset (10)	20	6	4	10	–	49	72	181
6	Middlesex (13)	20	7	5	8	–	45	56	171
7	Surrey (2)	20	6	4	10	–	42	69	171
8	Lancashire (12)	20	5	0	15	–	47	66	163
9	Warwickshire (7)	20	5	5	10	–	44	65	159
10	Kent (4)	20	5	8	7	–	33	63	146
11	Yorkshire (14)	19	4	7	8	–	37	69	146
12	Essex (8)	20	4	3	12	1	44	52	141
13	Sussex (15)	20	4	9	6	1	29	63	137
14	Gloucestershire (5)	19	4	9	6	–	29	55	124
15	Nottinghamshire (17)	20	1	9	10	–	42	66	118
16	Glamorgan (11)	19	2	7	10	–	28	56	104
17	Derbyshire (16)	20	1	6	13	–	23	62	95

Figures in brackets show the 1973 positions.
The matches between Hampshire and Yorkshire at Bournemouth (August 31, September 2, 3) and Gloucestershire and Glamorgan at Bristol (September 4, 5, 6) were abandoned without a ball being bowled.

THE GILLETTE CUP
Won by Kent who beat Lancashire by 4 wickets in the Final at Lord's on Monday, 9 September.

THE BENSON AND HEDGES CUP
Won by Surrey who beat Leicestershire by 27 runs in the Final at Lord's on 20 July.

THE 1974 SEASON

JOHN PLAYER LEAGUE

	FINAL TABLE	P	W	L	T	NR	Pts	Run-rate	6s	4w
1	LEICESTERSHIRE (5)	16	12	1	1	2	54	4·79	20	3
2	Somerset (11)	16	12	2	–	2	52	4·72	49	3
3	Kent (1)	16	10	4	–	2	44	4·50	13	2
4	Northamptonshire (17)	16	10	6	–	–	40	4·35	20	6
	Hampshire (3)	16	9	5	–	2	40	4·52	30	3
6	Sussex (7)	16	8	6	1	1	36	4·24	18	5
	Yorkshire (2)	16	8	6	–	2	36	4·33	42	4
8	Middlesex (7)	16	7	7	1	1	32	4·32	20	2
	Worcestershire (15)	16	7	7	–	2	32	4·57	19	2
10	Surrey (9)	16	7	8	–	1	30	4·41	23	5
	Warwickshire (15)	16	7	8	–	1	30	4·42	28	6
12	Lancashire (4)	16	5	9	1	1	24	4·09	21	2
	Gloucestershire (6)	16	4	8	–	4	24	4·22	21	3
14	Glamorgan (13)	16	5	10	–	1	22	3·94	26	5
15	Derbyshire (12)	16	4	11	–	1	18	4·17	29	2
	Essex (9)	16	4	11	–	1	18	3·89	18	4
17	Nottinghamshire (13)	16	3	13	–	–	12	4·08	12	2

Figures in brackets show the 1973 positions. Run-rate no longer being the deciding factor, counties with an equal number of points now share that particular placing.

FIRST-CLASS AVERAGES 1974

BATTING (Qualifications: 8 innings, average 10) *Not out

	M	I	NO	HS	Runs	Av	100	50
C. H. Lloyd	20	31	8	178*	1458	63·39	4	7
B. A. Richards	19	27	4	225*	1406	61·13	4	6
G. M. Turner	20	31	9	202*	1332	60·54	3	5
G. Boycott	21	36	6	160*	1783	59·43	6	8
R. T. Virgin	23	39	5	144*	1936	56·94	7	10
D. L. Amiss	18	31	3	195	1510	53·92	5	4
J. H. Edrich	16	23	2	152*	1126	53·61	3	6
J. H. Hampshire	14	23	6	158	901	53·00	2	3
R. B. Kanhai	14	22	4	213*	936	52·00	3	4
J. A. Jameson	24	42	2	240*	1932	48·30	6	7
G. St. A. Sobers	15	27	4	132*	1110	48·26	4	6
D. Lloyd	15	22	2	214*	958	47·90	3	3
B. F. Davison	24	39	3	142	1670	46·38	4	11
Zaheer Abbas	21	30	4	240	1182	45·46	5	2
M. J. Khan	20	35	3	164	1451	45·34	5	6
B. L. D'Oliveira	18	26	3	227	1026	44·60	2	4
M. J. Harris	23	41	3	133	1690	44·47	6	7
M. J. Smith	22	38	4	170*	1468	43·17	3	7
J. M. Brearley	21	36	5	173*	1324	42·70	2	7
Sadiq Mohammad	19	32	2	106	1278	42·60	2	10
H. Pilling	19	28	7	144	869	41·38	2	3
M. H. Denness	15	21	2	118	760	40·00	3	1
P. J. Watts	21	33	7	104*	1040	40·00	1	7
S. J. Storey	17	23	4	111	744	39·15	2	3
P. J. Graves	21	39	6	145*	1282	38·84	3	7
M. J. K. Smith	23	38	8	105	1159	38·63	1	8

	M	I	NO	HS	Runs	Av	100	50
R. D. V. Knight	23	40	5	144	1350	38·57	4	4
K. W. R. Fletcher	16	25	4	123*	809	38·52	3	3
M. C. Cowdrey	21	30	3	122	1027	38·03	5	3
R. M. C. Gilliat	21	29	3	106	977	37·57	1	8
M. J. Kitchen	13	24	2	88	819	37·22	–	7
D. B. Close	24	40	9	114*	1153	37·19	1	5
B. Dudleston	24	41	5	135	1337	37·13	4	4
J. C. Balderstone	14	23	2	140	775	36·90	1	6
R. G. A. Headley	19	31	2	137	1064	36·68	3	5
L. G. Rowe	17	30	1	94	1059	36·51	–	7
Imran Khan	19	31	3	170	1016	36·28	4	1
D. R. Turner	21	29	2	152	977	36·18	3	5
A. Hill	10	19	4	140*	539	35·93	2	2
L. W. Hill	14	24	4	96*	718	35·90	–	6
F. C. Hayes	25	39	2	187	1311	35·43	3	7
A. I. Kallicharran	24	39	2	132	1309	35·37	3	7
C. G. Greenidge	22	33	2	273*	1093	35·25	2	6
C. T. Radley	24	40	5	111*	1231	35·17	3	5
K. L. Snellgrove	11	17	4	75*	454	34·92	–	1
M. J. Procter	19	33	3	157	1033	34·43	2	6
B. R. Hardie	21	36	2	133	1168	34·35	2	5
E. J. O. Hemsley	10	15	2	120*	442	34·00	1	2
G. R. J. Roope	21	33	6	119	907	33·59	1	4
J. Simmons	20	25	11	75	466	33·28	–	2
P. J. Sainsbury	21	26	8	98	599	33·27	–	4
S. Turner	22	33	4	118*	963	33·20	1	6
I. V. A. Richards	23	38	1	107	1223	33·05	2	6
M. J. Smedley	23	41	6	118*	1134	32·40	1	6
F. M. Engineer	15	26	5	108	680	32·38	1	4
B. W. Luckhurst	22	35	2	148	1067	32·33	2	4
N. G. Featherstone	22	35	4	125	996	32·12	2	4
A. Jones	20	36	1	113	1121	32·02	2	6
Mushtaq Mohammad	21	34	3	101*	973	31·38	1	6
Younis Ahmed	19	33	4	116	907	31·27	1	4
D. S. Steele	21	36	3	104	1022	30·96	1	7
A. Kennedy	16	26	2	81	742	30·91	–	6
G. A. Greenidge	21	42	3	147	1187	30·43	2	4
K. S. McEwan	22	37	2	126	1056	30·17	2	4
B. Leadbeater	19	31	4	99*	804	29·77	–	5
R. W. Tolchard	24	34	9	103	743	29·72	1	3
C. J. C. Rowe	14	16	8	58*	237	29·62	–	1
G. W. Johnson	23	37	2	158	1029	29·40	1	8
J. M. Parker	17	27	1	140	760	29·23	2	3
T. R. Glover	5	10	1	103*	262	29·11	1	–
G. A. Gooch	15	25	3	114*	637	28·95	1	2
R. M. O. Cooke	18	29	4	100	718	28·72	1	3
P. R. Thackeray	8	15	4	65*	315	28·63	–	2
T. J. Yardley	22	31	8	66*	656	28·52	–	5
C. J. Aworth	17	29	2	97	767	28·40	–	6
D. J. S. Taylor	23	40	5	179	994	28·40	1	5
R. A. Woolmer	23	34	4	112	840	28·00	3	1
J. B. Bolus	22	38	6	112	892	27·87	1	5
D. Breakwell	19	28	7	67	585	27·85	–	2
Asif Iqbal	16	24	2	80	611	27·77	–	4
B. Hassan	23	43	6	83*	1009	27·27	–	9

THE 1974 SEASON

	M	I	NO	HS	Runs	Av	100	50
J. T. Murray	22	28	4	82*	654	27.25	–	4
G. P. Howarth	17	30	2	98	751	26.82	–	4
R. G. D. Willis	19	22	16	24	159	26.50	–	–
J. F. Steele	24	41	5	116*	953	26.47	1	5
C. M. Old	18	22	2	116	529	26.45	1	2
R. G. Lumb	18	31	2	123*	763	26.31	2	2
B. Wood	22	35	1	101	893	26.26	1	4
A. J. Harvey-Walker	17	29	1	117	727	25.96	1	4
H. T. Tunnicliffe	11	19	5	87	357	25.50	–	2
J. N. Shepherd	21	30	6	79	609	25.37	–	2
D. R. Shepherd	19	30	0	101	747	24.90	2	3
A. W. Greig	18	28	1	106	669	24.77	1	4
R. N. Abberley	14	23	0	99	567	24.65	–	2
R. B. Nicholls	13	23	2	68	512	24.38	–	6
D. Nicholls	16	22	2	77	487	24.35	–	2
R. C. Davis	19	34	3	73	752	24.25	–	6
S. J. Rouse	9	13	3	55	242	24.20	–	1
A. W. Stovold	15	28	1	102	652	24.14	1	2
J. Birkenshaw	23	29	7	70*	530	24.09	–	1
G. D. Barlow	12	21	2	70	457	24.05	–	4
M. G. Griffith	11	20	3	121*	408	24.00	1	2
E. E. Hemmings	23	32	5	74	645	23.88	–	3
M. J. J. Faber	15	28	3	112*	593	23.72	1	2
R. Illingworth	21	27	8	67	448	23.57	–	2
F. W. Swarbrook	20	32	11	65	490	23.33	–	2
P. Willey	23	37	3	100*	790	23.23	1	2
T. W. Cartwright	7	8	0	68	185	23.12	–	1
J. M. Parks	22	36	5	66	717	23.12	–	2
C. A. Milton	12	19	1	76	413	22.94	–	2
G. R. Stephenson	21	24	7	69*	390	22.94	–	2
R. D. Jackman	20	27	6	92*	481	22.90	–	5
A. G. E. Ealham	22	33	3	73	686	22.86	–	4
Sarfraz Nawaz	17	21	7	53	317	22.64	–	1
J. W. Solanky	15	25	5	71	452	22.60	–	3
G. P. Ellis	10	18	2	116	356	22.25	1	–
M. H. Page	18	29	0	91	645	22.24	–	4
D. L. Murray	22	34	2	78	707	22.09	–	2
T. E. Jesty	21	28	2	90	571	21.96	–	3
N. M. McVicker	24	25	5	64	438	21.90	–	3
R. I. Smyth	10	20	0	61	438	21.90	–	3
M. N. S. Taylor	21	24	2	68	479	21.77	–	3
R. E. East	22	31	6	64	544	21.76	–	4
A. R. Lewis	13	23	1	95	477	21.68	–	3
R. O. Butcher	5	8	1	53*	150	21.42	–	1
G. Cook	23	37	2	85	746	21.31	–	5
D. W. Randall	22	42	4	105	804	21.15	1	4
J. D. Morley	22	43	2	85	864	21.07	–	6
B. E. A. Edmeades	19	33	1	54*	673	21.03	–	2
J. A. Ormrod	22	34	2	82	673	21.03	–	3
Intikhab Alam	20	28	3	62	525	21.00	–	5
A. Tait	16	26	0	99	545	20.96	–	4
K. D. Boyce	12	16	0	75	335	20.93	–	1
B. K. Gardom	14	20	2	79*	374	20.77	–	2
L. E. Skinner	10	18	0	84	364	20.22	–	2
N. G. Cowley	11	13	1	43	242	20.16	–	–

	M	I	NO	HS	Runs	Av	100	50
P. Carrick	12	13	3	46	196	19.60	–	–
D. P. Russell	8	16	1	56*	291	19.40	–	2
A. C. Smith	18	23	4	39	368	19.36	–	–
G. Miller	19	29	2	53	518	19.18	–	1
A. G. Nicholson	16	16	8	50	153	19.12	–	1
H. Cartwright	7	11	2	43*	172	19.11	–	–
P. H. Edmonds	22	31	7	57	453	18.87	–	1
H. G. Wilcock	14	19	3	44	302	18.87	–	–
P. W. Denning	21	35	1	60	641	18.85	–	2
R. A. Hutton	18	25	5	102*	376	18.80	1	–
M. J. Llewellyn	9	17	0	61	318	18.70	–	1
E. W. Jones	19	30	6	67	445	18.54	–	2
E. D. Fursdon	11	18	5	55	239	18.38	–	1
D. L. Bairstow	23	32	3	79	533	18.37	–	4
D. A. Francis	9	15	5	52*	183	18.30	–	1
F. J. Titmus	22	26	6	81*	366	18.30	–	1
P. J. Squires	13	21	3	67	329	18.27	–	2
J. G. Tolchard	19	26	3	64*	419	18.21	–	2
R. K. Baker	11	20	0	51	364	18.20	–	1
D. P. Hughes	22	29	7	62	399	18.13	–	2
A. S. Brown	21	34	2	62	572	17.87	–	2
R. V. Lewis	10	15	1	136	250	17.85	1	–
G. I. Burgess	21	33	0	90	588	17.81	–	4
J. A. Snow	22	34	3	63	552	17.80	–	1
G. Sharp	23	32	7	48	443	17.72	–	–
K. Shuttleworth	20	15	6	44	158	17.55	–	–
P. J. Sharpe	17	29	2	83	474	17.55	–	2
A. W. Mansell	20	33	6	72*	470	17.40	–	1
U. C. Joshi	6	8	5	20	51	17.00	–	–
I. T. Botham	18	29	3	59	441	16.96	–	1
N. Smith	19	27	3	77	406	16.91	–	1
T. M. Lamb	12	12	6	40*	101	16.83	–	–
R. W. Taylor	22	33	4	54	488	16.82	–	1
G. Richards	15	28	2	61	436	16.76	–	1
K. V. Jones	14	17	2	52	251	16.73	–	1
T. J. Murrills	11	20	0	43	334	16.70	–	–
K. R. Pont	8	14	1	40	213	16.38	–	–
G. A. Cope	22	24	7	43	275	16.17	–	–
M. J. Edwards	15	27	2	63	402	16.08	–	2
R. A. White	23	38	3	83	563	16.08	–	3
J. C. Foat	10	16	1	62*	241	16.06	–	1
A. R. Butcher	15	16	3	57	207	15.92	–	1
M. S. T. Dunstan	6	9	0	52	143	15.88	–	1
S. Venkataraghavan	21	28	6	33*	349	15.86	–	–
A. J. Borrington	7	12	1	58	174	15.81	–	1
R. Swetman	6	8	4	14*	63	15.75	–	–
C. Johnson	8	12	1	60*	173	15.72	–	1
D. R. Owen-Thomas	16	25	4	35	328	15.61	–	–
M. E. J. C. Norman	12	20	3	40*	265	15.58	–	–
N. D. Botton	10	20	4	38*	249	15.56	–	–
J. Davey	14	20	11	37*	137	15.22	–	–
P. I. Pocock	21	25	6	41	289	15.21	–	–
J. Abrahams	13	22	2	78	304	15.20	–	2
C. J. Tavaré	9	11	1	31	152	15.20	–	–
J. K. Lever	21	19	13	19*	91	15.16	–	–

	M	I	NO	HS	Runs	Av	100	50
J. D. Inchmore	16	16	4	113	181	15·08	1	–
W. A. Bourne	12	16	2	29	210	15·00	–	–
B. S. Bedi	24	23	6	61	253	14·88	–	1
A. Long	21	22	6	42	232	14·50	–	–
J. A. Hopkins	9	15	2	44*	183	14·07	–	–
S. P. Coverdale	10	18	0	52	250	13·88	–	2
H. C. Latchman	20	29	7	78	302	13·72	–	1
N. P. D. Ross	6	11	1	30	137	13·70	–	–
P. A. Todd	10	18	1	37	232	13·64	–	–
E. J. W. Jackson	10	18	3	33	203	13·53	–	–
G. D. McKenzie	21	20	4	50	214	13·37	–	1
G. R. Cass	8	9	1	39	105	13·12	–	–
A. Mitra	4	8	0	30	104	13·00	–	–
N. Gifford	22	27	6	30	270	12·85	–	–
C. Milburn	12	17	4	39*	167	12·84	–	–
D. A. Graveney	18	25	3	50*	282	12·81	–	1
A. P. E. Knott	15	21	1	83	254	12·70	–	1
W. Snowden	11	20	0	52	253	12·65	–	1
A. J. Hignell	8	14	1	27	161	12·38	–	–
M. J. Vernon	10	12	4	27	99	12·37	–	–
H. A. Gomes	12	19	1	85	222	12·33	–	1
J. D. Bond	17	24	4	65*	245	12·25	–	1
M. N. Field	10	15	5	39*	122	12·20	–	–
J. Lyon	16	16	2	48	170	12·14	–	–
P. E. Russell	20	28	8	26*	241	12·05	–	–
M. J. D. Stallibrass	11	16	6	24	119	11·90	–	–
J. B. Mortimore	21	30	4	63	308	11·84	–	1
M. A. Buss	16	25	3	31	260	11·81	–	–
A. Hodgson	13	15	4	30	128	11·63	–	–
J. Spencer	18	26	5	37	243	11·57	–	–
D. L. Acfield	12	9	3	31	69	11·50	–	–
W. H. Hare	5	9	1	36	92	11·50	–	–
P. A. Wilkinson	15	21	8	28*	148	11·38	–	–
G. G. Arnold	14	12	3	23	102	11·33	–	–
P. B. Fisher	7	13	1	29	136	11·33	–	–
M. W. W. Selvey	15	16	7	37*	102	11·33	–	–
J. J. Groome	9	16	0	59	181	11·31	–	1
J. R. T. Barclay	11	21	0	28	237	11·28	–	–
R. M. H. Cottam	14	10	2	62*	88	11·00	–	1
V. A. Holder	21	23	4	29	204	10·73	–	–
J. M. Ward	10	16	0	37	170	10·62	–	–
D. W. Jarrett	7	13	0	51	138	10·61	–	1
D. L. Underwood	16	16	5	43	116	10·54	–	–
W. Blenkiron	12	15	1	28	147	10·50	–	–
K. Stevenson	9	10	2	33	83	10·37	–	–
B. M. Brain	22	22	7	35	154	10·26	–	–
A. E. Cordle	14	23	3	37	201	10·05	–	–
M. A. Nash	17	25	3	46	220	10·00	–	–

BOWLING (Qualifications: 10 wickets in 10 innings)

	O	M	R	W	Av	BB	5wI	10wM
A. M. E. Roberts	727·4	198	1621	119	13·62	8– 47	6	–
G. G. Arnold	487	140	1069	75	14·25	6– 32	4	1
V. A. Holder	659	146	1493	94	15·88	7– 40	5	1

	O	M	R	W	Av	BB	5wI	10wM
M. J. Procter	311·3	80	776	47	16·51	5– 29	1	–
B. L. D'Oliveira	345·3	105	697	40	17·42	5– 49	1	–
M. N. S. Taylor	541	147	1259	72	17·48	6– 26	3	–
H. R. Moseley	661·5	198	1420	81	17·53	5– 24	3	–
R. Illingworth	535·1	204	1014	57	17·78	7– 18	4	–
P. Carrick	405·4	167	840	47	17·87	6– 43	2	1
S. Turner	615·5	166	1317	73	18·04	6– 87	4	–
S. J. Rouse	164·5	34	489	27	18·11	4– 26	–	–
D. L. Underwood	563	229	1181	65	18·16	8– 51	7	3
J. C. Balderstone	134·4	33	351	19	18·47	4– 19	–	–
R. P. Baker	210·2	48	511	27	18·92	6– 29	1	–
G. D. McKenzie	531·3	131	1345	71	18·94	5– 36	4	–
C. M. Old	526·3	132	1366	72	18·97	5– 21	3	–
R. A. Woolmer	467·4	134	1065	56	19·01	5– 41	2	–
N. Gifford	617	197	1333	69	19·31	7– 15	3	–
R. S. Herman	657·4	201	1426	73	19·53	6– 15	3	–
R. M. H. Cottam	454	115	1101	56	19·66	6– 88	4	–
M. Hendrick	531·1	127	1288	65	19·81	5– 13	1	–
Sarfraz Nawaz	559	153	1356	68	19·94	8– 27	4	–
J. A. Snow	569·1	122	1517	76	19·96	6– 14	6	2
D. J. Brown	495	135	1143	56	20·41	5– 45	1	–
A. L. Robinson	375·5	103	880	43	20·46	6– 61	2	–
Asif Iqbal	79	20	205	10	20·50	4– 46	–	–
D. B. Close	104	30	287	14	20·50	5– 70	1	–
B. Wood	405·4	136	892	43	20·74	6– 33	3	–
R. D. Jackman	664·1	146	1744	84	20·76	6– 58	4	–
B. M. Brain	633·1	121	1752	84	20·85	6– 58	2	–
Mushtaq Mohammad	370·3	103	1106	53	20·86	7– 59	3	–
A. Ward	400·4	82	1174	56	20·96	7– 42	5	1
J. S. E. Price	153	33	451	21	21·47	6– 54	1	–
D. A. Graveney	384·5	105	1014	47	21·57	8– 85	3	1
G. A. Cope	743·5	260	1681	77	21·83	7–101	5	1
J. C. J. Dye	541·1	110	1512	69	21·91	5– 54	2	–
J. D. Inchmore	283·2	54	858	39	22·00	5– 50	1	–
E. E. Hemmings	738	213	1855	84	22·08	7– 57	6	1
R. G. D. Willis	471·2	92	1369	62	22·08	5– 85	1	–
F. J. Titmus	941·2	312	1953	88	22·19	7– 39	6	2
N. M. McVicker	511·1	113	1357	61	22·24	6– 19	2	–
B. A. Langford	412·1	153	937	42	22·30	5– 51	3	–
T. W. Cartwright	273	130	493	22	22·40	4– 45	–	–
A. A. Jones	565	120	1539	67	22·97	6– 37	5	–
M. A. Nash	539·5	124	1463	63	23·22	7–126	3	–
P. J. Sainsbury	425·2	196	813	35	23·22	4– 30	–	–
R. A. White	704·4	196	1909	79	24·16	6– 41	4	1
A. Hodgson	284·2	63	751	31	24·22	5– 36	1	–
G. Miller	380	90	1020	42	24·28	5– 88	1	–
P. H. Edmonds	815·5	266	1888	77	24·51	7– 38	3	1
P. Lever	557·1	142	1401	57	24·57	4– 20	–	–
H. C. Latchman	351·3	66	1158	47	24·63	6– 31	3	–
B. S. Bedi	1085·3	306	2760	112	24·64	7– 25	8	1
K. D. Boyce	313·4	55	868	35	24·80	6– 76	3	1
M. A. Buss	350	123	797	32	24·90	6– 74	2	–
A. G. Nicholson	471	152	1100	44	25·00	5– 74	1	–
S. J. Storey	180	49	401	16	25·06	3– 2	–	–
Intikhab Alam	489	119	1459	58	25·15	5– 60	4	–

THE 1974 SEASON

	O	M	R	W	Av	BB	5wI	10wM
J. Simmons	601·1	178	1467	58	25·29	5– 79	2	–
K. Higgs	421·1	107	996	39	25·53	5– 53	2	–
R. A. Hutton	259·2	70	620	24	25·83	6– 85	1	–
I. T. Botham	309	76	779	30	25·96	5– 59	1	–
W. Taylor	303·5	58	885	34	26·02	5– 83	1	–
P. I. Pocock	651·5	192	1576	60	26·26	5– 30	3	–
E. D. Fursdon	330·3	79	870	33	26·36	6– 60	1	–
A. S. Brown	348·4	86	925	35	26·42	5– 49	1	–
J. Spencer	464·3	112	1243	47	26·44	6– 19	3	–
A. R. Butcher	188	42	478	18	26·55	3– 31	–	–
G. W. Johnson	468·2	140	1172	44	26·63	5– 51	1	–
K. Shuttleworth	566·1	162	1418	53	26·75	7– 61	2	–
G. R. J. Roope	315·2	76	857	32	26·78	3– 5	–	–
J. Birkenshaw	514·2	135	1262	47	26·85	7– 56	4	–
P. Booth	124·5	17	380	14	27·14	3– 57	–	–
C. P. Phillipson	189	50	439	16	27·43	5– 30	1	–
Sadiq Mohammad	96·5	25	357	13	27·46	5–126	1	–
D. Wilson	157·4	39	469	17	27·58	5– 36	1	–
B. Stead	628	147	1713	62	27·62	6– 65	1	1
T. M. Lamb	395·5	87	997	36	27·69	5– 57	2	–
G. I. Burgess	437·1	114	1140	41	27·80	3– 18	–	–
D. P. Hughes	591·3	196	1428	51	28·00	5– 38	2	–
A. C. Smith	291·4	68	729	26	28·03	4– 49	–	–
J. Cumbes	243·5	49	595	21	28·33	4– 25	–	–
R. E. East	571·1	151	1431	50	28·62	5– 27	1	–
T. E. Jesty	321·1	96	749	26	28·80	4– 47	–	–
K. V. Jones	278·5	69	778	27	28·81	5– 78	1	–
D. L. Williams	511	93	1586	55	28·83	5– 67	2	–
J. F. Steele	397·5	136	866	30	28·86	4– 38	–	–
J. N. Graham	465·3	107	1138	39	29·17	5– 60	1	–
M. J. Vernon	155	19	586	20	29·30	6– 58	2	1
C. Milburn	146	29	353	12	29·41	3– 25	–	–
Imran Khan	610·3	126	1808	60	30·13	5– 44	4	1
A. E. Cordle	289	40	914	30	30·46	5–101	1	–
A. W. Greig	551·5	123	1677	55	30·49	6– 50	1	–
J. N. Shepherd	641	154	1691	55	30·74	6– 42	2	–
P. Lee	341·2	85	902	29	31·10	5– 62	1	–
D. S. Steele	161	59	405	13	31·15	3– 68	–	–
R. N. S. Hobbs	368·1	98	1061	34	31·20	5– 73	1	–
J. Davey	286	46	812	26	31·23	3– 49	–	–
W. Blenkiron	160·4	34	473	15	31·53	5– 45	1	–
G. St. A. Sobers	350·4	82	925	29	31·89	4– 48	–	–
P. E. Russell	554·3	154	1413	44	32·11	5– 75	1	–
B. E. A. Edmeades	170·4	35	419	13	32·23	3– 19	–	–
R. D. V. Knight	388·3	88	1127	34	33·14	6– 44	1	–
C. E. Waller	582·5	150	1580	47	33·61	5– 69	2	–
W. A. Bourne	166	29	578	17	34·00	3– 31	–	–
P. A. Wilkinson	377·1	98	953	28	34·03	4– 46	–	–
M. N. Field	268·4	51	827	24	34·45	4– 76	–	–
D. Breakwell	345·1	109	957	27	35·44	4– 56	–	–
M. W. W. Selvey	414·3	83	1246	35	35·60	6–109	2	–
K. Stevenson	171·2	16	654	18	36·33	4–127	–	–
J. W. Solanky	290	59	880	24	36·66	5– 78	1	–
R. B. Elms	290·4	68	870	23	37·82	5– 76	1	–
S. Venkataraghavan	667·2	136	1923	49	39·24	7–102	2	–

	O	M	R	W	Av	BB	5wI	10wM
D. L. Acfield	303.2	82	709	18	39.38	5– 52	1	–
P. Willey	238.1	69	595	15	39.66	3– 94	–	–
B. K. Gardom	195.2	31	696	17	40.94	6–139	1	–
R. C. Davis	444.5	136	956	22	43.45	4– 92	–	–
J. K. Lever	492.2	78	1355	31	43.70	3– 38	–	–
E. J. W. Jackson	250.2	50	849	19	44.68	4– 48	–	–
J. B. Mortimore	529.2	110	1481	33	44.87	4– 26	–	–
J. A. Jameson	205.5	42	641	12	53.41	4– 47	–	–
F. W. Swarbrook	427.4	138	1168	21	55.61	4– 51	–	–

The following bowlers took ten wickets but bowled in less than ten innings:

	O	M	R	W	Av	BB	5wI	10wM
R. Senghera	107	32	276	15	18.40	5– 81	1	–
J. W. Swinburne	80	20	219	10	21.90	5– 22	1	–
B. D. Julien	93	21	266	12	22.16	5– 91	1	–
D. R. Doshi	130	39	327	10	32.70	2– 49	–	–
U. C. Doshi	182	54	431	13	33.15	4– 79	–	–
B. J. Griffiths	110	23	385	10	38.50	3– 54	–	–

FIELDING

- 62 D. I. Bairstow (51ct, 11st), G. R. Stephenson (61ct, 1st)
- 55 R. W. Taylor (52ct, 3st)
- 53 R. W. Tolchard (46ct, 7st)
- 51 J. T. Murray (37ct, 14st)
- 50 D. L. Murray (47ct, 3st), G. Sharp (44ct, 6st), D. J. S. Taylor (45ct, 5st)
- 47 D. Nicholls (47ct, 0st)
- 46 A. Long (41ct, 5st)
- 45 A. P. E. Knott (41ct, 4st)
- 41 H. G. Wilcock (40ct, 1st)
- 34 A. W. Mansell (32ct, 2st), C. T. Radley, T. J. Yardley
- 33 G. Cook
- 31 E. W. Jones (29ct, 2st), J. A. Ormrod, N. Smith (28ct, 3st)
- 30 M. J. Harris (25ct, 5st), J. Lyon (29ct, 1st)
- 28 G. R. J. Roope, J. F. Steele
- 27 F. M. Engineer (26ct, 1st)
- 26 M. J. Smedley
- 25 D. B. Close
- 24 M. C. Cowdrey, P. H. Edmonds, A. W. Greig, J. A. Jameson, Sadiq Mohammad, R. T. Virgin
- 23 G. R. Cass (23ct, 0st), C. G. Greenidge, B. Hassan, B. W. Luckhurst, B. A. Richards, M. J. K. Smith
- 22 B. F. Davison
- 21 B. Dudleston, M. J. Khan
- 20 R. K. Baker (19ct, 1st), J. M. Brearley, D. S. Steele

Fielding statistics for overseas players include their figures for their respective touring team.

The Prudential Cup
Christopher Martin-Jenkins

I can think of only one possible reason why the Prudential Cup competition should not be an absolutely resounding success; and it is something which the world's best cricketers, the organisers of the eight nations, and even the Prudential Assurance Company itself can do nothing about: the weather.

In some respects one-day cricket is even more at the mercy of the weather than the fuller forms of cricket, because its essential excitement lies in achieving a finish within a single day's play. If a one-innings match is begun on one day and continued the next, the second act is almost inevitably an anti-climax. So let us pray that there will not be a wet June, as well as insuring against it! If the sun shines as it should, we shall all be able to witness this summer the most exciting experiment in the game since the brave introduction of the Gillette Cup in England twelve years ago.

Perhaps one should say at the outset that no one will be claiming that the winners of the Prudential Cup Final at Lord's on 21 June will be Cricket's World Champions. Test matches played over five days and two innings will always (I hope) be counted as the true yardstick of international cricket standing. But the winners of the Prudential Cup will be the *limited-over* World Champions, and that is no empty title. Limited-over cricket, in a nutshell, has been the financial saviour of English Cricket, and since Rothmans and Gillette pioneered the idea, with the blessing of the Lord's authorities, it has spread quickly to the other cricket-playing countries. The International Cricket Conference has recognised one-day cricket's growing importance by sanctioning this competition and the considerable profit one hopes they will make from it will benefit the game throughout the world. As for the teams taking part, and the thousands of spectators who will watch them, the fun this June is going to be 'bustin' out all over'.

It all begins on 7 June. All eight contestants will be in action that day, but it is at Lord's and at Headingley that the two really crucial games take place. The prospect of taking on England at Lord's has always been one which visiting teams view with particular relish. This time the Indian side will have a special reason for wanting to do well. For it was at Lord's last year that with a suddenness and completeness that was quite bewildering at the time, they collapsed against very good swing bowling by Chris Old and Geoff Arnold and went down to defeat by an innings and 285 runs. India's second innings total of 42 was the lowest in their Test history and unless in the twelve months they have unearthed much more penetrating seam bowling support for the consistent Abid Ali, or Chandrasekhar has rediscovered his old accuracy and rapid spin, the millions of Indian people sure to be following their progress in the Prudential Cup this summer seem doomed to disappointment. Not that Bishan Bedi at his best isn't capable of upsetting the safest predictions, or class batsmen like Viswanath or Gavaskar of making plenty of runs. England will certainly be favourites to win this opening match and take a firm stride towards the semi-final but it will be fascinating to see if the selectors, knowing how much prestige is at stake, will make rather more concessions to limited-over cricket than they have done in the past. In the One-day Internationals of the last few seasons the choice of Bob Woolmer of Kent has been about the only one made solely because a player is a limited-over specialist. Writing before the England squad is known, I wonder whether men like John Hampshire, Graham Roope, Chris Balderstone, Barry Wood, Ken Higgs and even a couple of Yorkshiremen named Boycott and Close will be seriously considered. All of course are very good players in their own right but apart from Boycott none was originally selected to make the recent trip to Australia. Yet on their consistent performances in England's various one-day competitions over the last few seasons, a good case could be made out for all of them – not to mention a few others.

The other decisive encounter on the opening day may well be the one between Australia and Pakistan. Just as India have a bone to pick with England, so do Pakistan with Australia, who twice recovered to beat them when the two countries met each other in Australia a couple of winters ago. In some ways Pakistan have the best equipped side of all. They revealed their immense potential for limited-over cricket when easily taking the Prudential Trophy against England last year when those two strapping fast bowlers from Lahore, Asif Masood and Sarfraz Nawaz, did so well. Like Australia, they have a number of good all-rounders such as Intikhab, Asif Iqbal and Mushtaq Mohammad, and if in addition batsmen like Sadiq Mohammad, Zaheer Abbas or Majid Khan are in the mood, all bowlers are likely to suffer. Australia themselves, with men like Doug Walters and the Chappell brothers – not to mention Thomson and Lillee, carry plenty of big guns and some of their team will be eager to erase the memory of traumatic events on the last occasion they were at Headingley! A great match in the making.

West Indies, of course, are the third very strong side in Group B, and, assuming they dispatch Sri Lanka as they should on the opening day, their matches with Pakistan at Edgbaston on 11 June and Australia at the Oval on 14 June will decide their fate. It was at the Oval in 1973 that the recent revival of West Indian cricket began and there will certainly be plenty of the customary exuberant Caribbean support for them drawn from the environs of Kennington! Those West Indian cricket followers who have settled over here have yet to see the best of Lawrence Rowe, and sadly it seems that his eye infirmity may keep him out of the competition. But with Clive Lloyd, Alvin Kallicharran, Roy Fredericks, Gordon Greenidge, Vivian Richards, Keith Boyce, Andy Roberts and company, there is no shortage of West Indian talent. On paper West Indies have an almost unbeatable combination.

You will gather from all this that it may just be a matter of luck and form on the day that decides which of the three giants of Group B go through to the semi-finals, but most people would place their money on West Indies and Australia. Indeed Australia *v* West Indies at the Oval on 14 June is the one-day match of the year – if not the century. For many people one of the most exciting things in the competition will be seeing Jeff

Thomson 'in the flesh'. He and Lillee will be quite a proposition even in limited-over cricket, and though they will be restricted to 12 overs each, Australia with Walker, Walters and Mallett will have a formidable attack. Quite apart from their confrontation with the West Indies batting galaxy, there will inevitably be comparisons between the pace of Thomson, Lillee and Andy Roberts.

In Group A, on the other hand, one would go with rather more confidence for England and New Zealand. These two meet on 11 June and there is special significance about the venue for it was at Trent Bridge two seasons ago that New Zealand staged one of the bravest Test recoveries of all time. Who can forget that wonderful stand by Bev Congdon and Vic Pollard and their glorious attempt to get nearly five hundred runs to win in the second innings after being dismissed for only 97 in the first? I certainly cannot, even though I had to rely on my radio colleagues for news of how the final day was going, having dashed south at close of play on the fourth day in time to see my son come into the world! (He had clearly decided that the match would be over in four days, but like many others he underestimated New Zealand – or perhaps he was fed up with listening to the commentary through his mother's tum and decided he would watch the last day on television!)

Whatever the outcome this time, New Zealand will have to dispose of India at Old Trafford on 14 June and this too will be a vital match. Any side containing Glenn Turner cannot be dismissed lightly.

What of the two underdogs, Sri Lanka and East Africa? Their presence adds a welcome extra dimension to the competition, gives spectators a chance to see some talented new players and the countries themselves a great chance to put themselves more firmly on the cricketing map. Who knows, indeed, whether good performances this June might in time persuade the I.C.C. that one or other of these teams is worthy of Test match status? Sri Lanka in particular have done well in recent years against visiting teams – notably India. Nor should one be too patronising. Major upsets *can* occur in cricket. Though neither of the conquered giants would like to be reminded of the fact, Yorkshire were once beaten by Durham and the West Indians by Ireland (they bowled out the 1969 West Indies touring team for 25 and won by nine wickets)!

For these reasons, if for no others, I personally won't be putting much money on predicting who will contest the semi-finals at Leeds and the Oval on 18 June. The rules are that the top team from each group plays the second team from the other and there could be a little luck involved in the way this works out. If England and New Zealand *do* get through from Group A for instance, I imagine that Australia, West Indies, or whichever country gets through, would *choose* to take on the less experienced New Zealanders. Whatever happens in the semi-finals, 21 June at Lord's will be a unique cricketing occasion, not to be missed for anything else in the world. We all know what a wonderful atmosphere there can be at the headquarters of cricket on a great occasion like a Test match or a Gillette Final. But Father Time will have seen nothing quite like this before and, like everyone else, he is going to enjoy it: weather permitting, of course!

COMPETING NATIONS

Group A: East Africa (EA); India (I); New Zealand (NZ); England (E).
Group B: Australia (A); Sri Lanka (SL); Pakistan (P); West Indies (WI).

PROGRAMME OF MATCHES

	LORD'S	OVAL	BIRMINGHAM	LEEDS	MANCHESTER	NOTTINGHAM
Sat. 7 June	E *v* I		NZ *v* EA	A *v* P	WI *v* SL	
Wed. 11 June		A *v* SL	P *v* WI	I *v* EA		E *v* NZ
Sat. 14 June		A *v* WI	E *v* EA		I *v* NZ	P *v* SL
Wed. 18 June		S/F		S/F		
Sat. 21 June Final						

THE RULES IN BRIEF

The competition will consist of two parts (i) a league competition with each team playing the other three in its group and

(ii) a knock-out competition consisting of two semi-finals and a final played between the two top teams in each of the Groups.

Playing Conditions:
  (i) Matches will consist of one innings per side, each innings being limited to 60 six-ball overs, as in the Gillette Cup.
  (ii) Matches should be completed in one day, but two days will be allocated in case of weather interference. Normal hours of play will be from 11.00 a.m. to 7.30 p.m.

IF YOU CAN'T GET A TICKET...

On television, BBC-1 and 2 will be covering two matches a day and Test Match Special on Radio 3 will have ball-by-ball commentary on the main games and reports on the others. For the exact times of broadcasts see *Radio Times*.

STOP PRESS

At the time of going to press the following teams had been announced:

AUSTRALIA: See pages 140-51.

EAST AFRICA: Harilal R. Shah (capt.), Frasat Ali, Zulfiquar Ali, Don Pringle, Mehmood Quaraishy, Ramesh Sethi, Jawahir Shah (all Kenya), Yunus Badat, Hamish McLeod, P. G. Nana (all Zambia), Praful Mehta, Shiraz Sumar (both Tanzania), J. Nagenda, S. Walusimba (both Uganda).

NEW ZEALAND: G. M. Turner (capt.), B. L. Cairns, R. O. Collinge, B. G. Hadlee, D. R. Hadlee, R. J. Hadlee, B. F. Hastings, G. P. Howarth, H. J. Howarth, B. J. McKechnie, J. F. M. Morrison, D. R. O'Sullivan, J. M. Parker, K. J. Wadsworth.

PAKISTAN: (14 from) Asif Iqbal (capt.), Asif Masood, Azam Khan, Imran Khan, Javed Miandad, Liaquat Ali, Majid Khan, Mudassar Nazar, Mushtaq Mohammad, Naeem Ahmed, Naseer Malik, Parvez Mir, Sadiq Mohammad, Sarfraz Nawaz, Shafiq Ahmed, Shahid Aziz, Wasim Bari, Wasim Raja, Zaheer Abbas.

WEST INDIES: C. H. Lloyd (capt.), K. D. Boyce, M. L. C. Foster, R. C. Fredericks, L. R. Gibbs, C. G. Greenidge, V. A. Holder, B. D. Julien, A. I. Kallicharran, D. L. Murray, I. V. A. Richards, A. M. E. Roberts, L. G. Rowe, G. St A. Sobers.

The following teams have not yet been announced but will probably be chosen from:

INDIA: S. Venkhataraghavan (capt.), M. Amarnath, B. S. Bedi, F. M. Engineer, A. D. Gaekwad, S. M. Gavaskar, K. Ghavri, H. S. Kanitkar, S. M. H. Kirmani, Madan Lal Sharma, A. V. Mankad, B. P. Patel, E. A. S. Prasanna, P. M. Salgaonkar, P. Sharma, E. D. Solkar, G. R. Viswanath.

SRI LANKA: A. Tennekoon (capt.), D. Chanmugam, A. De Silva, S. De Silva, R. Fernando, S. Fernando, D. Heyn, S. Jeganathan, L. Kaluperuma, D. Mendis, T. Opatha, G. Pathmanathan, M. Peiris, N. Samarasekera, J. Seneviratne, M. Tissera, B. Warnapura, S. Wettimuny.

County Championship

Seventeen counties compete in the Championship, each playing twenty matches. Each county plays twelve of the counties once, and the other four twice. This is by mutual arrangement based largely on tradition (e.g. Yorkshire *v* Lancashire). The county which has gained the most points at the end of the season is the Champion county. If two or more sides are equal on points the side with most wins is the winner.

The two first innings are limited to a total of 200 overs, of which the side batting first is limited to not more than 100 overs. So if the side fielding first dismisses their opponents in *under* 100 overs, they may add the balance to their own innings (e.g. if A bowls out B in 90 overs, A may bat for 110 overs, but Bonus Points will still only apply to the first 100 of these overs).

AWARD OF POINTS
10 points for a win.
5 points each for a tie.
NO points for first innings lead.
Bonus Points: Batting and bowling points are awarded only for performances in *the first 100* overs of each first innings and are retained whatever the result of the match.

(1) *Maximum of four batting points* – as follows:
150–199 runs – 1 point.   200–249 runs   – 1 point.
250–299 runs – 1 point.   300 runs or more – 1 point.

(2) *Maximum of four bowling points* – as follows:
3–4 wickets taken – 1 point.   5– 6 wickets taken – 1 point.
7–8 wickets taken – 1 point.   9–10 wickets taken – 1 point.

N.B. If play starts when less than eight hours *playing* time remains, it will become a one-innings match with no bonus points.

The Gillette Cup

A knock-out competition started in 1963 and competed for by the seventeen First-Class Counties and the five leading Minor Counties (excluding First-Class County 2nd XI's) in the previous season. The five Minor Counties and seven First-Class Counties (decided on a rota basis) contest the first round. The draw for the first two rounds is made in October of the previous year. Matches are played on the grounds of the teams drawn first, except the Final which is always played at Lord's. The matches are NOT considered first class.

AWARDS

The winners	£2000
The losing Finalists	£500

PLAYING CONDITIONS

(i) The Playing Conditions for First-Class matches in the United Kingdom will apply, except where specified in these Playing Conditions.

(ii) *Duration:*

The matches will consist of one innings per side and each innings will be limited to 60 overs. The matches are intended to be completed in one day, but three days (four days, if Sunday play is scheduled) will be allocated in case of weather interference. Matches scheduled to start on Saturday, but not completed on that day, may be continued or, if necessary, started on the Sunday during the hours of 2 p.m. to 7 p.m. Umpires may order extra time until 7.30 p.m. on the Sunday, if in their opinion a finish can be obtained that day.

Cup Final only:

In the event of the match starting not less than half an hour nor more than one and a half hours late, owing to weather or the state of the ground, each innings shall be limited to 50 overs. If, however, the start of play is delayed for more than one and a half hours, the 60 over limit shall apply.

(iii) *Hours of Play:*

Normal hours will be 11 a.m. to 7.30 p.m. The Umpires may order extra time if, in their opinion, a finish can be obtained on any day. The Captains of the two teams in the Final will be warned that heavy shadows may move across the pitch towards the end of the day and that play cannot be stopped because of these.

(iv) *Intervals:*

(a) All Rounds other than Semi-Finals and Final: Lunch 1 p.m.–1.40 p.m.

This may be varied if, owing to the weather or state of the ground, an alteration has been agreed upon by the Captains or ordered by the Umpires.

Between Innings 10 minutes.

Tea (20 minutes).

(i) In an uninterrupted match, the tea interval will be taken at 4.30 p.m. or after 25 overs of the innings of the side batting second, whichever is the later.

(ii) In a match where the start is delayed or play is suspended for such a length of time as to make it impracticable to adopt (i) above, owing to the unlikelihood of completing the match on that day, the tea interval will be taken at 4.30 p.m., except in the following circumstances:

(a) If nine wickets are then down or no more than six overs of an innings remain to be bowled, the tea interval will be taken at the end of the innings, or after 30 minutes play, whichever is the earlier.

(b) If, between the hours of 3.45 p.m. and 4.30 p.m. play is suspended (this includes a suspension which may be in progress at 3.45 p.m.) the tea interval of 20 minutes will then be taken.

(b) Semi-Finals and Final:
Start of play   10.30 a.m.
Lunch   12.30 p.m.–1 p.m.

Between innings 10 minutes
Tea (15 minutes) As before, except that the timings shall be 30 minutes earlier.

NOTE: The timing of any interval may be delayed for a maximum of 15 minutes on the second or third day of a match, if the Umpires consider that a finish can be obtained within that time.

(v) *Covering the Pitch:*

The pitch will be completely covered in the event of rain.

(vi) *Limitation of Overs by any one Bowler:*

No bowler may bowl more than 12 overs in an innings. If, in the Cup Final, the duration of each innings is reduced to 50 overs under Rule 3 (ii) no bowler may bowl more than 10 overs in an innings. In the event of a bowler breaking down and being unable to complete an over, the remaining balls will be bowled by another bowler. Such part of an over will count as a full over only in so far as each bowler's limit is concerned.

(vii) *The Result:*

 (a) *A Tie*

 In the event of a tie, the following shall apply:

  (a) The side losing the lesser number of wickets is the winner.

  (b) If both sides are all out, the side with the higher overall scoring rate is the winner.

  (c) If the result cannot be decided by (a) or (b), the winner is the side with the higher score (i) after 30 overs, or if still equal (ii) after 20 overs, or if still equal (iii) after 10 overs.

 (b) *Unfinished Match:*

If a match remains unfinished after three days (four days, if Sunday play is scheduled) the winner will be the side which has scored the faster in runs per over throughout the innings, provided that at least 20 overs have been bowled at the side batting second. If the scoring rate is the same, the side losing the lesser number of wickets in the first 20 overs of each innings will be the winner.

 If, however, at 3 p.m. on the third day (fourth day if Sunday play is scheduled) in the opinion of the Umpires no result can be achieved in the match, whatever the weather, the Umpires will order a match of 10 overs each side to be started, if to do so is humanly possible.

If no play is possible on the first and second days (and third day, if Sunday play is scheduled) the Captains, bearing in mind the time remaining, will be empowered to rearrange the number of overs to be bowled by each side to achieve a result. In the event of the number of overs being rearranged, a minimum of 10 overs for each innings will apply.

If, owing to conditions, it is not possible to obtain a result, the two Captains will arrange another match of a minimum of 10 overs each side, to be played within 10 days on a ground to be mutually agreed. Such a match may be played on a Sunday.

In the event of two Competitors having great difficulty in arranging another match within 10 days, the matter shall be referred to the Chairman of the Special Competitions Sub-Committee and the Secretary of the T.C.C.B. for decision.

The Benson and Hedges Cup

Twenty teams compete, divided into four zones. Each team plays the others in its zone once, on a league basis, the top two teams in each zone qualifying to go into a draw for the quarter-finals. From then on the competition is played on a knock-out basis. The twenty teams consist of the First-Class Counties, two from the Minor Counties Cricket Association, and a combined team of Oxford and Cambridge Universities.

THE FOUR ZONES

North
Derbyshire
Lancashire
Nottinghamshire
Yorkshire
Minor Counties (North)

South
Essex
Kent
Middlesex
Sussex
Minor Counties (South)

Midlands
Leicestershire
Northamptonshire
Warwickshire
Worcestershire
Oxford and Cambridge Universities

West
Glamorgan
Gloucestershire
Hampshire
Somerset
Surrey

Each team will play two matches at home and two away as decided by the Fixtures Sub-Committee. The knock-out matches are played on the grounds of the teams drawn first. The Final is played at Lord's on a Saturday at the end of July.

(1) *Awards:*

Winner of the Competition	£3000
Losing Finalist	£1500
Each Losing Semi-finalist	£1000

Each Losing Quarter-finalist £600
'Team of the Week' during each of the five weeks in
  which zonal league matches played £300
Winners of individual zonal league matches £200
  In addition the following individual 'Gold Awards' will be made:
In each of 40 zonal league matches £30
Quarter-finals £60
Semi-finals £75
Final £150

(2) *Playing Conditions:*
As for first-class cricket except as shown.
  (i) *Duration:*
The matches will consist of one innings per side, each innings being limited to 55 overs. All matches will be completed in one day, if possible, but three days (four days if Sunday play is scheduled) will be allocated in case of weather interference.

  Matches scheduled to start on Saturday, but not completed on that day, may be continued or, if necessary, started on the Sunday.

  (ii) *Hours of Play:*
Normal hours will be 11 a.m. to 6.30 p.m. (start at 2 p.m. on Sundays). The umpires may order extra time if they consider a finish can be obtained on any day, or in order to give the team batting second an opportunity to complete 20 overs, bearing in mind that play should not normally be extended beyond 7.30 p.m.

  (iii) *Intervals:*
Lunch   – 1 p.m.–1.40 p.m.
Between innings   – 10 minutes.
Tea (20 minutes) – To be taken at 4.15 p.m. except in the following circumstances:

  (a) If nine wickets are then down or no more than six overs of an innings remain to be bowled, the tea interval will be taken at the end of the innings, or after 30 minutes play, whichever is the earlier.

  (b) If the team batting second commences its innings before 2.45 p.m., tea will be taken after one and a half hours of that innings, provided that there is no interruption.

(c) If, between the hours of 3.30 p.m. and 4.15 p.m., an innings closes or play is suspended (this includes a suspension which may be in progress at 3.30 p.m.), the tea interval of 20 minutes (to include the interval between innings) will then be taken.

NOTE: The timing of any interval may be delayed for a maximum of 15 minutes on the second or third day of a match, if the umpires consider that a finish can be obtained within that time.

(iv) *Covering of the Pitch:*

The pitch will be fully covered in the event of rain.

(v) *Boundary:*

The distance of the boundary, measured from the centre of the pitch, shall not be less than 50 yards.

(vi) *Limitation of Overs by any one Bowler:*

No bowler may bowl more than 11 overs in an innings.

In the event of a bowler breaking down and being unable to complete an over, the remaining balls will be bowled by another bowler. Such part of an over will count as a full over only in so far as each bowler's limit is concerned.

(vii) *The Result:*

(a) *Unfinished Match:*

If a match remains unfinished after three days (four days if Sunday play is scheduled) the winner will be the side which has scored the faster in runs per over throughout the innings, provided that at least 20 overs have been bowled at the side batting second. If the scoring rate is the same, the side losing the lesser number of wickets in the first 20 overs of each innings will be the winner.

If, however, at 3 p.m. on the third day (fourth day if Sunday play is scheduled), in the opinion of the umpires, no result can be achieved in the match, whatever the weather, the umpires will order a match of 10 overs each side to be started, if it is humanly possible to do so.

If no play is possible on the first and second days (and third day if Sunday play is scheduled), the umpires, bearing in mind the time remaining, will be empowered to rearrange the number of overs to be bowled by each side to achieve a result. In the event of the number of overs being rearranged, a minimum of 10 overs for each innings will apply.

If it is impossible to achieve a result in a zonal league match, it shall be declared 'No Result'.

If it is impossible to achieve a result in a knockout match, another match of a minimum of 10 overs each side will be arranged, to be played within seven days on a ground to be mutually agreed. Such a match may be played on a Sunday. If it is not possible to arrange another match within seven days, the matter shall be referred to the Chairman of the Special Competitions Sub-Committee and the Secretary of the T.C.C.B. for decision.

(b) *A Tie:*

In the event of a tie, the following shall apply:

    (a) The side taking the greater number of wickets shall be the winner.

    (b) If both sides are all out, the side with the higher overall scoring rate shall be the winner.

    (c) If the result cannot be decided by (a) or (b), the winner shall be the side with the higher score (i) after 30 overs, or if still equal (ii) after 20 overs, or if still equal (iii) after 10 overs.

(viii) *Points Scoring System for Zonal League Matches:*

    (a) The team winning the match to score 3 points.

    (b) In a 'No Result' match, each team to score 1 point.

    (c) In the event of two or more teams in any zone having an equal number of points, their positions in the table shall be based on the faster rate of taking wickets in all zonal league matches (to be calculated by total balls bowled, divided by wickets taken).

The John Player League

Started in 1969 and restricted to the 17 First-Class Counties, who all play each other once. The matches are played on Sundays and are NOT considered first-class.

SCORING OF POINTS
(a) The team winning the match to score 4 points.
(b) In the event of a 'Tie' each team to score 2 points.
(c) In a 'No Result' match, each team to score 2 points.
(d) If at the end of the season there is a tie at the top of the table the winner of the League will be the team with the most number of wins. Or failing that, the most *away* wins. And if still level after that, the team with the best run-rate throughout the season will be the winner.

(1) AWARDS

Winner of the Competition	£2000
Runner-up	£1000
Third	£500
Winner of each match	£50
Individual batting award	£1000

For each six hit, the striker will qualify for one share of the award, the hitter of most sixes in the season to receive a bonus of £150

Individual bowling award £1000

A bowler taking four or more wickets in an innings will qualify for one share of the award, the holder of the most shares receiving a bonus of £150

Fastest 50 in a televised match £250

(2) PLAYING CONDITIONS
As for First-Class Cricket except as shown.

(A) *Hours of Play:*

All matches shall commence at 2 p.m., with a tea interval of 20 minutes at 4.10 p.m. or between innings, whichever is the earlier. The duration and time of the tea interval can be varied in the case of an interrupted match. Close of Play shall normally be at 6.40 p.m., but play may continue after that time, if, in the opinion of the Umpires, the overs remaining to be bowled can be completed by 7 p.m.

(B) *Length of Innings:*

  (i) In an uninterrupted match:

    (a) Each team shall bat for 40 overs unless all out earlier.

    (b) In the possible event of the team fielding first failing to bowl 40 overs by 4.10 p.m., the over in progress shall be completed and the innings of the team batting second shall be limited to the same number of overs as the innings of the team batting first. See NOTE 1.

  (ii) In matches where the start is delayed or play is suspended:

    (a) The object shall always be to rearrange the number of overs so that both teams have the opportunity of batting for the same number of overs (minimum 10 overs each team). The calculation of the number of overs to be bowled shall be based on an average rate of 18 overs per hour (one over per $3\frac{1}{3}$ minutes or part thereof) in the time remaining before Close of Play at 6.40 p.m. See NOTE 2.

    (b) If the number of overs of the side batting first is reduced, no fixed time will be specified for the close of their innings.

    (c) If, owing to a suspension of play during the innings of the team batting second, it is not possible for that team to have the opportunity of batting for the same number of overs as the team batting first, they will bat for a number of overs calculated as in (ii) (a).

    (d) The team batting second shall not bat for a

greater number of overs than the first team, unless the latter has been all out in less than the agreed number of overs.

NOTE 1: All teams are normally required to bowl at an average rate of 20 overs per hour. It is appreciated, however, that in certain exceptional circumstances it may not be possible to attain this average, and a short additional period for each innings is allowed in the Hours of Play. If, at 6.40 p.m., more than three overs remain to be bowled, play may continue as in Rule 2 (A) above, but the matter will be referred to the Discipline Sub-Committee.

NOTE 2: Umpires will notify the Home Authority of the time of resumption of play, following any delay or suspension, immediately they have reached a decision. The Home Authority will provide a representative who will be responsible for assisting Umpires in calculating the revised number of overs to be played in the match and for notifying the decision of the Umpires immediately to all concerned.

(C) *The Result:*

(i) A result can be achieved only if both teams have batted for at least 10 overs, unless one team has been all out in less than 10 overs or unless the team batting second scores enough runs to win in less than 10 overs. All other matches in which one or both teams have not had an opportunity of batting for a minimum of 10 overs shall be declared 'No Result' matches.

(ii) In matches in which both teams have had an opportunity of batting for the agreed number of overs (i.e. 40 overs each, in an uninterrupted match, or a lesser number of overs in an interrupted match – see Playing Conditions (B) (ii)), the team scoring the higher number of runs shall be the winner. If the scores are equal, the result shall be a 'Tie' and no account shall be taken of the number of wickets which have fallen.

(iii) If the team batting second has not had the opportunity to complete the agreed number of overs, and has neither been all out, nor has passed its opponent's score, the following shall apply:

(a) If the match is abandoned before 6.40 p.m., the result shall be decided on the average run-rate throughout both innings.

(b) If, due to suspension of play, the number of overs in the innings of the side batting second has to be revised, their target score shall be calculated by multiplying the reduced number of overs by the average runs per over scored by the side batting first.

(iv) In the event of the team batting first being all out in less than their full quota of overs, the calculation of their average run-rate shall be based on the full quota of overs to which they would have been entitled and not on the number of overs in which they were dismissed.

(D) *Number of Overs per Bowler:*

No bowler shall bowl more than eight overs in an innings. In the event of a bowler breaking down and being unable to complete an over, the remaining balls will be bowled by another bowler. Such part of an over will count as a full over only in so far as each bowler's limit is concerned.

(E) *Limitation of the Bowler's Run-up:*

The bowler's run-up, including his preliminary approach, shall be limited to 15 yards, to be measured from the wicket.

A white line will mark the maximum distance allowed.

(F) *Covering the Pitch:*

The pitch shall be fully covered in the event of rain.

(G) *Boundary:*

The distance of the boundary, measured from the centre of the pitch, shall not be less than 50 yards.

The 1975 Australians
Richie Benaud

Chappell, **Ian** Michael (South Australia) – Captain
b 26 Sep 43. RHB, LB. Début v Tasmania 1961–2. HS 209 Australians v Barbados 1972–3. BB 5–29 v NSW 1972–3.
Tours: South Africa 1966–7, 1970; England 1968, 1972; India 1969; West Indies 1973; New Zealand 1974.
One of Australia's greatest ever captains and an outstanding batsman, Ian Chappell has led Australia back to the top of the international cricket table since taking over the job at the end of 1970–1 series in Australia.

At that point Australia's stocks were low and, in fact, in his first game against England as captain, he was defeated in the deciding Test by Ray Illingworth. From that time on, Australia has beaten Pakistan, West Indies, New Zealand and has regained the Ashes. It has been a top-class performance by Chappell who, with his down-to-earth approach, has rejuvenated the Australian side.

His own batting has slumped a little by his high standards in the series just completed in Australia but he bats well in England and will be a force this summer.

In a team of brilliant fieldsmen he stands as one of the finest slip fieldsmen Australia has produced in Test cricket.

Chappell, **Gregory** Stephen (Queensland)
b 7 Aug 48. RHB, RM. Début for South Australia v Victoria 1966–7; for Queensland v NSW 1973–4. Played for Somerset

1968–9. HS 247* Australia v New Zealand 1974. BB 7–40 Somerset v Yorkshire 1969.
Tours: New Zealand 1969–70, 1974; England 1972; West Indies 1973.

Talk of great Australian batsmen and these days it is a question of just where Greg Chappell stands, not a question of his inclusion. His batting has been so magnificent in recent summers that I would rate him with South African Barry Richards as one of the top pair of batsmen in cricket today. The pity is that they are not seen on the same ground in international competition. English audiences who watched Chappell's innings at Lord's and The Oval in 1972 will have been suitably impressed – he is an even better player now.

By his own high standards, he failed as a run-getter in the series against England in Australia – he was never 100% fit – but there was no question of which batsman the English bowlers feared most. His technique prospered by means of the cricket he played with Somerset in English conditions and he is just about the complete batsman at this stage of his career.

He established a new catching record for catches in a Test in the Perth match of the series played in Australia in 1974–5 and in any position he is a wonderful exponent of the art. He generally fields at second slip although he is equally brilliant in the gully or the covers.

He has not bothered with his bowling in recent times – one of the bonuses for his batting has been that the Australian attack is so strong now that his right-arm medium-pace deliveries are not needed.

Edwards, Ross (Western Australia)
b 1 Dec 42. RHB, occasional WK. Début v Queensland 1964–5.
HS 170* Australia v England 1972.
Tours: England 1972; West Indies 1973.

One of the finest cover fieldsmen Australia has ever produced and one able to rank with any 'away from the slips area' fieldsmen in the world today. Ross Edwards is a completely dedicated cricketer, practising his fielding along the same lines as Colin Bland and Clive Lloyd, and is an ideal middle-order batsman for Australia.

He is not the dashing stroke player to be compared with the Chappell brothers, Walters or Marsh, but he is a sound partner for them with his cutting and on-side strokes and very quick running between the wickets. Since making his century at Trent Bridge in 1972, he has turned in mixed performances for Australia but he always has the advantage of starting with a bonus of 30 runs from his fielding.

He is a competent wicket-keeper who was Australia's second string 'keeper to the West Indies in 1973.

Gilmour, Gary John (New South Wales)
b 26 Jun 51. LHB, LFM. Début v South Australia 1971–2. HS 122 v South Australia 1971–2. BB 5–59 v Queensland 1974–5. Tours: New Zealand 1974.

This talented left-hand all-rounder could come back from the tour as one of Australia's finest players. A good opening bowler, he has the ability to *swing* the ball both ways, rather than simply push it away to the slips as an alternative delivery.

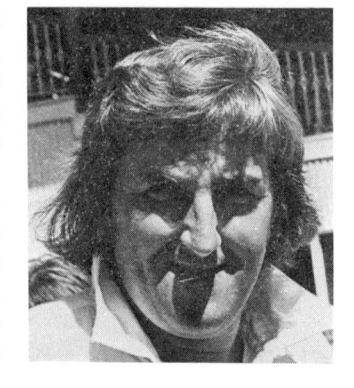

He has one of the best throwing arms in Australia and his batting is based on attack – his only problem may be a diffidence on the field that sometimes sees him not playing to his full capacity. There is no doubting his ability and, if he takes full advantage of the tour, he could return to Australia having solved all the selectors' problems over a late-order all-rounder.

In only three seasons of first-class cricket, he has hit a century in his début match and has taken over 100 wickets and scored more than 1000 runs, having previously toured West Indies with the Australian Schoolboys' side in 1969–70.

Higgs, James Donald (Victoria)
b 11 Jul 50. RHB, LB. Début *v* Western Australia 1970–1. HS 21 *v* Western Australia 1974–5. BB 8–66 *v* Western Australia 1974–5.

One of the younger brigade of spin bowlers in Australia, Jim Higgs beat the more experienced Terry Jenner of South Australia for a place in this team.

English cricket followers will see immediately that his basic bowling action is along the lines of speedster Jeff Thomson, in that he starts the ball from behind the right thigh. From a good side-on action, he spins the ball a considerable amount and is a genuine wrist-spinner.

He topped the list of wicket-takers of all the leg-spin bowlers in Australia for the past summer but, to date, has played no Test cricket. His inclusion is clearly for the future for, in a team bristling with pace bowlers plus Ashley Mallett, he will find it difficult to gain a place in a Test in this brief programme of matches.

Hurst, Alan George (Victoria)
b 15 Jul 50. RHB, RF. Début *v* Western Australia 1972–3. HS 18 *v* South Australia 1973–4. BB 5–22 *v* South Australia 1974–5.
Australia is fortunate to have Hurst as a back-up man for the speed pair Thomson and Lillee, and this tour could provide

another really fast bowler for the Australian selectors.

He began the season in moderate fashion, missing some games through injury, but then fought back well in the latter half, finishing with 29 wickets. Against this was Dymock's effort of 46 first-class wickets but Hurst's extra pace gained him the selectors' nod.

He is a very good fieldsman but an ordinary batsman – if Lillee and Thomson remain fit, his main job will be to take the new ball in the county games.

There is tremendous promise there, however, and a good side-on action makes him one of Australia's best prospects.

Laird, **Bruce** Malcolm (Western Australia)
b 21 Nov 50. RHB. Début v Victoria 1972–3. HS 127 v Queensland 1974–5.

It is unusual for one Sheffield Shield opener to displace his batting partner in an Australian touring team but Laird has done that this year to Wally Edwards. A compact right-hander, he is a good stroke-player who plays fast bowling well and looks the type to do well either opening or going in down the list. He finished third in the first-class averages for the season just concluded and played some most attractive innings.

A brilliant gully fieldsman, he will probably have to make way there for Mallett in the Tests but he is equally versatile away from the wicket.

With Redpath an absentee, there will be great pressure on Laird and the other two prospective openers to get the innings away to a good start.

Lillee, Dennis Keith (Western Australia)
b 18 Jul 49. RHB, RF. Début v Queensland 1969–70. HS 46 v New South Wales 1974–5. BB 8–29 Australia v World XI 1971–2.
Tours: New Zealand 1969–70; England 1972; West Indies 1973.
For Australia to retrieve the Ashes from England in 1974–5, it was necessary that Dennis Lillee should be fit and able to take his place at the head of the bowling attack. They had an added bonus in the end when Jeff Thomson came good, but Lillee and his back were the important features before a ball was bowled.

He first damaged the back in England in 1972 and then didn't play in the West Indies after the first Test in Jamaica – there was doubt that he would play Test cricket again, having sustained three stress fractures of the lower part of the back. Yet by the end of this last series he had made such a successful comeback that watchers were able to rank him with the former great Australian fast bowler Ray Lindwall.

This is high praise but I believe, having played with Lindwall and watched Lillee, that even 'Lindy' could not have bowled better than Dennis in the Sydney and Adelaide Tests. His bowling in both the Prudential Cup and the Tests this summer will be the difference between Australia and their opposition and, now that his back seems completely recovered, Australia's chances are that much improved.

His batting came on very well in the recent series and he is a good, safe fieldsman, mostly away from the close-catching positions.

McCosker, Richard Bede (New South Wales)
b 11 Dec 46. RHB. Début v South Australia 1973–4. HS 164 v Victoria 1974–5.
Not many Australian players make their début as batsmen at

the ripe old age of 28 – normally the youngsters are noted at the latest in their early twenties and brought into the Test arena soon after.

Rick McCosker is one of the exceptions, a phlegmatic right-hander well suited to opening, although beginning his first-class career in the middle of the order. He has never been outstanding in Sydney Grade cricket but was given his chance by the State selectors when brittle middle-order batting was posing problems in the 1973–4 summer. He seized the opportunity at number six, was promoted to number three the next year and then, when Wally Edwards failed, McCosker was pushed in as Redpath's opening partner.

It was a gamble by the Australian selectors but his technique is well suited to playing against the new ball. He is a solidly-built right-hander, very strong off his pads and is a safe rather than brilliant fieldsman.

Mallett, **Ashley** Alexander (South Australia)
b 13 Jul 45. RHB, OB. Début v New Zealanders 1967–8. HS 92 v Western Australia 1970–1. BB 8–59 Australia v Pakistan 1972–3.
Tours: England 1968, 1972; India 1969; South Africa 1970; New Zealand 1974.
It took the tall Australian off-spinner a long time to establish himself in Test match ranks and even in the recent series in Australia he was left out of the opening Test in Brisbane. Later in the summer, however, his bowling proved to be of great importance to Ian Chappell in balancing his attack, and in the Sydney and Adelaide Tests Mallett was in top form.

His height allows him a little extra bounce and, although he will not get that out of English pitches, his accuracy and ability to turn the ball and, as well, drift it away from the right-hander, makes him difficult to handle.

The surprising feature of his cricket in recent times has been his emergence as a wonderful gully fieldsman. The catches he took in that position against England a few months ago could be ranked with anything seen in Test match cricket – for a wearer of contact lenses, some of them were astonishing. His batting has fallen away lately and it is as a bowler and fieldsman that he makes this trip to England. He will be a key man in the Australians' plans for battle in both the Prudential Cup and the four Tests against England.

Marsh, **Rodney** William (Western Australia)
b 4 Nov 47. LHB, WK. Début *v* West Indians 1968–9. HS 236 *v* Pakistanis 1972–3.
Tours: England 1972; West Indies 1973; New Zealand 1974.
English camp followers in 1970–1 dubbed Rodney Marsh as 'iron gloves' – by the time the recent series was completed in Australia, Australian camp followers were wanting to dub him 'Sir Rodney'.

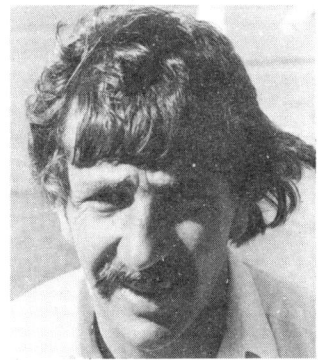

He had a torrid time against the fast bowlers Lillee and Thomson but I thought his keeping was outstanding in a team where brilliance was the operative word in their out-cricket. He took some great catches and made some great saves in what was an inspiring effort behind the stumps for Australia.

He is one of the finest all-round cricketers I have seen play for Australia since the war – with his batting he is a formidable opponent for all classes of bowler. He ranks with any overseas player as a hard hitter of the ball but that is not just against the spin bowlers in the opposition. He is an equally powerful striker against pace, probably with a preference for on-side stroking. Whenever credit is to be apportioned for Australia's revival in international cricket, Marsh's name must be very high on the list.

Robinson, Richard Darrel (Victoria)
b 9 Jul 46. RHB, WK. Début v New South Wales 1971–2. HS 99 v New Zealanders 1973–4.
Richie Robinson beat New South Wales's young 'keeper, Steve Rixon, for a position with some good all-round efforts during the past season, and his first-class career batting figures make him an ideal all-rounder as second wicket-keeper, in case anything happens to Rod Marsh by way of injury.

He has an aggressive approach to the game and has been one of the main reasons for Victoria's successful challenges for the Sheffield Shield in recent seasons in Australia.

Thomson, Jeffrey Robert (Queensland)
b 16 Aug 50. RHB, RF. Début for NSW v Queensland 1972–3; for Queensland v NSW 1974–5. HS 61 v Victoria 1974–5. BB 7–85 v Queensland 1973–4.
There have been many sensational débuts by Australian players in Test cricket, none more so than the one made by former Sydney fast bowler, Jeff Thomson, in the Test match to open the recent series. Bowling on a Brisbane pitch where the ball bounced at varying heights at one end, Thomson worked up great pace and, with Lillee, formed what I thought was the fastest combination I have seen in Test cricket. Whether they were as good as Frank Tyson and Brian Statham or Ray Lindwall and Keith Miller is a matter for argument but they were extremely fast and dangerous.

Thomson, with his slinging action akin to that of a javelin

throw, was very deceptive, and took 33 wickets in the series. Batsmen say that one of the great difficulties with him is that the ball doesn't start at face height but suddenly appears from behind his body.

The shoulder injury he sustained playing tennis during the Adelaide Test may pose problems for him, particularly in the chill English weather in some of the early games of the tour, but if he is back to full fitness I believe he will bowl extremely well in English conditions. Even in Australia he was able to move the ball off the seam and I don't agree with some of the verdicts that slower English pitches will sort him out.

Apart from his pace, I believe he could be a very useful performer for Ian Chappell. He is a good fieldsman with a fast flat throwing arm and, batting at number eleven, posed some problems for the English bowlers.

Turner, Alan (New South Wales)
b 23 Jul 50. LHB. Début *v* Victoria 1968–9. HS 127 *v* Western Australia 1971–2.
Tours: New Zealand 1969–70.

Turner, like Gary Gilmour, is a product of the Australian Schoolboys' Cricket Tours, having made the trip to South Africa in 1967–8.

Ian Redpath's decision not to tour left the way open for a number of young players to catch the selectors' eyes and Turner, a left-hander, was chosen as the extra opener. Although his overall first-class figures in the past six years are not outstanding, he has tightened his game considerably in the past twelve months.

A good double against MCC in Sydney last November gave him a start on his fellow contenders and, at 24 years of age, he has a bright future. His fielding is safe rather than spectacular, generally in the areas away from close-catching positions.

Walker, **Maxwell** Henry Norman (Victoria)
b 12 Sep 48. RHB, RMF. Début v Queensland 1968–9. HS 53 v New Zealanders 1973–4. BB 8–143 Australia v England 1974–5. Tours: West Indies 1973; New Zealand 1974.

English crowds may believe by the end of this summer that Max Walker is the ugliest bowler they have ever seen – I shall be most surprised if they do not also consider him one of the finest.

Suddenly put in the situation of being first change for Australia, Walker needed to adopt a different technique in the last series but he bowled extremely well. Before that he had been outstanding against Pakistan, New Zealand and West Indies and I rate him so highly that I feel he will be talked about in years to come as a bowler who has approached the skills of Alec Bedser. Certainly he is the finest medium pacer Australia has sent to England in many years and cricket-watchers should not be deceived by his ungainly action.

He bowls a tight line and a very good length and is constantly moving the ball a little in the air and off the seam. In the field he is safe but not as athletic as some, though his batting in the series in Australia several times saved Australia from a possible late order collapse. He plays very straight and, if he has a batting weakness, it is against spin rather than pace.

Walters, Kevin **Douglas** (New South Wales)
b 21 Dec 45. RHB, RM. Début v Queensland 1962–3. HS 253 v

South Australia 1964–5. BB 7–63 v South Australia 1964–5.
Tours: England 1968, 1972; India 1969; South Africa 1970; West Indies 1973; New Zealand 1974.

There is no greater batting enigma in cricket than Doug Walters, who made his début against England in the 1965–6 series in Australia and proceeded to rip off a century in each of his first two games against England. Only Bill Ponsford of Australia has done the same, but Walters's form fell away after a stint in the Army two years after he began his Test career.

There is no greater man in a crisis for Australia and he seems to play his best cricket when the team is in trouble. Two innings that will always live in the memory are the century he made against New Zealand in Auckland in 1974 when the Australians were caught on a bad pitch and the 55 he made on another soft strip against England in Adelaide in 1975. Both times the bowlers were on top – both times he swung the game Australia's way with a brilliant exhibition.

In the last series against England in England, he was a failure but England bowlers have a most healthy respect for his ability. He is quite outstanding in the field, almost ranking with Ross Edwards in the cover area, and has a safe pair of hands in close-catching positions.

The manager of the touring side is F. W. Bennett.

AUSTRALIAN FIRST-CLASS CAREER RECORDS
Complete to 24 June 1975

	Matches	I	NO	Runs	Av	100s	Ct/St	Runs	Wkts	Av
G. S. Chappell	187	322	42	13830	49·39	38	202	5976	204	29·29
I. M. Chappell	223	379	36	16413	47·85	48	277	6270	165	38·00
R. Edwards	109	182	19	6346	38·93	13	104/11	48	1	48·00
G. J. Gilmour	35	54	8	1341	29·15	1	36	4025	135	29·81
J. D. Higgs	31	31	12	106	5·57	—	16	2957	100	29·57
A. G. Hurst	23	24	6	165	9·16	—	10	2477	85	29·14
B. M. Laird	10	20	1	767	40·36	2	9	5	0	—
D. K. Lillee	74	87	28	702	11·89	—	27	7154	305	23·45
R. B. McCosker	19	33	3	1600	53·33	4	16	—	—	—
A. A. Mallett	123	155	38	1632	13·94	—	64	12207	506	24·12
R. W. Marsh	110	174	17	5629	35·85	7	317/39	13	0	—
R. D. Robinson	34	55	9	1552	33·73	—	118/15	—	—	—
J. R. Thomson	20	25	9	245	15·31	—	10	1975	89	22·19
A. Turner	61	112	6	3304	31·16	3	43	10	1	10·00
M. H. N. Walker†	57	79	22	998	17·50	—	21	5729	224	25·57
K. D. Walters	187	311	38	12161	44·54	37	101	5867	169	34·71

†excluding matches played for Derrick Robins's XI in South Africa in March and April 1975.

TEST CAREER RECORDS
Complete to 9 July 1975

BATTING & FIELDING	Tests	I	NO	HS	Runs	Av	100	50	Ct	St
G. S. Chappell	30	52	6	247*	2431	52·84	9	11	46	—
I. M. Chappell	62	112	7	196	4309	41·03	12	21	94	—
R. Edwards	16	26	2	170*	918	38·25	2	6	7	—
G. J. Gilmour	3	4	—	52	60	15·00	—	1	2	—
A. G. Hurst	1	1	—	16	16	16·00	—	—	—	—
D. K. Lillee	17	22	7	26	132	8·80	—	—	5	—
R. B. McCosker	3	5	—	80	202	40·40	—	2	1	—
A. A. Mallett	25	35	8	43*	304	11·25	—	—	16	—
R. W. Marsh	31	50	6	132	1598	36·31	2	8	112	7
J. R. Thomson	6	6	3	24*	84	28·00	—	—	3	—
M. H. N. Walker	17	21	8	41*	331	25·46	—	—	7	—
K. D. Walters	53	91	10	242	4016	49·58	12	25	20	—

BOWLING	Balls	M	R	W	Av	5wI	10wM	BB
G. S. Chappell	2740	97	1022	24	42·58	1	—	5– 61
I. M. Chappell	2597	75	1180	17	69·41	—	—	2– 21
G. J. Gilmour	768	11	347	15	23·13	1	—	5– 64
A. G. Hurst	232	5	73	1	73·00	—	—	1– 56
D. K. Lillee	4421	148	1828	76	24·05	4	1	6– 66
A. A. Mallett	7217	316	2602	105	24·78	6	1	8– 59
J. R. Thomson	1553	35	702	33	21·27	2	—	6– 46
M. H. N. Walker	5056	183	1792	77	23·27	5	—	8–143
K. D. Walters	2970	66	1277	43	29·69	1	—	5– 66

*not out

The Cricket Follower's Guide
Brian Johnston

APPEALS: If the fielding side believes that a batsman is out they appeal to the umpire with the call 'How's that?' It covers all ways of being out unless a specific way of getting out is stated by the person asking. Although the ball is 'dead' on 'over' being called, an appeal can still be made before the first ball of the following over is bowled, provided the bails have not been removed by both umpires after 'Time' has been called, either for close of play or for the lunch or tea intervals.

ASHES: The mythical trophy for which all Test matches between England and Australia are played. The origin of the term goes back to August 1882, when Australia defeated England by seven runs at the Oval and so secured their first Test victory in England. On the following day the *Sporting Times* published an obituary for English cricket, as follows:

In affectionate remembrance

of

English Cricket

which died at the Oval, 29 August, 1882, deeply lamented by a large circle of sorrowing friends and

acquaintances.

R.I.P.

N.B. The body will be cremated and the Ashes taken to

Australia.

In the following winter (1882–3) the Hon. Ivo Bligh took a team to Australia and won two of three Test matches arranged. At the end of the third match some ladies burnt a stump and sealed the Ashes in a small urn and presented it to the England captain, later Earl Darnley. The urn was his private property until his death in 1927 when it was bequeathed to the MCC, and is now kept at Lord's. The Ashes, therefore, exist, but are not actually played for and do not change hands.

BACKING UP: The non-striker is said to be backing up when he advances a few paces up the pitch after the delivery of the ball, with the expectation of a possible run. By so doing he makes it easier to 'steal' a quick single. Backing up is also applied to the fielding side, when one fielder covers another in case he misses the ball. This is especially the case when the ball is returned to the wicket-keeper or bowler when the batsmen are running.

BACK-STROKE: Usually made off a short pitched ball. The batsman steps back with the weight on the right foot which is moved back and across in front of the stumps. It should be kept parallel to the popping crease while the batsman's body stays as sideways as possible.

BACKWARD POINT: (see page 183).

BAILS: The two bails are each $4\frac{3}{8}''$ long and when in position at the top of the stumps must not project more than $\frac{1}{2}''$ above them. For a batsman to be out, a bail has to fall from the top of the stumps. He is *not* out if it is only disturbed but not dislodged.

BALL: Made of red leather with the interior of cork bound with twine. Weight not less than $5\frac{1}{2}$ nor more than $5\frac{3}{4}$ ounces. Circumference not less than $8^{13}/_{16}''$ nor more than $9''$.

BAT: Made of willow and shall not exceed $4\frac{1}{4}''$ in the widest part, and not be more than $38''$ in length.

BATTING CREASE: (see POPPING CREASE).

BEAMER: A full pitch bowled at a batsman's head, either intentionally or unintentionally.

BENEFITS: Counties normally award a benefit or testimonial to a capped player at least once in his career. Some still allow him to choose a match from which he takes all the proceeds, after paying all expenses for the match and for the return fixture against the same county. Because of the weather this is always a gamble and some beneficiaries have actually lost on their match. So now many counties rely on a subscription list and an agreed number of collections at matches to be chosen by the player. In addition, most players arrange Sunday matches and sell brochures, ties, and raffle tickets etc.

BENSON & HEDGES CUP: (*see* page 132).
A league/knockout competition in which all the first-class counties, two representative teams from the minor counties and a combined team from Oxford and Cambridge universities compete.

BLOCK: A very defensive batsman, who does not try to hit the ball but merely to stop it, is said to block.

BLOCK HOLE: The hole made by a batsman on or just behind the popping crease, when he marks the position of his guard given by the umpire.

BOSIE: The Australian name for the googly – after its inventor B. J. T. Bosanquet.

BOUNCER: A short pitched ball (*see* BUMPER).

BOUNDARY: This is the outside limit of the playing area, usually marked by a white line or a rope. There is no specified distance from the pitch to the boundary. Its length is decided by the 'Home' ground authority. But in first-class cricket, grounds are encouraged to make the boundaries as long as possible with a maximum of 90 yards. Four runs are scored if the ball *crosses* the boundary line and six if it is hit *over* and clear of the line. If *more* than four runs are completed at the instant the ball reaches the boundary then the batsman is credited with these *instead* of the boundary four. But if a boundary results from an overthrow, kicking or throwing the ball over the line, any runs already run are *added* to the boundary four.

N.B. (1) If a ball hits an obstacle or person within the playing area, or one of the umpires, and does not cross the boundary line, it is *not* counted as a boundary.

(2) It is *not* a six if the ball hits a sightscreen full pitch, if the sightscreen is on or inside the boundary line.

BOWLED: A batsman is dismissed 'bowled' if the ball breaks the wicket, even if the ball first touches his bat or person.

BOWLING CREASE: This crease is in line with the stumps and

is 8'8" in length, with the stumps in the centre. Before the recent change in the No Ball law a bowler had to have some part of one foot behind the bowling crease at the moment of delivery. Now it is the front foot which matters (*see* NO BALL).

BREAK-BACK: Another name for an off-break.

BUMP BALL: A ball which the batsman hits hard into the ground, and when fielded by a fielder close to the wicket gives the appearance of being a catch.

BUMPER: A short pitched ball which rises sharply. The persistent bowling of fast short-pitched balls is unfair if, in the opinion of the umpire at the bowler's end, it constitutes a systematic attempt at intimidation. In such event he must adopt the following procedure:
(a) When he decides that such bowling is becoming persistent, he forthwith 'cautions' the bowler and informs his captain and the other umpire.
(b) If this 'caution' is ineffective, he repeats it and again informs the captain and the other umpire.
(c) Should the above prove ineffective, the umpire at the bowler's end must:
    (i) At the first repetition and when the ball is 'dead' call 'Over'. The over shall then be regarded as having been completed.
    (ii) Direct the captain of the fielding side to take the bowler off forthwith. The captain shall take the bowler off as directed.
    (iii) Report the occurrence to the captain of the batting side as soon as an interval of play takes place.
A bowler who has been 'taken off' as above may not bowl again during the same innings.

BYE: A run scored from a ball which passes the wicket without touching the bat or batsman and which the wicket-keeper fails to stop. If the ball touches any part of the batsman, except his hands, the runs are scored as leg-byes.

CARRY ONE'S BAT: If an opening batsman is still not out when the last wicket falls he is said to have 'carried his bat'.

CAUGHT: A batsman is out 'caught' if a ball from a stroke of the bat or off a hand holding the bat, *but not the wrist*, is caught by a fielder before the ball touches the ground. The ball may be hugged to the body of the catcher, or be accidently lodged in his dress. The fielder must have both his feet entirely within the playing area at the instant the catch is completed, but he may go over the boundary line afterwards. Provided the ball does not touch the ground, the hand holding it may do so in making the catch.

CHAMPIONSHIP PENNANT: A flag to denote the holders of the County Cricket Championship. Instituted by Warwickshire in 1951 the pennant is given by the county holding the Championship to the winners in the following season. Warwickshire gave a pennant to Surrey at the end of the 1952 season, and after winning the Championship for seven years running, they in turn gave one to Yorkshire in 1959, and so on. The pennant shows the year of the Championship, the holders' badge in the centre and the badges of the other sixteen counties around the edge. You will always see this pennant flying over the pavilion wherever last year's Champions are playing.

CHINAMAN: The left-arm bowler's off-break to a right-handed batsman.

CHOP: A form of late cut, made by bringing the bat *down* sharply on the ball just as it is about to pass the batsman on the off-side.

CHUCKER: Someone who breaks law 26. In other words he throws instead of bowls.

CLOSE FIELD: The fielding positions close to the batsman, i.e. slips, gully, short-legs, silly point, silly mid off and mid on, etc.

CLOSE OF PLAY: The time arranged for play to finish. In Tests in this country it is 6.30 p.m. on the first four days and 5.30 p.m. (with an option of an extra half-hour at the request of either captain) on the fifth day. *But* in the event of play being suspended for one hour or more on any of the first four days, due to weather interference, play may be extended by one hour on that day, provided that play is still in progress at 6.30 p.m.

N.B. 'Play' includes an interval between innings.

In County matches on the first two days it can vary from 6.30 p.m. to 7.30 p.m., which is the latest allowed: on the third day, play cannot be scheduled to end later than 6.30 p.m. or before 4.30 p.m.

N.B. (1) In County cricket, if, in the opinion of both captains, thirty minutes extra at the end of the first or second day could bring about a definite result on that day, the umpires must order play to go on for half an hour after the advertised time. Once started, this thirty minutes must be completed. If the captains disagree, the umpires must decide.

(2) Remember that an over in progress at the advertised time for Close of Play on the *final* day of a match, must be completed at the request of either captain, even if a wicket falls after 'time' has been reached.

COVERING THE PITCH:

For Test Matches: The *whole* pitch shall be covered:

(1) On the night before the match and, if necessary, until the first ball is bowled. Also at any time whenever necessary before that during the preparation of the pitch.

(2) On each night of the match and, if necessary, throughout Sunday.

(3) On any day as soon as play is abandoned for the day, because in the umpire's opinion sufficient rain has fallen on the pitch to ensure no further play being possible on that day.

N.B. If rain stops play temporarily, the bowling ends *only* can be covered to a distance of 4 feet in front of the popping crease.

For other First-Class Matches: The whole pitch must be covered before the match and, if necessary, until the first ball is bowled. After that the pitch itself must remain *un*covered for the duration of the match. But the bowling ends will be covered to a distance of 4 feet in front of the popping creases:

(1) On each night of the match, and if necessary, over the weekend.

(2) Whenever, during the hours of play, the match is suspended.

COW SHOT: A swipe *across* the flight of a ball, from off to leg, sending the ball anywhere on the leg-side.

CROSS BAT: A stroke made with the bat when out of the true perpendicular.

CRUMBLING WICKET OR PITCH: A pitch which, due to the absence of rain, is dry and breaks up on the surface owing to wear. On a pitch of this nature a ball can turn and lift sharply, therefore being of more assistance to the spinners.

CUT: A stroke. (*See* under LATE- and SQUARE-.)

CUTTER: A batsman who cuts the ball. Also a type of ball bowled. (*See* OFF- and LEG-.)

DEAD BALL: The ball is 'dead':
(1) On being, in the opinion of the umpire, finally settled in the hands of the wicket-keeper or of the bowler.
(2) On reaching or pitching over the boundary.
(3) On lodging in the dress of either a batsman or umpire, whether it has been played or not.
(4) On the call of 'Over' or 'Time' by the umpire.
(5) On a batsman being out for any cause.
(6) In the case of unfair play or of a serious injury to a player.
In addition an umpire can also call 'Dead Ball':
(1) If satisfied that the striker is not ready to receive the ball.
(2) If the bowler drops the ball accidentally before delivery or if the ball does not leave his hand for any reason.
(3) If one or both bails fall from the striker's wicket before he receives the delivery.
(4) If the batsmen attempt to steal a run during the bowler's run-up, unless the bowler throws the ball at either wicket.

N.B. A ball does *not* become dead when it strikes an umpire, when the wicket is broken (unless a batsman is out) or when an unsuccessful appeal is made.

DECLARATION OF AN INNINGS: The batting captain may declare an innings closed at any time during a match irrespective of its duration. A captain can forfeit his *second* innings instead of having to make a time-wasting declaration like 1 for 0 declared, as has happened in the past. In this event there will be the usual 10 minutes between innings and he must inform the opposing captain and the umpire in time to allow seven minutes rolling of the pitch.

DONKEY DROP: A ball bowled very high in the air.

DRAG: Under the old No-Ball law bowlers used to be no-balled for dragging their back foot over the bowling crease before delivering the ball. Since the introduction of the front-foot experiment (*see* NO-BALL) this no longer applies.

DRAW: An unfinished match. Also used to describe an old-fashioned stroke, where the batsman cocked his left leg up and deflected the ball underneath – down towards long-leg.

DRINKS ON THE FIELD: Drinks can only be taken to the same team in the field *once* in each session.

DUCK: The dreaded score of 0.

EXTRAS: Are runs added to the score, but not actually scored by the batsman. They are byes, leg-byes, wides and no-balls.

FIRST-CLASS COUNTY: A team which competes in the County Cricket Championship. These are seventeen in number: Derbyshire, Essex, Glamorgan, Gloucestershire, Hampshire, Kent, Lancashire, Leicestershire, Middlesex, Northamptonshire, Nottinghamshire, Somerset, Surrey, Sussex, Warwickshire, Worcestershire and Yorkshire.

FIRST-CLASS MATCH: Is a match of three or more days duration between two sides of eleven players officially adjudged first class. The Governing Body in each country shall decide the status of the teams. A match *cannot* be first class if either team has more than eleven players or if the duration of the match is shorter than three days.

FLIGHT: The term used for a ball so delivered that in its passage through the air the batsman is deceived as to the spot on which it will touch the ground. Spin aids flights as the ball is inclined to dip just before hitting the ground.

FLIPPER: A type of delivery which is said to have been invented by Clarrie Grimmett and also bowled by Bruce Dooland, Richie Benaud, Bob Barber, and Intikhab amongst others. It is a ball held in the tips of the first and third fingers of the right hand. It is squeezed or flipped out of the hand from underneath the wrist – rather like flipping a cherry stone.

Pitched outside the off-stump it hurries through off the pitch, usually straight but sometimes from off to leg. A very useful surprise weapon if bowled occasionally, especially at a batsman who tends to play off the back foot or one who likes the pull shot off slow bowlers.

FOLLOW-ON: The side which bats first and leads by 200 runs in a five-day match, by 150 runs in a three- or four-day match, by 100 runs in a two-day match, or by 75 runs in a one-day match, has the option of asking the other side to follow-on, i.e. to bat again.

FORWARD STROKE: A stroke played by advancing the front foot down the wicket.

FULL TOSS OR FULL PITCH: A ball which reaches the batsman at the popping crease without pitching, or a ball made into a full toss by a batsman advancing down the pitch and hitting the ball before it touches the ground.

GARDENING: On a wet pitch when small divots are removed by the ball when it is pitched, the batsmen often prod or pat the pitch with the bat to try to level it.

GILLETTE CUP: (*see* page 128).
A knock-out competition in which all the First-Class Counties and the top five Minor Counties of the previous year compete. One innings each of a maximum of sixty overs. No bowler can bowl more than twelve overs.

GOOGLY: A ball bowled out of the back of the right hand with what looks like a leg-break action, but which spins as an off-break when hitting the ground and so turns 'the wrong way' to what the batsman is expecting.

GO AWAY: A ball which leaves a batsman, i.e. moves from leg to off either in the air or off the pitch, is said to 'go away'.

GO WITH THE ARM: A term for a ball which appears to go with the direction of the bowler's arm, i.e. for a right-arm bowler it is, in fact, a continuation of an outswinger, and for a left-arm bowler, the continuation of an inswinger, when both are bowling to a right-handed batsman.

GREEN WICKET: A pitch well covered with plenty of grass which early in the day contains quite a lot of moisture. This is sometimes caused because the pitch has been covered all night and has 'sweated'. The greenness helps the pace-bowler to get extra life, lift and movement off the pitch.

GROUND, PITCH, WEATHER AND LIGHT: The fitness of the ground and pitch before and during play, and the fitness of the weather and light for play are all matters for the umpires to decide. This means that there are now no more appeals by batsmen against the light. But if *both* captains wish to start or continue when the umpires consider conditions are unfit, then play will go on. Similarly, if the batting side wish to continue after the umpires have judged the light too bad, they may do so.

GRUB: An underhand ball which shoots along the ground. Also called a 'sneak'.

GUARD: Given to the batsman by the bowler's umpire so that the batsman knows the position of his bat and feet in relation to the three stumps which he is guarding. Guard is given from behind the bowler's wicket unless otherwise asked for. The usual guards are: middle, middle and leg, or leg stump.

HALF VOLLEY: A ball which the bat strikes just after the ball leaves the ground.

HANDLED BALL: Either batsman may be dismissed 'handled ball' if he touches the ball, while in play, with his hands, unless he does so at the request of the fielding side.

HAT TRICK: The feat of a bowler taking three wickets with three consecutive deliveries, either in one over or spread over two. By long-standing custom three wickets in three balls spread over two innings of the same match is regarded as a 'hat trick', but the limit ends there and three wickets in three balls spread over two matches do not qualify for a 'hat trick'.

HIT THE BALL TWICE: A batsman is out if he hits the ball twice, unless the stroke is made in defence of his wicket. No runs can be scored off this second stroke except from an overthrow. The bowler does *not* get credit for the wicket if a batsman is given out *hit the ball twice*.

HIT WICKET: A batsman is out Hit Wicket if he hits down his wicket with his bat or any part of his person, in the following circumstances:
(1) At any time when playing at the ball.
(2) In setting off for his first run.

N.B. (1) 'When playing at the ball' means the action of a batsman receiving a bowler's delivery, which has not been called No Ball, regardless of whether such action is, in the opinion of the umpire, an attempt by the batsman to hit the ball or not.
(2) Any part of the batsman's dress will be considered part of his person.
(3) A batsman is 'Not Out' if he breaks his wicket in trying to avoid being run out or stumped.

HOOK: A stroke made to a short rising ball, usually on the wicket or leg-side, which is hit to leg.

INSWINGER: A ball which swings from off to leg in flight, thus moving into the batsman while still in the air.

KING PAIR: If a batsman is out first ball for 0 in each innings, he is said to have taken a 'king pair'.

LAP: An expression used by modern cricketers to describe a cross-bat stroke. The batsman hits across the flight of the ball and even though it pitches on or outside the off-stump, he hits it somewhere between square-leg and mid-on.

LAST OVER: The over in progress at the close of play on the final day of the match shall be completed at the request of either captain, even if a wicket falls after 'Time' has been called. The last over before close of play or an interval shall be started provided that the umpire standing at square leg, after walking at his normal pace, has arrived at his position behind the stumps at the bowler's end before time has been reached. This will also apply if a batsman is out or 'Retires' after the last ball of an over when less than two minutes remain for play at the end of the match.

LATE CUT: A stroke played late to a short ball outside the off-stump by stepping across with the right foot and hitting the ball down with a wristy action, so sending it past the slips.

LEG BEFORE WICKET: This method of dismissal causes much more trouble than the rest of the laws put together, and it is essential to point out that the only person who is really in a position to make a decision is the umpire at the bowler's end. From the boundary it is impossible to judge.

The umpire has five questions to ask himself in every l.b.w. appeal and the answer must be 'yes' in each case before the batsman can be given out:

(1) Would the ball have hit the wicket?
(2) Did the ball pitch on a straight line between wicket and wicket (this includes a ball played full pitch by the batsman) or did it pitch on the off-side of the wicket?
(3) Was it part of the striker's person, other than the hand or hands holding the bat, which first intercepted the ball?
(4) Was that part of the striker's person in a straight line between wicket and wicket at the moment of impact, irrespective of the height of point of impact?
(5) If the part of the striker's person was *outside* the line of the off-stump, was he *not* attempting to play a stroke?

The actual law reads as follows:

The striker is out l.b.w. if with any part of his person except his hand, which is in a straight line between wicket and wicket, even though the point of impact be above the level of the bails, he intercepts a ball which has not first touched his bat or hand, and which in the opinion of the umpire, shall have or would have pitched on a straight line from the bowler's wicket to the striker's wicket, or shall have pitched on the off-side of the striker's wicket, provided always that the ball would have hit the wicket.

N.B. 'Part of the striker's person' includes his head, and the 'hand' referred to must be holding the bat. To make things even more complicated there is now an experimental law in force whereby: A batsman is out l.b.w. even if the part of his body hit is *outside the line of the off-stump, if he has in the umpire's opinion made no attempt to play the ball with his bat. (See diagram.)*

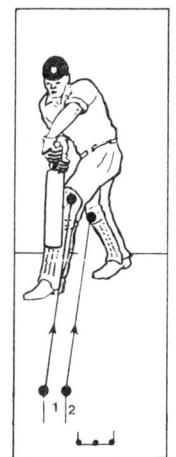

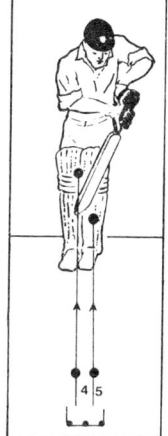

THE CRICKET FOLLOWER'S GUIDE 165

Ball 1
NOT OUT – as Batsman made a genuine attempt to play the ball with his bat, even though his left leg is outside line of off-stump.

Ball 2
OUT – as Batsman's right leg is in line between wicket and wicket.

Ball 3
OUT – as although Batsman's left leg is *outside* line of off-stump he has made *no* attempt to play the ball with his bat.

Balls 4 and 5
OUT – ball pitched in straight line between wicket and wicket.

Ball 6
NOT OUT – ball pitched outside Batsman's leg stump.

LEG BREAK: A ball which turns on the pitch from the leg side to the off. The orthodox spin for a left-arm bowler is a leg break to a right-handed batsman.

LEG-BYES: Leg-byes are scored when the ball is *unintentionally* deflected by the batsman with any part of his person except his hand or hands holding the bat. But in the opinion of the umpire the batsman must either have been trying to play the ball, or trying to avoid being hit by it. If he has played no stroke or deliberately deflects the ball the umpire must call Dead Ball as soon as one run has been completed or the ball has reached the boundary. These runs are then cancelled. Runs scored from leg-byes are counted as extras and are not debited against the bowler's analysis.

LEG-CUTTER: Is really a fast leg-break which is bowled by 'cutting' the fingers across the seam of the ball rather than by the normal wrist-spin.

LEG-SIDE: The side of the pitch *behind* the batsman as he takes his stand at the wicket. The number of fielders on the leg-side *behind the popping crease* must not exceed two at the instant of the bowler's delivery. If there are more than two the square-leg umpire must call No Ball. But there is no limit to the number of fielders allowed on the legside as a whole.

LEG THEORY: A method of bowling where the ball is pitched consistently on or just outside the leg stump with an array of fielders on the leg side. These fielders are usually known as the leg trap. This type of bowling restricts the batsman's strokes and is responsible for much dull cricket.

LEG-TRAP: A term used to describe a cluster of fielders in the short-leg positions.

LENGTH: A good-length ball is one which pitches on the pitch at such a distance from the batsman as to make him uncertain whether to play a backward or forward stroke. It is a ball which he cannot reach comfortably by playing forward, or adequately deal with by playing back, as the ball is too far up for this type of stroke.

LOB: A method of bowling which is rarely seen in first-class cricket today. Bowled under-arm, it is a survivor of the earliest known form of bowling. If the ball is returned under-arm by the fielder he is said to 'lob' it.

LONG FIELD: The part of the outfield in front of the sight-screen in the region of long-off and long-on.

LONG HANDLE: The aggressive batsman who is hitting out is sometimes said to be 'taking the Long Handle'.

LONG HOP: A very short-pitched ball.

LUNCH INTERVAL: In Tests from 1.30 p.m.–2.10 p.m. and in the County Championship from 1.15 p.m.–1.55 p.m. This can now be varied in both Tests and first-class cricket, if due to the weather or state of the ground an alteration is agreed upon by the captains, or ordered by the umpires. The interval is limited to forty minutes if an innings ends within ten minutes of the scheduled start of the interval, i.e. if an innings closes at 1.10 p.m. play resumes at 1.50 p.m.

MAIDEN OVER: An over off which no runs are scored by the batsmen.

MIDDLE: The centre of the ground or the square upon which the pitches are prepared.

NEW BALL: Either captain can demand a new ball at the start of each innings. The captain of the fielding side has the option of taking another new ball after 85 overs have been bowled with the old one in Tests, and all first-class matches except the County Championship when it is after 100 overs. This taking of the new ball can be delayed but the counting of overs for another new ball does not start until this new ball has been taken (i.e. if a Test captain delays taking a new ball until 100 overs have been bowled, the next new ball is due after 185th over).

N.B. In Australia, the new ball can be taken after 65 of the eight-ball overs.

NIGHT WATCHMAN: A lower-order batsman sent in to play out time when a wicket falls shortly before close of play. This saves the risk of a better batsman losing his wicket – often in failing light.

NO BALL:
(1) For a delivery to be fair, the ball must be bowled, not thrown; if, in the opinion of either umpire, a delivery is unfair in this respect, he shall call and signal 'No Ball' instantly upon delivery. The umpire at the bowler's wicket shall call and signal 'No Ball' if, in the delivery stride, the bowler's *front foot lands clear beyond the popping crease*, or if he is not satisfied that the bowler's back foot has landed within and not touching the return crease or its forward extension.

N.B. A bowler's front foot may touch or straddle the popping crease. The heel need *not* be grounded. *(See diagram, overleaf.)*

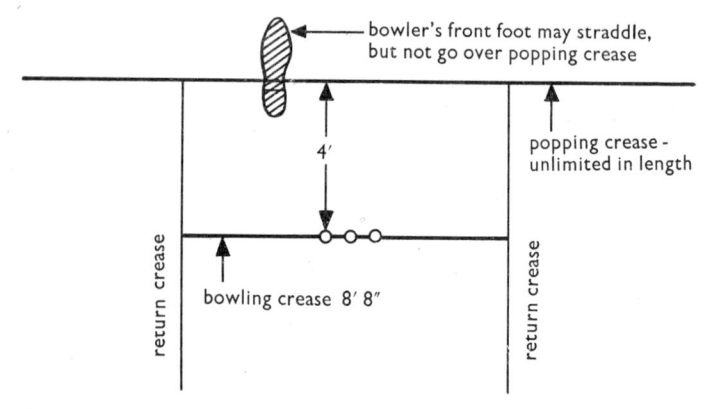

Figure: bowler's front foot may straddle, but not go over popping crease. 4′. popping crease – unlimited in length. return crease. bowling crease 8′ 8″. return crease.

(2) A ball shall be deemed to have been thrown if, in the opinion of either umpire, the process of straightening the bowling arm, whether it be partial or complete, takes place during that part of the delivery swing which directly precedes the ball leaving the hand. This definition shall not debar a bowler *from straightening an over-extended arm* nor from the use of the wrist in the delivery swing.

(3) In conjunction with the above-mentioned Experimental Law the following conditions shall apply: (i) The length of the return crease shall be four feet. (ii) The popping crease shall extend six feet either side of the line of stumps. (iii) The popping crease and return crease shall be redrawn during each interval.

The umpire will also call No Ball: (i) If the bowler fails to notify the batsman that he is changing his delivery i.e. from over to round the wicket, from over-arm to lobs, etc. (ii) If there are more than two fielders behind the popping crease on the leg-side. (iii) If a bowler, before delivery, throws the ball at the striker's wicket even in an attempt to run him out.

N.B. (1) A batsman may be out in four ways off a No Ball: Run out, handling the ball, obstructing the field, hitting the ball twice.

(2) The ball does *not* become dead upon the call of No Ball, and if runs are scored by the batsman they are credited to the score and debited to the bowler. If no runs are scored, then one No Ball is added to the extras.

(3) Any byes or leg-byes made off a No Ball are scored as No Balls.
(4) A No Ball does *not* count in the over so an extra ball has to be bowled for every No Ball bowled, in order that the over may consist of six legitimate deliveries.

OBSTRUCTING THE FIELD: Either batsman can be dismissed 'obstructing the field' if he *wilfully* obstructs the other side. If the obstruction prevents the ball from being caught then it is the striker who is out. The only question the umpire has to ask himself is, 'Was the obstruction wilful?'

OFF BREAK: A ball which after pitching turns from off to leg. Bowled by a right-arm bowler, it is referred to as orthodox spin. Spun mainly by the first finger of the right hand, the action is like turning a door handle.

OFF-CUTTER: A fast off-break bowled by 'cutting' the fingers across the seam of the ball rather than by orthodox finger spin.

OFF-DRIVE: A drive made off the front foot, usually from a half-volley, in the arc between cover-point and long-off.

OFF SIDE: The side of the field 'in front' of the batsman as he takes his stand at the wicket.

ON-DRIVE: A drive made off the front foot in the arc between mid-wicket and long-on.

ON SIDE: The same as the leg side, i.e. the side of the field behind the batsman.

OUTFIELD: That portion of the playing area which is some distance from the pitch. The fielding positions are nearer the boundary than the pitch (e.g. long-off, long-on, deep third man, long leg, deep mid wicket etc.).

OVER: An over of six balls is bowled from each wicket alternately. For first-class cricket in Australia the eight-ball over is in force. In the County Championship all Counties are required to achieve an overall average of at least 18·50 overs per hour. Any County failing to attain this average will be liable to a fine of £1000, of which the Club will pay £500 and the players £500.

OUT OF HIS GROUND: The batsman must have some part of his bat or his foot on the ground behind the popping crease in order to avoid being run out or stumped.

N.B. The foot placed on the line is 'out'. It is not enough for a batsman to have a foot or the bat in the air behind the crease, *it must be grounded*.

OUTSWINGER: A ball which swings from leg to off in flight, often described as 'leaving the bat'.

OVER THE WICKET: A method of delivery where the bowler faces the stumps at the bowler's end as he delivers the ball, i.e. a right-arm bowler bowls on the left-hand side of the stumps, a left-arm bowler on the right side.

OVERTHROW: A throw in from the field which eludes the wicket-keeper or bowler and travels beyond the stumps to the other side of the field, so that the batsmen may take further runs. If a ball hits the stumps with a batsman in his crease, and then ricochets off to the outfield, overthrows may still be taken even though the wicket is broken. All such runs scored are credited to the striker and (rather bad luck this) debited to the bowler, unless of course they are extras.

PAIR OF SPECTACLES: A term used to describe the performance of a batsman who fails to score in both innings of a match, thereby collecting two 'ducks'.

PAYMENTS OF PLAYERS AND UMPIRES IN TEST MATCHES:

Players	£180 per match
Twelfth Man on duty throughout	£95
Twelfth Man (1st and 2nd day)	£60
Twelfth Man (3rd, 4th, 5th day)	£36
Umpires	£150 per match
Scorers	£25 per match
Emergency Fielders	£7 per day

PITCH: 22 yards long and 5 feet in width on either side of a line joining the two middle stumps. A pitch may not be changed *during* a match unless it becomes unfit for play, and then only with the consent of *both* captains.

PLAYED ON: A term used for a batsman who is dismissed

'bowled' through hitting the ball into his own wicket with the bat.

PLAYING BACK: A stroke played by the batsman with his weight on the back foot, i.e. the foot nearest the stumps, the right foot in the case of a right-handed batsman. This stroke is usually used when playing a ball short of a length.

PLUMB PITCH OR WICKET: A perfect surface which has not been affected by either rain or wear. It gives no help to swing or spin bowlers as the ball comes off at a uniform height and pace, without any real change of direction. Ideal for batting.

POLISHING THE BALL: (1) No one, other than the bowler, may polish the ball. (2) No one (including the bowler) may rub the ball on the pitch or ground or interfere in any way with the natural condition of the ball. Wiping and cleaning is allowed under the umpire's supervision.

POP: A ball which lifts sharply off the pitch is said to Pop.

POPPING CREASE: A line four feet in front of the wicket parallel to the bowling crease, which is the forward limit of the batsman's safety area against stumping and run out decisions. When the wicket is broken the batsman's foot or bat must be behind the crease and not actually on the line.

The popping crease is now the line which determines a No Ball (see NO BALL).

PULL: A stroke made by hitting across the flight of a ball delivered on the stumps or off-side of the wicket and driving it away to the on-side. This is technically a forward stroke off the front foot. The bat remains perpendicular throughout as distinct from the cow-shot.

QUICKIE: A slang term for a fast bowler.

QUICK WICKET: A hard pitch from which the ball comes off very quickly. Usually produced by much rolling with the heavy roller.

REGISTRATION AND QUALIFICATION RULES: These are rather complicated but put in simple terms are:

(1) *Home-born Player* can play: (a) For the county of his birth. (b) For the county in which he has lived for the previous 12 consecutive months. (c) For the county for which he is specially registered. (A county can apply for special registration for up to two cricketers in any one calendar year and must give a contract for a minimum of three years.)

If a cricketer wants to leave his county to play for another against the wishes of his county, then he can only qualify for the other county by living in it for up to a maximum of 12 consecutive months – the exact period to be decided by the Registration Committee.

(2) *Overseas-born Player:* Each county may register one overseas-born player immediately without any qualification period being required. But they can only have two registered overseas players on their books at any one time, and can only make another immediate registration of another overseas player after three years.

Once an overseas player has been immediately registered by a county he can *never* be so registered again. If he wishes to play for another county he must qualify by a 12-month residence.

N.B. (1) An overseas-born player becomes a home-born player when he has lived in this country for 10 years.

(2) An overseas-born player playing for a county must be made available to play in Test matches for the country of his birth, either here in England, or in his own country.

RETIREMENTS: A batsman may retire at any time but cannot resume his innings without the consent of the fielding captain and then only *at the fall of a wicket*. A batsman is regarded as *not out* if he retires as a result of injury or illness but it counts as *out* if he retires for any other reason.

RETURN CREASE: A line which turns back at right angles at each end of the bowling crease and is deemed to be of unlimited length. Since the introduction of the front foot rule for calling no balls, the return crease is extended from the bowling crease to the popping crease.

ROLLING, MOWING AND WATERING: (1) The pitch cannot be rolled during a match except before the start of each innings and of each day's play, when, if the captain of the batting side chooses, it can be swept and rolled for *not more than seven minutes*. It can be rolled for less if the batting captain so wishes. Rolling before play must take place not *more* than thirty minutes before play is due to start, and the captain of the batting side can delay this rolling until ten minutes before the start if he wishes. But if the captain of the batting side only declares his innings closed just before the start, the time for sufficient rolling must be taken out of the normal playing period, if necessary. This also applies if a declaration is made later than fifteen minutes after the start of the lunch interval. Play will then not restart until 2.20 p.m.

(2) The pitch will be mown under the supervision of the umpires before play begins on alternate days after the start of a match. This means that in a Test in this country starting on a Thursday the pitch *can* be mown before the start and then *must* be mown on the Saturday and Monday. (Sunday counting as a day.) If owing to rain the pitch is not mown on the appointed day, it must be mown on the first day on which play is resumed and then on alternate days for the rest of the match. In first-class matches of three days the pitch must be mown on the third day. In weekend matches Sunday counts as a day so that the pitch must be mown on Monday.

(3) If conditions permit the outfield will be mown before the start of play on each morning of the match.

(4) The pitch *cannot* under any circumstances be watered during a match.

ROUND THE WICKET: A method of delivery where the bowler has his back to the stumps at the bowling end as he delivers the ball, i.e. a right-arm bowler bowls on the right-hand side of the stumps, a left-arm bowler on the left side.

RUNNER: (*see* SUBSTITUTES).

RUN OUT: A batsman is 'run out' if a fielder breaks the wicket while the batsman is out of his ground. The batsman nearest to the broken wicket is the one dismissed if they are in the act of running.

N.B. If the batsman plays the ball so that it breaks the wicket at the other end, the non-striker, if he is out of his crease, is only run out if the ball has been touched by a fielder before it breaks the wicket.

RUN-UP: To cut out time-wasting the bowler is not now allowed a trial run-up.

SEAM BOWLER OR SEAMER: A bowler – normally of medium pace or over – who 'moves' the ball in the air or off the pitch.

SELECTORS: The T.C.C.B. appoint four selectors each year to choose the Test teams in this country. Any of the counties can nominate a candidate for election at the bi-annual meeting of the T.C.C.B. in March. For tours overseas, although the Team is still known as M.C.C., it is selected by the four T.C.C.B. selectors assisted by the captain, manager and usually the chairman of the T.C.C.B. Cricket Committee. The 1975 selectors are A. V. Bedser (chairman), K. F. Barrington, C. S. Elliott and Sir Leonard Hutton.

SESSION: A session is one of the three official periods of play, i.e. from start to lunch, from lunch to tea, from tea to close of play.

SET: A batsman is said to be 'Set' when he has got his 'eye in' or has 'played himself in'. Some take longer than others!

SHINE: 'Shine on the ball' means that it still retains some of the smooth polished surface which it had when new. A smooth surface helps the ball to swing, which is why you see seam bowlers polishing the ball. (*See* POLISHING THE BALL.)

SHOOTER: A ball which does not rise after hitting the ground.

SHORT RUN: When a batsman fails to make good his ground at one end when running two or more runs. The umpire signals this *(see diagram, page 176)* and the scorers delete one or more runs from those actually run by the batsmen.

SHOULDER ARMS: An expression used to describe a batsman's action when he holds the bat aloft over his shoulder as he allows the ball to go by on the off-side without attempting a stroke.

THE CRICKET FOLLOWER'S GUIDE 175

SIGHT-SCREEN: In Test matches in this country sight-screens must now be provided at both ends of the ground.

SIGNALS:

Byes: by raising the open hand above the head.
Leg-byes: by touching a raised knee with the hand.

No-balls: by extending one arm horizontally.
Out: by raising the index finger above the head.

One short: by raising the arm upwards and by touching the
shoulder nearest to the scorers with the tips of the fingers.

Wides: by extending both arms horizontally.

Six: by raising both hands above the head.

Boundaries: by waving the hand from side to side.

SQUARE CUT: A stroke made to a short ball outside the off stump by stepping across the wicket and hitting the ball down with a wristy action as it is level with the batsman. This stroke will normally send the ball between Cover Point and Gully down towards Third Man.

START OF PLAY: In Test matches in this country it is always at

11.30 a.m. on the first four days and at 11 a.m. on the fifth day. In other first-class matches play now starts at 11 a.m. each day.

STICKY WICKET: Describes a pitch which has been affected by rain and subsequently drying out under the sun turns into a 'glue pot'. Only the top crust becomes harder with the underneath still soft and this allows the ball to bite into the pitch and turn more sharply and lift more abruptly than is usually the case.

STUMPS: Must be of equal size and placed into the ground so that the ball cannot pass between them. When in position the three stumps are 9 inches wide, each stump being 28 inches above the ground.

STUMPED: A batsman may be stumped if he is out of his ground when the wicket-keeper breaks the wicket with the ball in the hand which removes the bails, or if the ball rebounds from the wicket-keeper's person on to the stumps.

A wicket-keeper may *not* take the ball in front of the wicket for the purpose of stumping unless the ball has first touched the bat or person of the striker.* A batsman *can* be stumped off a wide.

*N.B. A batsman is out *stumped* after *hitting* the ball, although it used to be recorded as run out.

SUBSTITUTES: A substitute is allowed to field or act as a runner, for any player, who may be incapacitated from illness or injury *during the match*, but not for any other reason. The consent of the opposing captain always has to be obtained for a person to act as substitute, and he may also indicate positions in which the substitute may *not* field. No substitute may bat or bowl. It is also generally accepted that a substitute may not keep wicket, but there is nothing to stop him doing so, provided the opposing captain has not indicated it as one of the positions he may not field in.

Under the laws a substitute is allowed only for injury *sustained in the match*, and if a player starts the match injured and then finds himself unable to carry on, the opposing captain has the perfect right to refuse a substitute. A player may still bat, bowl or field, even though a substitute has acted for him earlier in the match.

When he is the striker a player with a substitute who is running for him can be out stumped or run out at the wicket-keeper's end. When not the striker the injured batsman is considered out of the game and stands out of the way near the square leg umpire.

SWEEP: A stroke played at a ball which is normally on or outside the leg stump, when the bat follows round and hits the ball behind the wicket on the leg side.

SWERVE: (*see* INSWINGER *and* OUTSWINGER).

TAIL: The players engaged more for their bowling or wicket keeping than for their talent as batsmen and who are not expected to score many runs are known as the 'Tail' or 'Tailenders'. They are also sometimes referred to as 'Rabbits'. One player was so notoriously bad as a batsman that he gained the nickname of 'Ferret' – the man who comes in after the 'Rabbits'.

TEA INTERVAL: The regulations governing this are the nightmare of commentators, spectators and even umpires! Tea will be taken at 4.15 p.m. in a match in which the drawing of stumps has been fixed for 6.30 p.m. unless: (1) Nine wickets are down, in which case play continues until the end of the innings, unless the two batsmen are still together at 4.45 p.m. in which case tea is taken; (2) If an innings ends at or after 3.45 p.m. tea is then taken, being combined with the ten minutes interval between innings, but limited to twenty minutes in all; (3) If an innings ends before 3.45 p.m., or the game is resumed after a stoppage, tea shall be taken after fifty minutes play, or at 4.15 p.m. whichever is the later. Summed up, this means that if an innings ends *after* 3.15 p.m. but *before* 3.45 p.m. tea will be taken one hour after the end of the innings. *If the drawing of stumps has been agreed at seven o'clock*, all the above timings are *fifteen minutes* later. And on the occasions when close of play is extended to 7.30 p.m. on any of the first four days in a Test the above timings are *twenty-five* minutes later. There is no interval: (1) If both captains agree to forgo it. (2) If the close of play (excluding any extra time) has been fixed at or before 5 p.m.

(3) If there has been no play at all between 2.45 p.m. and 3.45 p.m.

TEAM: A first-class match is played between two teams of eleven players each. Before tossing for choice of innings the two captains must exchange lists of their teams *in writing*, together with the twelfth men. Afterwards no alteration can be made in either team without the consent of the opposing captain. In practice this will probably be given in the event of sudden illness or injury *before the match starts*.

TESTIMONIAL: Awarded by counties to players of long standing; unlike a Benefit Match it does not include the proceeds of a special match and is limited to a subscription list, collections and special Sunday games.

TEST MATCHES: These are matches played between full representative teams of the members of the International Cricket Conference. The present members are: England, Australia, West Indies, New Zealand, India and Pakistan. The Associate members who do not yet qualify for Test Cricket are: The United States, Fiji, Sri-Lanka, Holland, Denmark, Bermuda, East Africa, Malaysia, Canada, Argentina, Israel and Singapore. South Africa, one of the founder members with England, and Australia, withdrew from the ICC when she left the Commonwealth in 1961. Since then *officially* any matches which South Africa has played against England, Australia and New Zealand have *not* been Test matches. But *unofficially* they have been called Tests and have been regarded as such by Wisden and BBC statisticians when compiling records.

THROWING: (*see* NO BALL).

TIE: A match which ends with an equal total of runs scored by each side, provided that the fourth innings is completed.

TOP SPIN: Spin which allows the ball to gain pace off the pitch when hitting the ground and then to continue on the same line. Bowled by leg-break bowlers in addition to the googly.

TOSS FOR INNINGS: The choice of innings is decided by the toss of a coin: the home captain tosses the coin and the away captain calls. The toss must be made not less than fifteen minutes before the time for start of play, and is, in fact, usually made at 11 a.m. for a match due to start at 11.30 a.m. If, owing to inclement weather, no start is made, the toss can be delayed until such time as the game can be started. But if the toss is made and rain then holds up the start of the match, the toss stands and the decision of the captain holds.

TRACK: A slang expression for the pitch. A batsman is sometimes said to 'go down the track' to a slow bowler.

TWELFTH MAN: The emergency fielder and 'drink waiter'.

UMPIRES: Two umpires are appointed and cannot be changed during a match without the consent of *both* captains. Before the toss for innings they must agree with the captains any special regulations and all conditions affecting the match, i.e. hours of play, intervals, which clock they are going by, choice of balls to be used and any local rule affecting the boundary.

They must also see that the wickets are properly pitched and that all instruments of play, such as bats, stumps, etc., conform to the laws. As shown elsewhere in addition to interpreting the laws, they have special powers to stop a bowler from bowling any more in an innings: (1) If he is guilty of bowling persistent bumpers. (2) If he causes damage to the pitch in his follow through. (The 'danger area' is an area contained by an imaginary line four feet from and parallel to the popping crease and within two imaginary and parallel lines drawn down the pitch from points one foot on either side of the middle stump.) (3) If he takes unnecessarily long to bowl an over.

N.B. An umpire may alter his decision provided that he does it promptly. He must also intervene if a batsman, not having been given out, has left his wicket under a misapprehension.

The various umpires' signals are shown on pages 175–6.

WASTING TIME: Umpires are reminded that any waste of time – such as a bowler wasting time; the fielders crossing over slowly between the overs and for left-handed batsmen; fielders throwing the ball to one another before returning it to the bowler, unless the bowler begins his walk back to his mark immediately after delivering the ball; captains being unduly deliberate in field placing and not starting such field placing until a new batsman has reached the wicket; incoming batsmen taking too long to reach the wicket – constitutes unfair play, and after consultation together and, where possible, after warning the captain concerned, they shall report such occurrences to the Secretary of the T.C.C.B. and to the Manager or Secretary of the team to which the offending player belongs.

In the event of a bowler taking unnecessarily long to bowl an over, the umpire at the bowler's end, after consultation with the other umpire, shall take the following immediate action: (1) Caution the bowler and inform the captain of the fielding side that he has done so. (2) Should this caution prove ineffective: (a) Direct the captain of the fielding side to take the bowler off at the end of the over in progress. The captain shall take the bowler off as directed. (b) Report the occurrence to the captain of the batting side as soon as an interval of play takes place. (c) Send a written report of the occurrence to the Secretary of the T.C.C.B. and to the Manager or Secretary of the team to which the offending player belongs. A bowler who has been 'taken off' as above may not bowl again during the same innings.

WET WICKET OR PITCH: A pitch affected by rain, where the ball leaves the turf slowly. The ball, as it pitches, usually takes divots out of the wicket, which causes the batsmen to undertake 'gardening' in an attempt to keep the wicket true. A pitch of this type becomes rather pitted if wet for a long time and the slight indentations allow the bowler to move the ball considerably as the wicket dries.

WICKET: The actual pitch (22 yards in length) between the two sets of stumps is often referred to as the wicket, but technically the wicket is the three stumps and two bails erected at each end of the pitch. The current size of the stumps is 28 inches high and 9 inches wide. The stumps must be of equal width and sufficient size to prevent a ball going through the wicket. The bails are $4\frac{3}{8}$ inches in width and when in position on the stumps must not project more than half an inch above them.

WICKET-KEEPER: A wicket-keeper must not have any part of his person in front of the wicket until the ball delivered by the bowler touches the bat or person of the batsman or passes the wicket, or until the batsman attempts a run. Otherwise the batsman *may* be given NOT OUT, bowled, caught, stumped or LBW. But if in the opinion of the umpire the encroachment by the wicket-keeper has not gained any advantage for the fielding side, nor in any way interfered with the right of the striker to play the ball with complete freedom, nor has had any effect whatsoever in the downfall of the striker, then the umpire shall disregard the infringement.

WICKET MAIDEN: An over off which no runs are scored by the batsman but in which the bowler takes one or more wickets.

WIDE BALL: The ball is called 'wide' if it is bowled so high over or wide of the wicket that in the umpire's opinion the ball is out of the reach of a batsman when taking guard *in the normal position*.

WISDEN TROPHY: A trophy which is played for by England and the West Indies. Presented by Wisden to celebrate their centenary.

WRONG-UN: Another term used to denote the googly, called a 'Bosie' in Australia after B. J. T. Bosanquet, the originator.

YORKER: A ball well pitched up so that it touches the ground at the batsman's feet and is liable to pass under the bat. A very useful ball for a pace-bowler at a new batsman.

THE CRICKET FOLLOWER'S GUIDE 183

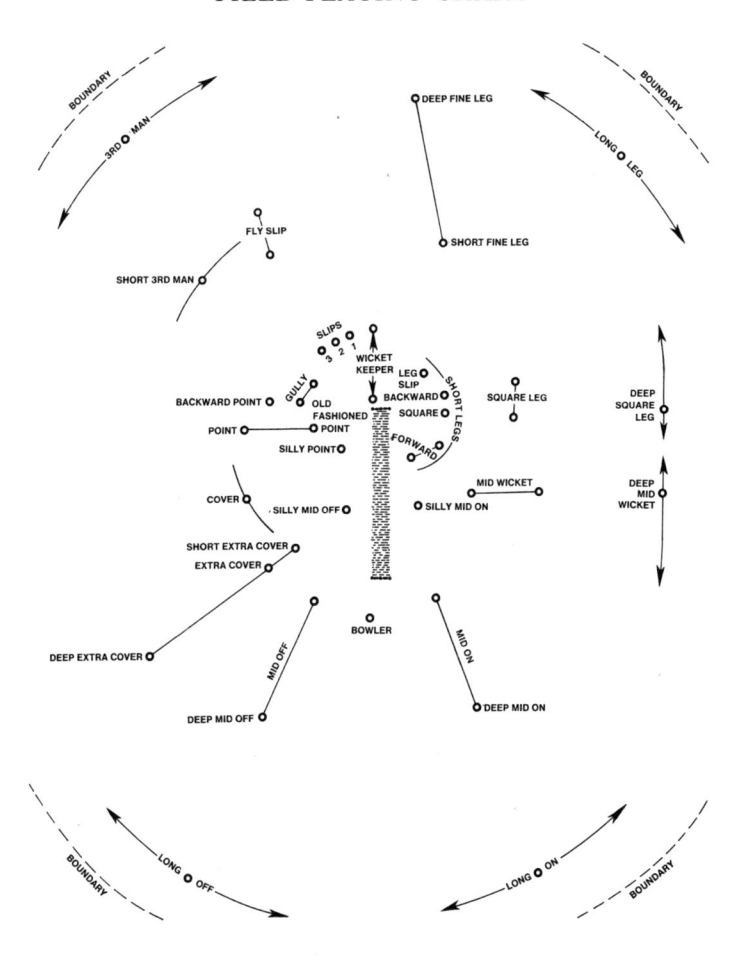

FIELD PLACING CHART

Test Grounds

BBC commentary positions shown on diagrams by X (Radio) and O (TV).

LORD'S
Opened 1814. First Test *v* Australia 1884.
Number of Tests 64. 5½ acres. Capacity approx. 26,000.

TRENT BRIDGE, NOTTINGHAM
Opened 1838. First Test *v* Australia 1899.
Number of Tests 29. 6½ acres. Capacity approx. 20,000.

THE OVAL
Opened 1845. First Test *v* Australia 1880 (first ever Test in England).
Number of Tests 58. 6½ acres. Capacity approx. 20,000.

OLD TRAFFORD, MANCHESTER
Opened 1857. First Test *v* Australia 1884.
Number of Tests 47. 4¾ acres. Capacity approx. 25,000.

EDGBASTON, BIRMINGHAM
Opened 1886. First Test *v* Australia 1902.
Number of Tests 17. 4¼ acres. Capacity approx. 24,000.

HEADINGLEY, LEEDS
Opened 1889. First Test *v* Australia 1899.
Number of Tests 38. 5 acres. Capacity approx. 20,000.

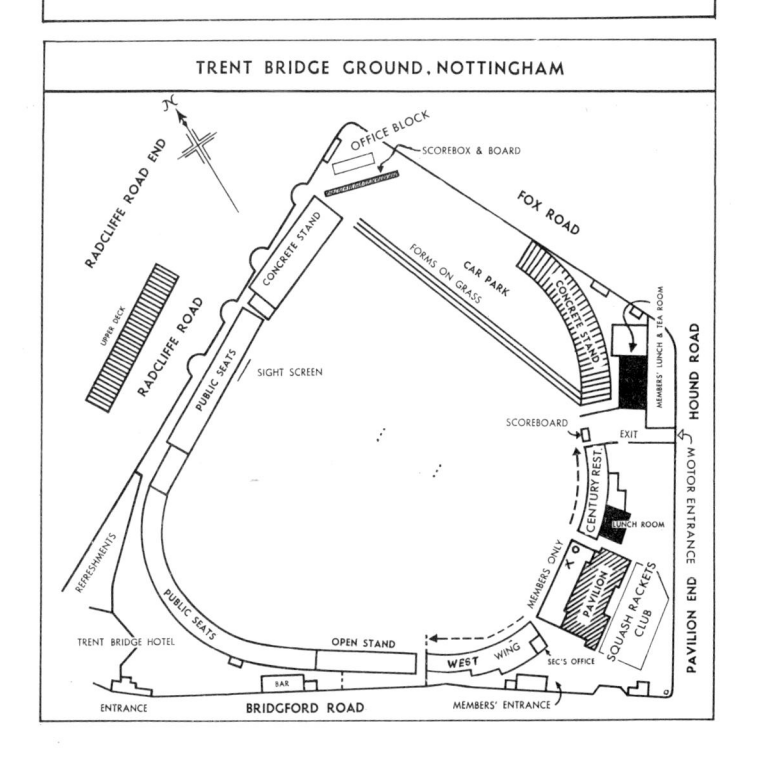

LORD'S CRICKET GROUND

TRENT BRIDGE GROUND, NOTTINGHAM

THE OVAL CRICKET GROUND

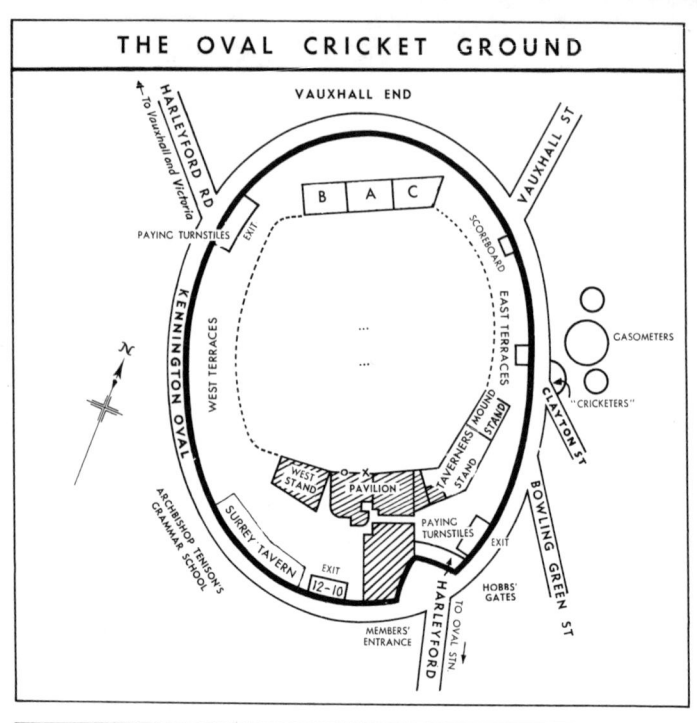

OLD TRAFFORD GROUND, MANCHESTER

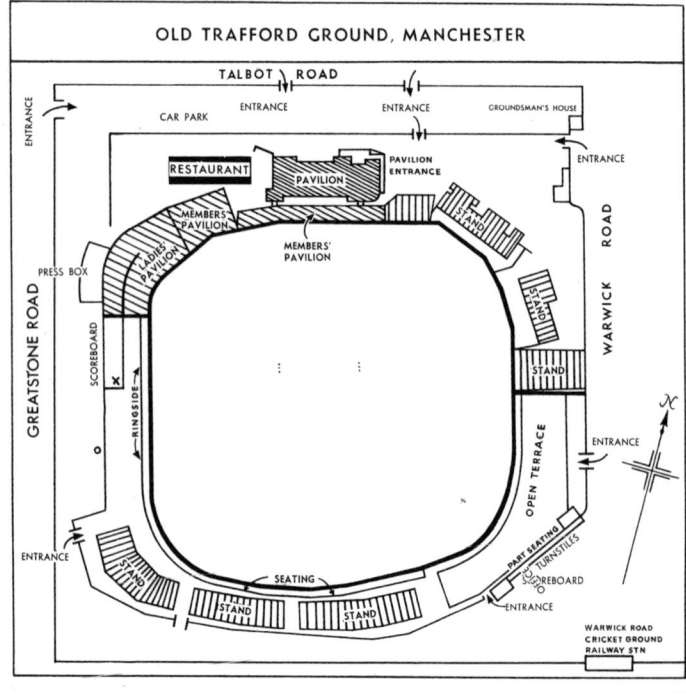

EDGBASTON (BIRMINGHAM) CRICKET GROUND

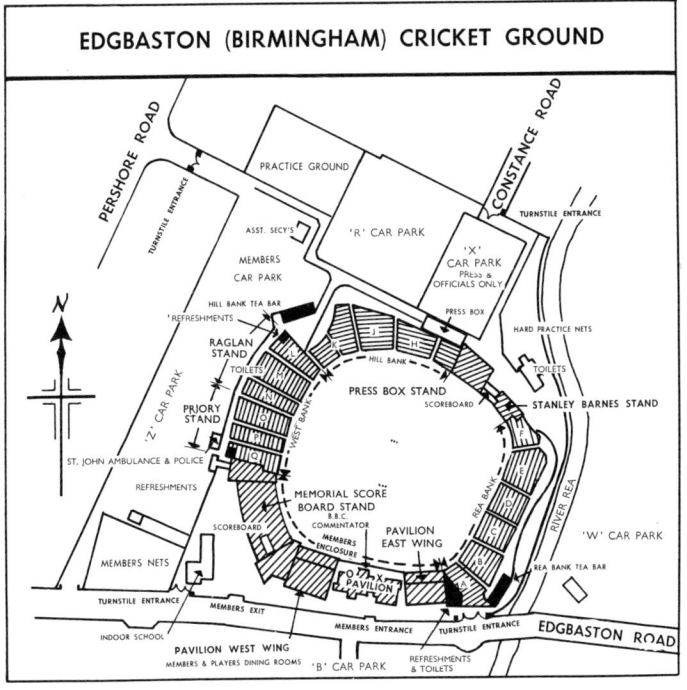

HEADINGLEY GROUND

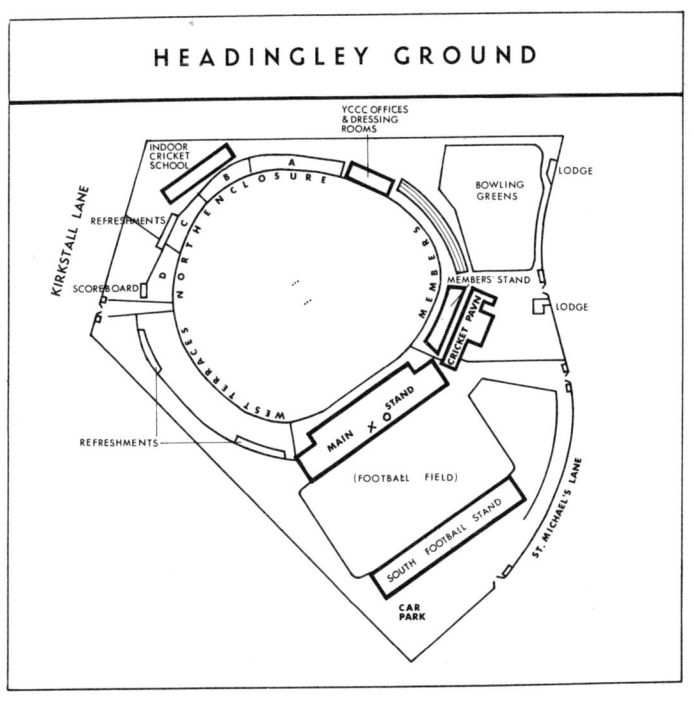

List of Matches – 1975

Abbreviations: BHC – Benson and Hedges Cup
GC   – Gillette Cup
JPL – John Player League
PC   – Prudential Cup
*   – Will continue on Sunday, if necessary
†   – Not first-class

Date	*Venue*	*Match*
April		
Sat. 19th	Cambridge	Cambridge University v Leicestershire
Wed. 23rd	Leicester	Leicestershire v Nottinghamshire† (Non-Championship)
	Lord's	M.C.C. v Worcestershire
	Oxford	Oxford University v Gloucestershire
	Cambridge	Cambridge University v Surrey
Sat. 26th (BHC)	Derby	Derbyshire v Minor Counties (North)
	*Southampton	Hampshire v Surrey
	Canterbury	Kent v Minor Counties (South)
	Old Trafford	Lancashire v Yorkshire
	Leicester	Leicestershire v Northamptonshire
	Lord's	Middlesex v Essex
	Taunton	Somerset v Glamorgan
	Worcester	Worcestershire v Warwickshire
Sat. 26th	Oxford	Oxford University v Sussex
Wed. 30th	Derby	Derbyshire v Worcestershire
	Bristol	Gloucestershire v Leicestershire
	Bournemouth	Hampshire v Essex
	Lord's	Middlesex v Kent
	Trent Bridge	Nottinghamshire v Glamorgan
	Taunton	Somerset v Sussex
	Edgbaston	Warwickshire v Lancashire
	Headingley	Yorkshire v Surrey
	Cambridge	Cambridge University v Northamptonshire
May		
Sat. 3rd (BHC)	Chelmsford	Essex v Kent
	Bristol	Gloucestershire v Hampshire
	Cambridge	Oxford & Cambridge Univs v Worcestershire
	The Oval	Surrey v Somerset
	Edgbaston	Warwickshire v Leicestershire

LIST OF MATCHES – 1975

May	Venue	Match
Sun. 4th (JPL)	Chelmsford	Essex v Somerset
	Moreton-in-Marsh	Gloucestershire v Warwickshire
	Old Trafford	Lancashire v Derbyshire
	Leicester	Leicestershire v Kent
	Lord's	Middlesex v Northamptonshire
	Trent Bridge	Nottinghamshire v Glamorgan
	Hove	Sussex v Surrey
	Worcester	Worcestershire v Hampshire
Mon. 5th (BHC)	Trent Bridge	Nottinghamshire v Lancashire
	Hove	Sussex v Middlesex
	Bradford	Yorkshire v Derbyshire
Wed. 7th	Chelmsford	Essex v Leicestershire
	Cardiff	Glamorgan v Gloucestershire
	Dartford	Kent v Yorkshire
	Northampton	Northamptonshire v Somerset
	The Oval	Surrey v Lancashire
	Worcester	Worcestershire v Nottinghamshire
	Oxford	Oxford University v Derbyshire
	Cambridge	Cambridge University v Warwickshire
Sat. 10th (BHC)	Chesterfield	Derbyshire v Nottinghamshire
	Cardiff	Glamorgan v Surrey
	Canterbury	Kent v Sussex
	Leicester	Leicestershire v Oxford & Cambridge Univs
	Scunthorpe (Appleby & Frodingham)	Minor Counties (North) v Yorkshire
	Bedford (Goldington Bury)	Minor Counties (South) v Essex
	Northampton	Northamptonshire v Warwickshire
	Street	Somerset v Gloucestershire
Sun. 11th (JPL)	Swansea	Glamorgan v Surrey
	Folkestone	Kent v Middlesex
	Northampton	Northamptonshire v Sussex
	Bristol (Imperial Ground)	Somerset v Gloucestershire
	Edgbaston	Warwickshire v Lancashire
	Huddersfield	Yorkshire v Derbyshire
Wed. 14th	Swansea	Glamorgan v Hampshire
	Leicester	Leicestershire v Sussex
	Lord's	Middlesex v Somerset
	Northampton	Northamptonshire v Warwickshire
	The Oval	Surrey v Derbyshire
	Worcester	Worcestershire v Yorkshire
	Oxford	Oxford University v Kent
	Cambridge	Cambridge University v Nottinghamshire
Sat. 17th (BHC)	Bristol	Gloucestershire v Glamorgan
	Bournemouth	Hampshire v Somerset
	Old Trafford	Lancashire v Derbyshire
	Lord's	Middlesex v Kent
	Northampton	Northamptonshire v Worcestershire

ARMCHAIR CRICKET 1975

May	*Venue*	*Match*
Sat. 17th (BHC)	Newark	Nottinghamshire v Minor Counties (North)
	Hove	Sussex v Minor Counties (South)
	Coventry (Courtaulds)	Warwickshire v Oxford & Cambridge Univs
Sun. 18th (JPL)	Chesterfield	Derbyshire v Middlesex
	Southampton	Hampshire v Sussex
	Canterbury	Kent v Yorkshire
	Trent Bridge	Nottinghamshire v Essex
	Yeovil	Somerset v Leicestershire
	The Oval	Surrey v Worcestershire
Wed. 21st (BHC)	Chelmsford	Essex v Sussex
	Swansea	Glamorgan v Hampshire
	Stoke-on-Trent (Longton)	Minor Counties (North) v Lancashire
	Amersham	Minor Counties (South) v Middlesex
	Oxford	Oxford & Cambridge Univs v Northamptonshire
	The Oval	Surrey v Gloucestershire
	Worcester	Worcestershire v Leicestershire
	Barnsley	Yorkshire v Nottinghamshire
Wed. 21st	Edgbaston	Warwickshire v Scotland†
Sat. 24th	Bristol	Gloucestershire v Somerset
	Southampton	Hampshire v Kent
	Old Trafford	Lancashire v Yorkshire
	Leicester	Leicestershire v Northamptonshire
	Trent Bridge	Nottinghamshire v Derbyshire
	The Oval	Surrey v Warwickshire
	Hove	Sussex v Middlesex
	Worcester	Worcestershire v Essex
	Oxford	Oxford University v Free Foresters†
Sun. 25th (JPL)	Ebbw Vale	Glamorgan v Essex
	Bristol	Gloucestershire v Northamptonshire
	Old Trafford	Lancashire v Nottinghamshire
	Leicester	Leicestershire v Worcestershire
	Lord's	Middlesex v Hampshire
	Edgbaston	Warwickshire v Yorkshire
Wed. 28th	Chesterfield	Derbyshire v Kent
	Bristol	Gloucestershire v Glamorgan
	Lord's	Middlesex v Essex
	Northampton	Northamptonshire v Lancashire
	Hove	Sussex v Hampshire
	Edgbaston	Warwickshire v Nottinghamshire
	Oxford	Oxford University v Somerset
Sat. 31st	Buxton	Derbyshire v Lancashire
	Colchester	Essex v Kent
	Bournemouth	Hampshire v Nottinghamshire
	Lord's	Middlesex v Surrey
	Northampton	Northamptonshire v Glamorgan

LIST OF MATCHES – 1975

May	*Venue*	*Match*
Sat. 31st	Hastings	Sussex *v* Warwickshire
	Worcester	Worcestershire *v* Gloucestershire
	Bradford	Yorkshire *v* Leicestershire
	Oxford	Oxford University *v* M.C.C.†

June		
Sun. 1st	Buxton	Derbyshire *v* Glamorgan
(JPL)	Colchester	Essex *v* Lancashire
	Southampton	Hampshire *v* Nottinghamshire
	Tring	Northamptonshire *v* Kent
	Guildford	Surrey *v* Somerset
	Hastings	Sussex *v* Warwickshire
	Worcester	Worcestershire *v* Gloucestershire
	Hull	Yorkshire *v* Leicestershire
Wed. 4th		BENSON & HEDGES CUP (Quarter-finals)
	Oxford	Oxford University *v* Combined Services†
Sat. 7th	Headingley	AUSTRALIA *v* PAKISTAN
(PC)	Lord's	ENGLAND *v* INDIA
	Edgbaston	NEW ZEALAND *v* EAST AFRICA
	Old Trafford	WEST INDIES *v* SRI LANKA
Sat. 7th	Ilford	Essex *v* Lancashire
	Swansea	Glamorgan *v* Warwickshire
	Southampton	Hampshire *v* Middlesex
	Leicester	Leicestershire *v* Worcestershire
	Bath	Somerset *v* Derbyshire
	Oxford	Oxford University *v* Northamptonshire
Sun. 8th	Swansea	Glamorgan *v* Warwickshire
(JPL)	Bristol	Gloucestershire *v* Middlesex
	Bournemouth	Hampshire *v* Kent
	Trent Bridge	Nottinghamshire *v* Sussex
	Bath	Somerset *v* Derbyshire
	The Oval	Surrey *v* Northamptonshire
	Worcester	Worcestershire *v* Yorkshire
Wed. 11th	The Oval	AUSTRALIA *v* SRI LANKA
(PC)	Trent Bridge	ENGLAND *v* NEW ZEALAND
	Headingley	INDIA *v* EAST AFRICA
	Edgbaston	PAKISTAN *v* WEST INDIES
Wed. 11th	Ilford	Essex *v* Nottinghamshire
	Bristol	Gloucestershire *v* Yorkshire
	Maidstone	Kent *v* Worcestershire
	Bath	Somerset *v* Surrey
	Cambridge	Cambridge University *v* Lancashire
	Oxford	Oxford University *v* Warwickshire
Sat. 14th	The Oval	AUSTRALIA *v* WEST INDIES
(PC)	Edgbaston	ENGLAND *v* EAST AFRICA
	Old Trafford	INDIA *v* NEW ZEALAND
	Trent Bridge	PAKISTAN *v* SRI LANKA

ARMCHAIR CRICKET 1975

June	Venue	Match
Sat. 14th	Cardiff	Glamorgan v Surrey
	Bristol	Gloucestershire v Hampshire
	Maidstone	Kent v Sussex
	Northampton	Northamptonshire v Derbyshire
	Scarborough	Yorkshire v Middlesex
	Cambridge	Cambridge University v M.C.C.†
Sun. 15th (JPL)	Ilford	Essex v Derbyshire
	Cardiff	Glamorgan v Hampshire
	Gloucester	Gloucestershire v Lancashire
	Canterbury	Kent v Worcestershire
	Leicester	Leicestershire v Warwickshire
	Bath	Somerset v Nottinghamshire
Wed. 18th	Headingley & The Oval	PRUDENTIAL CUP (Semi-finals)
Wed. 18th	Swansea	Glamorgan v Kent
	Old Trafford	Lancashire v Middlesex
	Leicester	Leicestershire v Somerset
	Trent Bridge	Nottinghamshire v Sussex
	Edgbaston	Warwickshire v Yorkshire
	Worcester	Worcestershire v Northamptonshire
Sat. 21st	Lord's	PRUDENTIAL CUP FINAL
Sat. 21st	Old Trafford	Lancashire v Derbyshire
	Leicester	Leicestershire v Hampshire
	Worksop	Nottinghamshire v Northamptonshire
	Hove	Sussex v Surrey
	Edgbaston	Warwickshire v Somerset
	Cambridge	Cambridge University v Essex
	Eastbourne	Derrick Robins' XI v Oxford University†
Sun. 22nd (JPL)	Old Trafford	Lancashire v Hampshire
	Northampton	Northamptonshire v Leicestershire
	Trent Bridge	Nottinghamshire v Gloucestershire
	The Oval	Surrey v Middlesex
	Hove	Sussex v Glamorgan
	Edgbaston	Warwickshire v Essex
	Bradford	Yorkshire v Somerset
Wed. 25th (GC 1st Round)	March	Cambridgeshire v Northamptonshire
	Lord's	Middlesex v Buckinghamshire
	Trent Bridge	Nottinghamshire v Sussex
	Oxford (Morris Motors)	Oxfordshire v Cornwall
	Stoke-on-Trent (Longton)	Staffordshire v Leicestershire
	The Oval	Surrey v Somerset
Wed. 25th	Burton-on-Trent	Derbyshire v Warwickshire
	Westcliff	Essex v Gloucestershire
	Canterbury	Kent v Australians
	Worcester	Worcestershire v Oxford University
	Sheffield	Yorkshire v Hampshire

LIST OF MATCHES – 1975

June	*Venue*	*Match*
Wed. 25th	Eastbourne	Derrick Robins' XI v Cambridge University†
	Edinburgh	Scotland v M.C.C.†
Sat. 28th	Burton-on-Trent (Bass Worthington)	Derbyshire v Oxford University
	Westcliff	Essex v Sussex
	Bristol	Gloucestershire v Northamptonshire
	Southampton	Hampshire v Australians
	Tunbridge Wells	Kent v Lancashire
	Leicester	Leicestershire v Glamorgan
	Lord's	Middlesex v Worcestershire
	Trent Bridge	Nottinghamshire v Surrey
	Harrogate	Yorkshire v Somerset
Sat. 28th	Portsmouth	Combined Services v Cambridge University†
Sun. 29th (JPL)	Chesterfield	Derbyshire v Gloucestershire
	Westcliff	Essex v Sussex
	Maidstone	Kent v Lancashire
	Leicester	Leicestershire v Glamorgan
	Lord's	Middlesex v Worcestershire
	Edgbaston	Warwickshire v Northamptonshire
	Scarborough	Yorkshire v Surrey

July		
Wed. 2nd		BENSON & HEDGES CUP (Semi-finals)
	Aldershot	Army v Oxford University†
	Lord's	M.C.C. v Australians
	Harrogate	Yorkshire v Derrick Robins' XI†
Sat. 5th	Ilkeston	Derbyshire v Essex
	Swansea	Glamorgan v Australians
	Bournemouth	Hampshire v Gloucestershire
	Old Trafford	Lancashire v Somerset
	Northampton	Northamptonshire v Kent
	Trent Bridge	Nottinghamshire v Middlesex
	The Oval	Surrey v Leicestershire
	Hove	Sussex v Yorkshire
	Worcester	Worcestershire v Warwickshire
	Lord's	Oxford University v Cambridge University
Sun. 6th (JPL)	Long Eaton (Trent College)	Derbyshire v Kent
	Southampton	Hampshire v Surrey
	Old Trafford	Lancashire v Somerset
	Lord's	Middlesex v Leicestershire
	Luton	Northamptonshire v Essex
	Hove	Sussex v Yorkshire
	Worcester	Worcestershire v Nottinghamshire
Wed. 9th	Basingstoke	Hampshire v Glamorgan
	Southport	Lancashire v Worcestershire
	Lord's	Middlesex v Gloucestershire
Thur. 10th	Edgbaston	ENGLAND v AUSTRALIA (First Test Match)

194 ARMCHAIR CRICKET 1975

July	*Venue*	*Match*
Sat. 12th	Chesterfield	Derbyshire v Yorkshire
	Dover	Kent v Nottinghamshire
	Leicester	Leicestershire v Essex
	Taunton	Somerset v Northamptonshire
	The Oval	Surrey v Middlesex
Sun. 13th	Chelmsford	Essex v Middlesex
(JPL)	Lydney	Gloucestershire v Glamorgan
	Basingstoke	Hampshire v Warwickshire
	Dover	Kent v Nottinghamshire
	Leicester	Leicestershire v Surrey
	Torquay	Somerset v Northamptonshire
	Headingley	Yorkshire v Lancashire
Wed. 16th	Bristol	Gloucestershire v Oxfordshire *or* Cornwall
(GC 2nd	Southampton	Hampshire v Glamorgan
Round)	Old Trafford	Lancashire v Cambridgeshire *or* Northamptonshire
	Trent Bridge *or* Hove	Nottinghamshire *or* Sussex v Kent
	The Oval *or* Taunton	Surrey *or* Somerset v Derbyshire
	Edgbaston	Warwickshire v Middlesex *or* Buckinghamshire
	Worcester	Worcestershire v Essex
	Headingley	Yorkshire v Staffordshire *or* Leicestershire
Wed. 16th	Trent Bridge *or* Hove	Nottinghamshire *or* Sussex v Australians (Loser of 1st Round GC Match)
Sat. 19th	Lord's	BENSON & HEDGES CUP FINAL
Sat. 19th	Chesterfield	Derbyshire (Gloucestershire *or* Worcestershire) v Australians
Sun. 20th	Burton-on-Trent	Derbyshire v Leicestershire
(JPL)	Chelmsford	Essex v Worcestershire
	Bournemouth	Hampshire v Gloucestershire
	Northampton	Northamptonshire v Yorkshire
	Trent Bridge	Nottinghamshire v Middlesex
	The Oval	Surrey v Lancashire
	Hove	Sussex v Somerset
	Edgbaston	Warwickshire v Kent
Wed. 23rd	Cardiff	Glamorgan v Derbyshire
	Old Trafford	Lancashire v Australians
	Northampton	Northamptonshire v Sussex
	Weston-super-Mare	Somerset v Worcestershire
	The Oval	Surrey v Essex
	Coventry (Courtaulds)	Warwickshire v Leicestershire
	Sheffield	Yorkshire v Nottinghamshire
Sat. 26th	Ilkeston	Derbyshire v Nottinghamshire
	Swansea	Glamorgan v Lancashire
	Cheltenham	Gloucestershire v Kent
	Leicester	Leicestershire v Australians

LIST OF MATCHES – 1975

July	*Venue*	*Match*
Sat. 26th	Northampton	Northamptonshire v Middlesex
	Weston-super-Mare	Somerset v Hampshire
	The Oval	Surrey v Yorkshire
	Edgbaston	Warwickshire v Essex
	Worcester	Worcestershire v Sussex
Sun. 27th	Ilkeston	Derbyshire v Nottinghamshire
(JPL)	Swansea	Glamorgan v Lancashire
	Cheltenham	Gloucestershire v Kent
	Leicester	Leicestershire v Sussex
	Lord's	Middlesex v Yorkshire
	Weston-super-Mare	Somerset v Hampshire
	Dudley	Worcestershire v Northamptonshire
Wed. 30th	Cheltenham	Gloucestershire v Warwickshire
	Canterbury	Kent v Hampshire
	Blackpool	Lancashire v Leicestershire
	Hove	Sussex v Glamorgan
Thur. 31st	Lord's	ENGLAND v AUSTRALIA (Second Test Match)
August		
Sat. 2nd	Cheltenham	Gloucestershire v Worcestershire
	Canterbury	Kent v Middlesex
	Old Trafford	Lancashire v Warwickshire
	Leicester	Leicestershire v Derbyshire
	Northampton	Northamptonshire v Essex
Sun. 3rd	Cardiff	Glamorgan v Yorkshire
(JPL)	Bristol	Gloucestershire v Essex
	Canterbury	Kent v Sussex
	Old Trafford	Lancashire v Leicestershire
	Byfleet	Surrey v Nottinghamshire
	Edgbaston	Warwickshire v Somerset
	Worcester	Worcestershire v Derbyshire
Wed. 6th		GILLETTE CUP (Quarter-finals)
Wed. 6th	Taunton	Somerset (*or* Surrey if Somerset still in Gillette Cup) v Australians
Sat. 9th	Leyton	Essex v Somerset
	Liverpool	Lancashire v Hampshire
	Leicester	Leicestershire v Nottinghamshire
	Lord's	Middlesex v Glamorgan
	Northampton	Northamptonshire v Australians
	Eastbourne	Sussex v Gloucestershire
	Edgbaston	Warwickshire v Kent
	Worcester	Worcestershire v Surrey
	Scarborough	Yorkshire v Derbyshire
	*Dublin	Ireland v Scotland
Sun. 10th	Chesterfield	Derbyshire v Surrey
(JPL)	Old Trafford	Lancashire v Worcestershire
	Leicester	Leicestershire v Essex

August	*Venue*	*Match*
Sun. 10th (JPL)	Lord's	Middlesex v Somerset
	Wellingborough	Northamptonshire v Glamorgan
	Trent Bridge	Nottinghamshire v Warwickshire
	Eastbourne	Sussex v Gloucestershire
	Bradford	Yorkshire v Hampshire
Wed. 13th	Leyton	Essex v Glamorgan
	Bournemouth	Hampshire v Surrey
	Lord's	Middlesex v Yorkshire
	Hove	Sussex v Derbyshire
Thur. 14th	Headingley	ENGLAND v AUSTRALIA (Third Test Match)
Sat. 16th	Cardiff	Glamorgan v Yorkshire
	Bournemouth	Hampshire v Northamptonshire
	Trent Bridge	Nottinghamshire v Lancashire
	Taunton	Somerset v Gloucestershire
	The Oval	Surrey v Sussex
	Edgbaston	Warwickshire v Worcestershire
Sun. 17th (JPL)	Cardiff	Glamorgan v Kent
	Southampton	Hampshire v Northamptonshire
	Old Trafford	Lancashire v Middlesex
	Trent Bridge	Nottinghamshire v Leicestershire
	The Oval	Surrey v Essex
	Arundel	Sussex v Derbyshire
	Edgbaston	Warwickshire v Worcestershire
Wed. 20th		GILLETTE CUP (Semi-finals)
Sat. 23rd	Ilkeston	Derbyshire v Gloucestershire
	Chelmsford	Essex v Australians
	Swansea	Glamorgan v Worcestershire
	Folkestone	Kent v Surrey
	Lord's	Middlesex v Sussex
	Northampton	Northamptonshire v Leicestershire
	Taunton	Somerset v Nottinghamshire
	Edgbaston	Warwickshire v Hampshire
	Headingley	Yorkshire v Lancashire
Sun. 24th (JPL)	Chelmsford	Essex v Hampshire
	Maidstone	Kent v Surrey
	Lord's	Middlesex v Warwickshire
	Northampton	Northamptonshire v Derbyshire
	Taunton	Somerset v Glamorgan
	Worcester	Worcestershire v Sussex
	Scarborough	Yorkshire v Gloucestershire
Wed. 27th	Chelmsford	Essex v Northamptonshire
	Folkestone	Kent v Somerset
	Lord's	Middlesex v Warwickshire
	Trent Bridge	Nottinghamshire v Leicestershire
	Edgbaston	Warwick Pool Under-25 County Cricket Competition

LIST OF MATCHES – 1975

August	Venue	Match
Thur. 28th	The Oval	ENGLAND *v* AUSTRALIA (Fourth Test Match)
Sat. 30th	Chesterfield Chelmsford Cardiff Bristol Southampton Tunbridge Wells Old Trafford Bradford	Derbyshire *v* Middlesex Essex *v* Worcestershire Glamorgan *v* Somerset Gloucestershire *v* Surrey Hampshire *v* Sussex Kent *v* Leicestershire Lancashire *v* Nottinghamshire Yorkshire *v* Northamptonshire
Sun. 31st (JPL)	Chelmsford Bristol Bournemouth Old Trafford Lord's Trent Bridge Edgbaston	Essex *v* Kent Gloucestershire *v* Surrey Hampshire *v* Leicestershire Lancashire *v* Northamptonshire Middlesex *v* Sussex Nottinghamshire *v* Yorkshire Warwickshire *v* Derbyshire

September		
Wed. 3rd	Leicester Trent Bridge Taunton Guildford Worcester Scarborough	Leicestershire *v* Middlesex Nottinghamshire *v* Warwickshire Somerset *v* Essex Surrey *v* Northamptonshire Worcestershire *v* Glamorgan Fenner Trophy Knock-Out Competition (3 days)
Sat. 6th	Lord's	GILLETTE CUP FINAL
Sat. 6th	Scarborough	T. N. Pearce's XI *v* Derrick Robins' Overseas XI
Sun. 7th (JPL)	Darley Dale Canterbury Leicester Brackley The Oval Hove Worcester	Derbyshire *v* Hampshire Kent *v* Somerset Leicestershire *v* Gloucestershire Northamptonshire *v* Nottinghamshire Surrey *v* Warwickshire Sussex *v* Lancashire Worcestershire *v* Glamorgan
Sun. 7th	Scarborough	T. N. Pearce's XI *v* Derrick Robins' Overseas XI (40 overs)†
Wed. 10th	Southampton Old Trafford Hove	Hampshire *v* Derbyshire Lancashire *v* Gloucestershire Sussex *v* Kent
Sat. 13th	Chesterfield Trent Bridge Taunton The Oval Hove Edgbaston	Derbyshire *v* Leicestershire Nottinghamshire *v* Gloucestershire Somerset *v* Glamorgan Surrey *v* Kent Sussex *v* Lancashire Warwickshire *v* Northamptonshire

September	*Venue*	*Match*
Sat. 13th	Worcester	Worcestershire *v* Hampshire
	Middlesbrough	Yorkshire *v* Essex
Sun. 14th	Cardiff	Glamorgan *v* Middlesex
(JPL)	Taunton	Somerset *v* Worcestershire
	Bradford	Yorkshire *v* Essex

*Will continue on Sunday, if necessary.

1975 Guide to the John Player League

Compiled by Bill Frindall

PART I – GENERAL RECORDS

TEAM RECORDS

Highest innings total

288–6	Sussex v Middlesex at Hove	1969
273–4	Sussex v Nottinghamshire at Worksop	1971
265–6	Essex v Lancashire at Chelmsford	1969
262–3	Somerset v Gloucestershire at Bristol	1974
262–6	Leicestershire v Somerset at Frome	1970
261–5	Kent v Somerset at Weston-super-Mare	1970
260–6	Derbyshire v Gloucestershire at Derby	1972
258–4	Worcestershire v Sussex at Dudley	1972
257–7	Kent v Northamptonshire at Brackley	1973
256–3	Leicestershire v Gloucestershire at Gloucester	1974
255–5	Lancashire v Somerset at Manchester	1970
254–7	Leicestershire v Sussex at Leicester	1969
253–7	Sussex v Leicestershire at Leicester	1969
252–5	Notts v Warwickshire at Birmingham	1971
251–3	Lancashire v Nottinghamshire at Nottingham	1972
251–9	Gloucestershire v Somerset at Bristol	1974
251	Hampshire v Glamorgan at Basingstoke	1974

Highest totals batting second (240 and over)

254–7	Leicestershire v Sussex at Leicester	1969
251–9	Gloucestershire v Somerset at Bristol	1974

This is the highest total by a side batting second and LOSING.

249–6	Warwickshire v Worcestershire at Birmingham	1972
243–6	Kent v Northamptonshire at Dover	1970

Highest match aggregates (500 and over)

519	Sussex (288–6) v Middlesex (231) at Hove	1969

513	Somerset (262–3) v Gloucs (251–9) at Bristol	1974
507	Sussex (253–7) v Leics (254–7) at Leicester	1969

Lowest innings totals (under 70)

23	Middlesex v Yorkshire at Leeds	1974
36	Leicestershire v Sussex at Leicester	1973
41	Northamptonshire v Middlesex at Northampton	1972
43	Hampshire v Essex at Basingstoke	1972
45	Northamptonshire v Essex at Ilford	1971
48	Middlesex v Gloucestershire at Lydney	1973
56	Middlesex v Worcestershire at Kidderminster	1969
59	Northamptonshire v Middlesex at Tring	1974
61	Somerset v Hampshire at Bath	1973
63	Sussex v Derbyshire at Hove	1969
65	Glamorgan v Surrey at The Oval	1969
66	Nottinghamshire v Yorkshire at Bradford	1969
67	Northamptonshire v Kent at Brackley	1973
69	Essex v Derbyshire at Chesterfield	1974

Lowest total batting first and winning

76	Middlesex v Northants (41) at Northampton	1972

Lowest total in complete 40 overs

74–9	Yorkshire v Hampshire at Hull	1970

Lowest match aggregate (20 wickets)

117	Middlesex (76) v Northamptonshire (41) at Northampton	1972

Shortest uninterrupted match

2 hr 13 min. Essex v Northamptonshire at Ilford 1971
Total overs: 40·3.

Teams dismissed in fewest overs

16·0	Northamptonshire (59) v Middlesex at Tring	1974
16·3	Derbyshire (97) v Notts at Chesterfield	1969
16·4	Lancashire (87) v Essex at Manchester	1971
16·5	Derbyshire (70) v Surrey at Derby	1972

Fewest overs to win uninterrupted match

11·4 Gloucestershire (87–1) v Surrey (86) at The Oval
  1969

Largest margins of victory

190 runs	Kent v Northamptonshire at Brackley	1973
170 runs	Worcestershire v Sussex at Dudley	1972
152 runs	Gloucestershire v Hampshire at Bristol	1970

10 wkts Glamorgan *v* Leicestershire at Llandudno 1969
Match reduced to 27 overs.
10 wkts Surrey *v* Warwickshire at Birmingham 1969
10 wkts Essex *v* Northamptonshire at Ilford 1971
10 wkts Hampshire *v* Warwickshire at Birmingham 1972
Match reduced to 10 overs each side.
10 wkts Leicestershire *v* Worcestershire at Dudley 1972
10 wkts Leicestershire *v* Glamorgan at Leicester 1972
10 wkts Warwickshire *v* Notts at Nottingham 1973

Tied matches (40-overs matches unless otherwise stated)
Nottinghamshire *v* Kent at Nottingham (20-overs) 1969
Gloucestershire *v* Hampshire at Bristol (39-overs) 1972
Gloucestershire *v* Northamptonshire at Bristol 1972
Surrey *v* Worcestershire at Byfleet 1973
Middlesex *v* Lancashire at Lord's 1974
Sussex *v* Leicestershire at Hove (39-overs) 1974

Smallest margins of victory (excluding 'faster run-rate results')
1 run   16 instances
1 wkt   13 instances

Most six-hits in an innings
14   Leicestershire *v* Somerset at Frome   1970

Most six-hits in a match
17   Somerset (9) *v* Yorkshire (8) at Bath   1974

Most six-hits in one Sunday's matches
48   16 June 1974 – in eight matches

Most six-hits by a county in one season
53   Kent in 1970

Summary of batting and bowling awards 1969–74

	Six-hits	*Four or more wkts*
1969	355	56
1970	438	58
1971	422	65
1972	384	62
1973	340	56
1974	409	59
Totals	2348	356
Average	391	59
Average value	£2·56 per six	£16·85 per award

Unusual dismissals
Obstructing the field
R. W. Tolchard (103): Leicestershire *v* Middlesex at Lord's 1972
Run out by bowler before ball has been bowled
P. Willey (1) by P. Lever: Northamptonshire *v* Lancashire at Northampton 1974

Similarities of dismissal
Five batsmen run out in an innings
Essex (168–9) *v* Surrey at Harlow 1972
Derbyshire (195–9) *v* Kent at Maidstone 1974
First four wickets in an innings falling to 'lbw' decisions
Warwickshire *v* Somerset at Taunton 1974

Most 'no result' matches in one season
21 in 1973

INDIVIDUAL RECORDS – BATTING
(* denotes not out or an unbroken partnership)

Highest individual innings
155* B. A. Richards – Hampshire *v* Yorkshire at Hull 1970

Two hundreds in successive innings
G. M. Turner (121 and 108) for Worcestershire in 1972
D. L. Amiss (100 and 110) for Warwickshire in 1974

Most hundreds in one season
3 B. A. Richards for Hampshire in 1970

Hundreds (63) (5 in 1969, 11 in 1970, 10 in 1971, 11 in 1972, 10 in 1973, 16 in 1974)

H. M. Ackerman	(1) 115*	Northamptonshire *v* Kent at Dover	1970
D. L. Amiss	(2) 100	Warwickshire *v* Lancashire at Manchester	1974
	100	Warwickshire *v* Surrey at Birmingham	1974
G. Boycott	(2) 104*	Yorkshire *v* Glamorgan at Colwyn Bay	1973
	108*	Yorkshire *v* Northamptonshire at Huddersfield	1974
M. A. Buss	(1) 121	Sussex *v* Nottinghamshire at Worksop	1971
G. S. Chappell	(1) 128*	Somerset *v* Surrey at Brislington	1969
A. Clarkson	(1) 102*	Somerset *v* Northamptonshire at Northampton	1969
D. B. Close	(2) 128	Somerset *v* Gloucestershire at Bristol	1974
	131	Somerset *v* Yorkshire at Bath	1974
P. W. Denning	(1) 100	Somerset *v* Northamptonshire at Brackley	1974
B. L. D'Oliveira	(1) 100	Worcestershire *v* Surrey at Byfleet	1973
B. Dudleston	(1) 109*	Leicestershire *v* Gloucestershire at Gloucester	1974
J. H. Edrich	(1) 108*	Surrey *v* Derbyshire at Derby	1972
B. C. Francis	(2) 107	Essex *v* Lancashire at Manchester	1971
	106	Essex *v* Lancashire at Leyton	1973

P. J. Graves	(1)	101*	Sussex v Middlesex at Eastbourne	1972
D. M. Green	(1)	127*	Gloucestershire v Hampshire at Bristol	1970
C. G. Greenidge	(1)	102	Hampshire v Sussex at Hove	1974
J. H. Hampshire	(4)	108	Yorkshire v Nottinghamshire at Sheffield	1970
		119	Yorkshire v Leicestershire at Hull	1971
		106*	Yorkshire v Lancashire at Manchester	1972
		111*	Yorkshire v Sussex at Hastings	1973
M. J. Harris	(1)	104*	Nottinghamshire v Hampshire at Nottingham	1970
R. G. A. Headley	(1)	112*	Worcestershire v Kent at Worcester	1974
J. A. Jameson	(2)	123*	Warwickshire v Notts at Nottingham	1973
		104	Warwickshire v Derbyshire at Buxton	1974
A. I. Kallicharran	(1)	101*	Warwickshire v Derbyshire at Chesterfield	1972
R. B. Kanhai	(4)	102	Warwickshire v Notts at Birmingham	1969
		112	Warwickshire v Northants at Birmingham	1971
		120	Warwickshire v Leicestershire at Birmingham	1972
		101*	Warwickshire v Kent at Birmingham	1973
C. H. Lloyd	(2)	134*	Lancashire v Somerset at Manchester	1970
		100*	Lancashire v Nottinghamshire at Nottingham	1974
D. Lloyd	(2)	103*	Lancashire v Northamptonshire at Bedford	1971
		101	Lancashire v Essex at Southport	1974
B. W. Luckhurst	(3)	142	Kent v Somerset at Weston-super-Mare	1970
		124	Kent v Essex at Chelmsford	1973
		104	Kent v Somerset at Canterbury	1973
R. W. Phillips	(1)	116*	Gloucestershire v Lancashire at Manchester	1970
M. J. Procter	(1)	109*	Gloucestershire v Warwickshire at Cheltenham	1972
C. T. Radley	(1)	133*	Middlesex v Glamorgan at Lord's	1969
B. A. Richards	(6)	155*	Hampshire v Yorkshire at Hull	1970
		104	Hampshire v Glamorgan at Southampton	1970
		132*	Hampshire v Kent at Bournemouth	1970
		105	Hampshire v Leicestershire at Leicester	1972
		101	Hampshire v Worcestershire at Worcester	1972
		123	Hampshire v Glamorgan at Basingstoke	1974
I. V. A. Richards	(1)	108*	Somerset v Nottinghamshire at Nottingham	1974
G. R. J. Roope	(1)	120*	Surrey v Worcestershire at Byfleet	1973
M. J. Smith	(2)	203	Middlesex v Surrey at Lord's	1969
		110	Middlesex v Lancashire at Lord's	1971
G. St A. Sobers	(1)	116*	Nottinghamshire v Worcestershire at Newark	1971
A. Tait	(1)	102*	Northants v Warwickshire at Peterborough	1974
B. Taylor	(1)	100	Essex v Derbyshire at Buxton	1971
R. W. Tolchard	(2)	103	Leicestershire v Middlesex at Lord's	1972
		100	Leicestershire v Worcestershire at Worcester	1974
G. M. Turner	(3)	121	Worcestershire v Sussex at Dudley	1972
		108	Worcestershire v Warwickshire at Birmingham	1972
		129*	Worcestershire v Glamorgan at Worcester	1973
R. T. Virgin	(2)	123*	Somerset v Surrey at The Oval	1970
		101*	Somerset v Surrey at Torquay	1971
P. Willey	(1)	102	Northamptonshire v Sussex at Hove	1971

Fastest hundreds

50 min. C. H. Lloyd 100* Lancashire v Nottinghamshire at Nottingham 1974

58 min. R. B. Kanhai 112 Warwickshire v Northants at Birmingham 1971

Kanhai scored his second fifty in nine minutes.

Hundred on début in John Player League
No instance. Highest innings on début:
70 J. M. Parks Sussex *v* Lancashire at Hove 1969
Twelve players have scored fifties in their first JPL innings.

Fastest fifties
Ideally this record should be measured in terms of the fewest balls received but not all county scorers use a method giving such information. In some cases the times for a batsman reaching 50 have not been recorded. The fastest recorded fifties are:

i) Fewest balls
26 balls A. P. E. Knott (52) Kent *v* Yorkshire at Maidstone 1971
29 balls K. D. Boyce (58*) Essex *v* Glamorgan at Pontypridd 1970
30 balls J. N. Shepherd (52*) Kent *v* Northamptonshire at Northampton 1971

ii) Fewest minutes
23 min. K. D. Boyce (50) Essex *v* Lancashire at Chelmsford 1969
25 min. P. T. Marner (99) Leicestershire *v* Sussex at Leicester 1969

Note: R. B. Kanhai (112) took his score from 50 to 100 in only nine minutes for Warwickshire *v* Northamptonshire at Birmingham in 1971.

Fastest fifties in a match televised on BBC2 (£250 award)
1969 K. D. Boyce   23 min.   Essex *v* Lancs at Chelmsford
1970 M. A. Nash   33 balls Glamorgan *v* Kent at Swansea
1971 J. N. Shepherd   30 balls Kent *v* Northants at Northampton
1972 G. M. Turner   32 balls Worcestershire *v* Northants at Worcester
1973 Asif Iqbal   38 balls Kent *v* Worcestershire at Canterbury
1974 B. F. Davison   43 balls Leicestershire *v* Surrey at Sunbury

Most fifties in successive innings
5 G. M. Turner (Worcs): 121, 108, 88, 83, 57*. 1972

Carrying bat through completed innings (side dismissed)
D. H. K. Smith (36*)   Derbyshire (109) v Kent at Chesterfield   1969

Most runs off an over
28   R. B. Kanhai off Sarfraz Nawaz: Warwickshire v Northamptonshire at Birmingham   1971
26   M. H. Denness off G. D. McKenzie: Kent v Leicestershire at Folkestone   1971
(a 14-ball over containing 8 no-balls)
26   J. N. Shepherd off H. R. Moseley: Kent v Somerset at Canterbury   1973

Most six-hits off successive balls
3   R. B. Kanhai off A. Buss – Warwickshire v Sussex at Birmingham   1971
3   M. J. Harris off A. E. Cordle – Nottinghamshire v Glamorgan at Nottingham   1972

Most six-hits in an innings
8   P. T. Marner   Leicestershire v Sussex at Leicester   1969
8   R. B. Kanhai   Warwickshire v Northamptonshire at Birmingham   1971
8   D. B. Close   Somerset v Yorkshire at Bath   1974

Most six-hits in a season
19   D. B. Close for Somerset   1974

Most six-hits in a career (40 and over)
49   C. H. Lloyd   Lancashire
48   K. D. Boyce   Essex
48   D. B. Close   Yorkshire and Somerset
44   B. A. Richards   Hampshire
43   J. A. Jameson   Warwickshire

Six runs (all run) from one hit
R. D. Jackman off R. A. Hutton   Surrey v Yorkshire at The Oval   1974

Most runs in a season (600 and over)

		Season	Innings	N.O.	Runs	Av	100
J. H. Hampshire	Yorkshire	1973	15	2	668	51·38	1
M. A. Buss	Sussex	1971	16	0	650	40·62	1
B. A. Richards	Hampshire	1972	14	2	643	53·58	2
G. M. Turner	Worcestershire	1972	15	1	642	45·85	2
H. Pilling	Lancashire	1970	15	3	625	52·08	0
C. T. Radley	Middlesex	1974	15	3	618	51·50	0

Most runs in a career (2000 and over)

		Innings	N.O.	Runs	H.S.	Av	100
B. A. Richards	Hampshire	79	7	2871	155*	39.87	6
B. W. Luckhurst	Kent	71	9	2626	142	42.35	3
M. J. Smith	Middlesex	86	1	2550	110	30.00	2
R. G. A. Headley	Worcestershire	79	9	2379	112*	33.98	1
C. T. Radley	Middlesex	85	8	2270	133*	29.48	1
B. Hassan	Nottinghamshire	88	8	2268	86*	28.35	0
M. J. Harris	Nottinghamshire	83	12	2236	104*	31.49	1
Younis Ahmed	Surrey	83	3	2175	96	27.18	0
G. Boycott	Yorkshire	57	5	2135	108*	41.05	2
G. M. Turner	Worcestershire	64	3	2130	129*	34.91	3
J. A. Jameson	Warwickshire	78	4	2069	123*	27.95	2

First batsman to score 2000 runs

B. A. Richards (Hampshire) on 27 August 1972 in his 53rd innings.

First batsman to score 1000 runs

H. Pilling (Lancashire) on 30 August 1970 in his 30th innings

Highest Partnerships for each wicket

1st	182	M. H. Denness, B. W. Luckhurst: Kent v Somerset, Weston-super-Mare	1970
	182	R. G. A. Headley, G. M. Turner: Worcestershire v Warwickshire, Birmingham	1972
2nd	179	B. W. Luckhurst, M. H. Denness: Kent v Somerset, Canterbury	1973
3rd	182	H. Pilling, C. H. Lloyd: Lancashire v Somerset at Manchester	1970
4th	175*	M. J. K. Smith, D. L. Amiss: Warwickshire v Yorkshire, Birmingham	1970
5th	128	G. Barker, K. D. Boyce: Essex v Surrey at The Oval	1971
6th	121	C. P. Wilkins, A. J. Borrington: Derbyshire v Warwickshire at Chesterfield	1972
7th	96*	R. Illingworth, J. Birkenshaw: Leicestershire v Somerset at Leicester	1971
8th	88	B. A. Davis, M. A. Nash: Glamorgan v Kent at Swansea	1970
9th	86	D. P. Hughes, P. Lever: Lancashire v Essex at Leyton	1973
10th	57	D. A. Graveney, J. B. Mortimore: Gloucestershire v Lancashire at Tewkesbury	1973

INDIVIDUAL RECORDS – BOWLING

Best analysis
8–26 K. D. Boyce Essex v Lancashire at Manchester 1971

Six or more wickets in an innings (19)

R. R. Bailey	6–22	Northamptonshire v Hampshire at Portsmouth	1972
C. J. R. Black	6–25	Middlesex v Surrey at The Oval	1971
K. D. Boyce	8–26	Essex v Lancashire at Manchester	1971
G. I. Burgess	6–25	Somerset v Glamorgan at Glastonbury	1972
M. A. Buss	6–14	Sussex v Lancashire at Hove	1973
R. E. East	6–18	Essex v Yorkshire at Hull	1969
A. W. Greig	6–28	Sussex v Middlesex at Hove	1971
M. Hendrick	6–7	Derbyshire v Nottinghamshire at Nottingham	1972
K. Higgs	6–17	Leicestershire v Glamorgan at Leicester	1973
R. N. S. Hobbs	6–22	Essex v Hampshire at Harlow	1973
V. A. Holder	6–33	Worcestershire v Middlesex at Lord's	1972
R. W. Hooker	6–6	Middlesex v Surrey at Lord's	1969
R. A. Hutton	7–15	Yorkshire v Worcestershire at Leeds	1969
Intikhab Alam	6–25	Surrey v Derbyshire at The Oval	1974
R. D. Jackman	6–34	Surrey v Derbyshire at Derby	1972
A. A. Jones	6–34	Somerset v Essex at Westcliff-on-Sea	1971
G. C. Kingston	6–36	Glamorgan v Derbyshire at Ebbw Vale	1969
A. G. Nicholson	6–36	Yorkshire v Somerset at Sheffield	1972
D. Wilson	6–18	Yorkshire v Kent at Canterbury	1969

Four wickets with consecutive balls
A. Ward   Derbyshire v Sussex at Derby   1970

Hat-tricks (7)
W. Blenkiron   Warwickshire v Derbyshire at Buxton 1974
K. D. Boyce   Essex v Somerset at Westcliff   1971
A. Buss   Sussex v Worcestershire at Hastings   1974
G. D. McKenzie Leicestershire v Essex at Leicester   1972
R. Palmer   Somerset v Gloucestershire at Bristol 1970
A. Ward   Derbyshire v Sussex at Derby   1970
R. G. D. Willis Warwickshire v Yorkshire at Birmingham 1973

Three wickets in four balls
A. M. E. Roberts Hampshire v Nottinghamshire at Nottingham 1974
K. Shuttleworth   Lancashire v Yorkshire at Manchester 1970
P. M. Walker   Glamorgan v Warwickshire at Birmingham 1970

Wicket with first ball in League
C. J. Armishaw   Derbyshire v Middlesex at Chesterfield 1973

Four or more wickets on début

C. J. Armishaw	4–31	Derbyshire v Middlesex at Chesterfield	1973
A. Brown	4–17	Kent v Warwickshire at Maidstone	1969
K. Ibadulla	4–13	Warwickshire v Gloucestershire at Bristol	1969
J. D. F. Larter	4–34	Northants v Glamorgan at Northampton	1969
D. A. Marriott	4–12	Middlesex v Surrey at Byfleet	1972
P. J. Plummer	5–44	Nottinghamshire v Yorkshire at Bradford	1969
D. J. Shepherd	5–31	Glamorgan v Northants at Northampton	1969
C. T. Spencer	5–13	Leicestershire v Somerset at Weston-super-Mare	1969
D. L. Underwood	4–26	Kent v Hampshire at Canterbury	1969

Note: T. E. Jesty took 4-11 for Kent v Hampshire (Canterbury) 1969 in his second match having not bowled in his first.

Most bowling awards in a season

4 D. A. Marriott   Middlesex   1973

Most bowling awards in a career

14 D. L. Underwood   Kent

Most economical bowling

O	M	R	W		
8—8—0—0				B. A. Langford: Somerset v Essex at Yeovil	1969
7—7—0—2				T. E. Jesty: Hampshire v Yorkshire at Hull	1970
8—6—2—3				F. J. Titmus: Middlesex v Northants at Northampton	1972
8—5—3—3				A. L. Robinson: Yorkshire v Derbyshire at Scarborough	1973
7·4—4—3—4				K. Shuttleworth: Lancashire v Somerset at Manchester	1970
8—5—4—3				J. C. J. Dye: Kent v Middlesex at Canterbury	1969
8—5—4—2				D. Wilson: Yorkshire v Glamorgan at Swansea	1972
8—6—4—1				D. P. Hughes: Lancashire v Leicestershire at Manchester	1972
8—6—5—1				T. W. Cartwright: Somerset v Essex at Chelmsford	1973
8—4—5—1				K. Higgs: Leicestershire v Northamptonshire at Leicester	1972
7—3—5—4				J. Denman: Sussex v Leicester at Leicester	1973

Most expensive bowling

O	M	R	W		
8—0—79—1				R. E. East: Essex v Glamorgan at Swansea	1969
8—0—78—2				R. D. Jackman: Surrey v Middlesex at The Oval	1971
7—0—75—3				T. J. P. Eyre: Derbyshire v Lancashire at Buxton	1970

Longest over

14 balls   G. D. McKenzie   Leicestershire v Kent at Folkestone 1971

No-balled eight times under front-foot law by umpire W. E. Alley.

Most overs in a season (Maximum possible: 128)

126·1	F. E. Rumsey	Derbyshire	1970
124·4	B. Stead	Nottinghamshire	1972
123·1	G. D. McKenzie	Leicestershire	1971

Most wickets in a season (30 and over)

		Season	O	M	R	W	Av	R/over
R. J. Clapp	Somerset	1974	92·4	5	448	34	13·17	4·83
K. D. Boyce	Essex	1971	121·4	16	419	33	12·69	3·44
D. L. Williams	Glamorgan	1971	93·3	4	409	33	12·39	4·37
V. A. Holder	Worcestershire	1971	116·1	10	390	32	12·18	3·36

1975 GUIDE TO THE JOHN PLAYER LEAGUE 209

		Season	O	M	R	W	Av	R/over
D. L. Williams	Glamorgan	1974	106.1	16	434	32	13.56	4.09
R. A. Woolmer	Kent	1970	121.1	7	540	32	16.87	4.46
K. D. Boyce	Essex	1972	108.2	17	370	31	11.93	3.42

Most wickets in a career (100 and over)

		O	M	R	W	Av	R/over
K. D. Boyce	Essex	562.1	84	1887	139	13.57	3.35
D. L. Underwood	Kent	496.2	74	1803	133	13.55	3.63
S. Turner	Essex	642.3	74	2469	122	20.23	3.84
R. A. Woolmer	Kent	575.5	53	2181	121	18.02	3.78
J. C. J. Dye	Kent & Northants.	627.2	79	2367	119	19.89	3.77
D. L. Williams	Glamorgan	544.2	52	2198	118	18.62	4.03
R. D. Jackman	Surrey	609.3	59	2536	117	21.67	4.16
J. K. Lever	Essex	627	76	2127	117	18.17	3.39
G. D. McKenzie	Leicestershire	644.2	80	2196	116	18.93	3.40
G. I. Burgess	Somerset	588.1	59	2506	114	21.98	4.26
J. S. E. Price	Middlesex	557.2	63	2020	112	18.03	3.62
A. G. Nicholson	Yorkshire	556.1	88	1874	110	17.03	3.36
V. A. Holder	Worcestershire	476	50	1579	109	14.48	3.31
P. J. Sainsbury	Hampshire	568.2	51	2258	109	20.71	3.97
T. E. Jesty	Hampshire	502.5	38	2291	106	21.61	4.55
J. N. Shepherd	Kent	570.3	52	2070	105	19.71	3.62
P. Lever	Lancashire	521.4	64	1914	104	18.40	3.66
N. M. McVicker	Warwicks. & Leics.	553.5	45	2356	104	22.65	4.25
M. N. S. Taylor	Notts. & Hants.	635.1	50	2717	104	26.12	4.27
J. A. Snow	Sussex	476.4	49	1780	102	17.45	3.73

First bowler to take 100 wickets

K. D. Boyce (Essex) on 11 June 1972 in his 51st match.

INDIVIDUAL RECORDS – ALL-ROUND PERFORMANCES

Five wickets and fifty runs in a match

C. J. R. Black	6–25 & 72*	Middlesex v Surrey at The Oval 1971
M. A. Buss	5–36 & 69	Sussex v Derbyshire at Eastbourne 1973
G. W. Johnson	5–26 & 50	Kent v Surrey at The Oval 1974

1000 runs and 100 wickets in a career

		Runs	Av	Wkts	Av	Matches for 'Double'
K. D. Boyce	Essex	1314	19.61	139	13.57	51
G. I. Burgess	Somerset	1431	21.04	114	21.98	71
T. E. Jesty	Hampshire	1049	18.40	106	21.61	80
J. N. Shepherd	Kent	1122	24.93	105	19.71	74
S. Turner	Essex	1354	19.34	122	20.23	78

First player to achieve the career 'double'

K. D. Boyce (Essex) on 11 June 1972 in his 51st match – an achievement marked by a special award of £100.

WICKET-KEEPING
Most dismissals in an innings
6 (all ct)	K. Goodwin	Lancashire v Worcestershire at Worcester 1969
5 (all ct)	A. P. E. Knott	Kent v Northamptonshire at Northampton 1969
5 (4ct 1st)	S. A. Westley	Gloucestershire v Somerset at Bristol 1971
5 (3ct 2st)	B. Taylor	Essex v Derbyshire at Leyton 1972
5 (all ct)	R. W. Tolchard	Leicestershire v Lancashire at Leicester 1974
5 (4ct 1st)	H. G. Wilcock	Worcestershire v Essex at Worcester 1974

Most dismissals in a season
25 (23ct 2st)	R. W. Taylor	Derbyshire	1974
24 (19ct 5st)	R. W. Taylor	Derbyshire	1970
24 (21ct 3st)	R. W. Tolchard	Leicestershire	1972

Most dismissals in a career (100 and over)
107 (85ct 22st)	R. W. Taylor (Derbyshire)
100 (88ct 12st)	R. W. Tolchard (Leicestershire)

First wicket-keeper to make 100 dismissals
R. W. Taylor (Derbyshire) on 21 July 1974 in his 81st match (78ct, 22st).

FIELDING
Most catches in an innings
4	A. J. Harvey-Walker	Derbyshire v Sussex at Hove 1971
4	C. Johnson	Yorkshire v Northamptonshire at Huddersfield 1974
4	P. J. Robinson	Somerset v Worcestershire at Worcester 1971

Most catches in a season
15	P. J. Watts for Northamptonshire	1970

Most catches in a career (40 and over)
46	C. T. Radley	Middlesex
43	M. H. Denness	Kent
40	C. H. Lloyd	Lancashire
40	G. R. J. Roope	Surrey

1975 GUIDE TO THE JOHN PLAYER LEAGUE

MISCELLANEOUS

Most appearances (maximum possible: 96)
92 S. Turner for Essex
Appearing for three counties in League matches
J. Cumbes for Surrey, Lancashire and Worcestershire.

PART II – COUNTY RECORDS

GENERAL RECORDS

John Player League Champions

		Points
1969	Lancashire	49
1970	Lancashire	53
1971	Worcestershire	44
1972	Kent	45
1973	Kent	50
1974	Leicestershire	54

Earliest date for winning League

12 August   Kent   1973

Most wins in a season

13   Lancashire   1970

Fewest wins in a season

2   Glamorgan   1972

Most defeats in a season

13   Nottinghamshire   1974

Fewest defeats in a season

1   Leicestershire   1974

Final positions 1969-74

Season	DERBYSHIRE	ESSEX	GLAMORGAN	GLOUCESTERSHIRE	HAMPSHIRE	KENT	LANCASHIRE	LEICESTERSHIRE	MIDDLESEX	NORTHAMPTONSHIRE	NOTTINGHAMSHIRE	SOMERSET	SURREY	SUSSEX	WARWICKSHIRE	WORCESTERSHIRE	YORKSHIRE
1969	15	3	10	6	2	4	1	11	7	14	13	16	5	17	9	12	8
1970	3	4	16	8	12	2	1	7	11	13	10	15	9	17	5	6	14
1971	11	2	10	16	6	8	3	4	13	14	12	5	9	7	17	1	15
1972	9	3	17	16	6	1	8	2	5	14	13	7	10	15	12	11	4
1973	12	9	13	6	3	1	4	5	7	17	13	11	9	7	15	15	2
1974	15	15	14	12	4	3	12	1	8	4	17	2	10	6	10	8	6
1975																	

INDIVIDUAL COUNTY RECORDS

DERBYSHIRE

Results 1969–74   Played 96   Won 39   Lost 49   No result 8
Highest Total   260–6   *v* Gloucestershire at Derby   1972
Lowest Total   70   *v* Surrey at Derby   1972
Highest Score   94   C. P. Wilkins *v* Warwickshire at Chesterfield   1972
Best Bowling   6–7   M. Hendrick *v* Nottinghamshire at Nottingham   1972
Playing Record against each County   (W=Won, L=Lost, T=Tied, A=No result)

Season	ESSEX	GLAMORGAN	GLOUCESTERSHIRE	HAMPSHIRE	KENT	LANCASHIRE	LEICESTERSHIRE	MIDDLESEX	NORTHAMPTONSHIRE	NOTTINGHAMSHIRE	SOMERSET	SURREY	SUSSEX	WARWICKSHIRE	WORCESTERSHIRE	YORKSHIRE
1969	L	L	W	L	L	L	L	W	L	L	W	L	W	A	W	L
1970	W	W	W	W	L	L	L	W	L	W	L	W	W	W	W	W
1971	L	A	L	L	W	L	W	W	W	W	L	W	W	L	L	W
1972	L	W	W	W	L	L	W	A	W	W	L	L	L	W	A	L
1973	L	W	W	A	L	L	L	W	A	W	L	W	L	A	L	L
1974	W	W	L	A	L	W	L	L	L	W	L	L	L	L	L	L
1975																

ESSEX

Results 1969–74   Played 96   Won 51   Lost 38   No result 7
Highest Total   265–6   *v* Lancashire at Chelmsford   1969
Lowest Total   69   *v* Derbyshire at Chesterfield   1974
Highest Score   107   B. C. Francis *v* Lancashire at Manchester   1971
Best Bowling   8–26   K. D. Boyce *v* Lancashire at Manchester   1971
Playing Record against each County

Season	DERBYSHIRE	GLAMORGAN	GLOUCESTERSHIRE	HAMPSHIRE	KENT	LANCASHIRE	LEICESTERSHIRE	MIDDLESEX	NORTHAMPTONSHIRE	NOTTINGHAMSHIRE	SOMERSET	SURREY	SUSSEX	WARWICKSHIRE	WORCESTERSHIRE	YORKSHIRE
1969	W	W	W	W	W	W	W	W	A	W	L	L	W	L	L	W
1970	L	W	W	W	L	L	W	W	W	W	A	A	A	L	W	L
1971	W	W	W	L	W	W	L	W	W	W	L	W	L	W	L	W
1972	W	W	L	W	L	A	L	L	W	W	L	W	W	W	W	W
1973	W	L	L	L	L	W	L	W	W	A	W	L	W	W	L	L
1974	L	L	L	W	L	L	A	L	L	W	L	L	W	W	L	L
1975																

1975 GUIDE TO THE JOHN PLAYER LEAGUE   213

GLAMORGAN

Results 1969–74   Played 96   Won 31   Lost 56   No result 9
Highest Total   234–6   *v* Worcestershire at Cardiff   1974
Lowest Total   65   *v* Surrey at The Oval   1969
Highest Score   90   A. Jones *v* Derbyshire at Buxton   1973
Best Bowling   6–36   G. C. Kingston *v* Derbyshire at Ebbw Vale   1969
Playing Record against each County

Season	DERBYSHIRE	ESSEX	GLOUCESTERSHIRE	HAMPSHIRE	KENT	LANCASHIRE	LEICESTERSHIRE	MIDDLESEX	NORTHAMPTONSHIRE	NOTTINGHAMSHIRE	SOMERSET	SURREY	SUSSEX	WARWICKSHIRE	WORCESTERSHIRE	YORKSHIRE
1969	W	L	L	W	L	L	W	L	W	W	W	L	L	W	L	L
1970	L	L	L	L	W	L	L	A	W	W	W	L	A	L	L	W
1971	A	L	L	L	W	W	W	L	L	W	A	L	L	W	W	W
1972	L	L	W	A	L	L	L	L	L	L	L	L	A	W	L	L
1973	L	W	W	A	L	L	L	W	W	L	L	L	W	A	L	L
1974	L	W	L	L	L	L	L	L	W	W	L	L	A	L	W	W
1975																

GLOUCESTERSHIRE

Results 1969–74   Played 96   Won 34   Lost 48   Tied 2   No result 12
Highest Total   251–9   *v* Somerset at Bristol   1974
Lowest Total   82   *v* Hampshire at Lydney   1974
Highest Score   127*   D. M. Green *v* Hampshire at Bristol   1970
Best Bowling   5–10   M. J. Procter *v* Sussex at Arundel   1972
Playing Record against each County

Season	DERBYSHIRE	ESSEX	GLAMORGAN	HAMPSHIRE	KENT	LANCASHIRE	LEICESTERSHIRE	MIDDLESEX	NORTHAMPTONSHIRE	NOTTINGHAMSHIRE	SOMERSET	SURREY	SUSSEX	WARWICKSHIRE	WORCESTERSHIRE	YORKSHIRE
1969	L	L	W	L	W	L	W	L	L	L	W	W	W	L	W	W
1970	L	L	W	W	L	L	A	L	W	L	W	W	W	A	L	W
1971	W	L	W	W	L	L	L	L	W	A	L	L	L	W	L	A
1972	L	W	L	T	L	L	L	L	T	W	L	L	W	A	L	L
1973	L	W	L	A	L	L	L	W	L	W	W	A	W	W	A	W
1974	W	W	W	L	A	L	L	L	L	W	L	A	L	L	A	A
1975																

HAMPSHIRE

Results 1969–74 Played 96 Won 52 Lost 35 Tied 1 No result 8
Highest Total 251 *v* Glamorgan at Basingstoke 1974
Lowest Total 43 *v* Essex at Basingstoke 1972
Highest Score 155* B. A. Richards *v* Yorkshire at Hull 1970
Best Bowling 5–13 A. M. E. Roberts *v* Sussex at Hove 1974
Playing Record against each County

Season	DERBYSHIRE	ESSEX	GLAMORGAN	GLOUCESTERSHIRE	KENT	LANCASHIRE	LEICESTERSHIRE	MIDDLESEX	NORTHAMPTONSHIRE	NOTTINGHAMSHIRE	SOMERSET	SURREY	SUSSEX	WARWICKSHIRE	WORCESTERSHIRE	YORKSHIRE
1969	W	L	L	W	L	W	W	W	W	W	W	W	W	L	W	W
1970	L	L	W	L	W	L	W	L	L	L	L	W	L	W	L	W
1971	W	W	W	L	L	W	L	W	L	W	L	L	W	W	L	W
1972	L	L	A	T	A	W	W	A	L	W	L	W	L	W	W	W
1973	A	W	A	A	W	W	L	W	W	W	W	L	W	L	W	L
1974	A	L	W	W	L	W	L	W	L	W	A	L	W	W	W	W
1975																

KENT

Results 1969–74 Played 96 Won 62 Lost 28 Tied 1 No result 5
Highest Total 261–5 *v* Somerset at Weston-super-Mare 1970
Lowest Total 84 *v* Gloucestershire at Folkestone 1969
Highest Score 142 B. W. Luckhurst *v* Somerset at Weston-super-Mare 1970
Best Bowling 5–19 D. L. Underwood *v* Gloucestershire at Maidstone 1972
Playing Record against each County

Season	DERBYSHIRE	ESSEX	GLAMORGAN	GLOUCESTERSHIRE	HAMPSHIRE	LANCASHIRE	LEICESTERSHIRE	MIDDLESEX	NORTHAMPTONSHIRE	NOTTINGHAMSHIRE	SOMERSET	SURREY	SUSSEX	WARWICKSHIRE	WORCESTERSHIRE	YORKSHIRE
1969	W	L	W	L	W	L	W	W	W	T	W	L	W	W	L	L
1970	W	W	L	W	L	W	L	W	W	W	W	W	W	W	W	L
1971	L	L	L	W	W	L	W	W	W	L	W	L	W	L	L	W
1972	W	W	W	W	A	L	W	L	W	L	L	W	W	W	W	W
1973	W	W	W	W	L	L	W	A	W	W	W	A	W	W	W	W
1974	W	W	W	A	W	W	W	A	L	W	W	L	W	W	L	L
1975																

1975 GUIDE TO THE JOHN PLAYER LEAGUE 215

LANCASHIRE

Results 1969–74	Played 96 Won 56 Lost 31 Tied 1 No result 8	
Highest Total	255–5 *v* Somerset at Manchester	1970
Lowest Total	76 *v* Somerset at Manchester	1972
Highest Score	134* C. H. Lloyd *v* Somerset at Manchester	1970
Best Bowling	5–13 K. Shuttleworth *v* Nottinghamshire at Nottingham	1972

Playing Record against each County

Season	DERBYSHIRE	ESSEX	GLAMORGAN	GLOUCESTERSHIRE	HAMPSHIRE	KENT	LEICESTERSHIRE	MIDDLESEX	NORTHAMPTONSHIRE	NOTTINGHAMSHIRE	SOMERSET	SURREY	SUSSEX	WARWICKSHIRE	WORCESTERSHIRE	YORKSHIRE
1969	W	L	W	W	L	W	W	W	W	W	W	W	W	W	L	A
1970	W	W	W	W	W	L	W	W	W	W	W	L	W	A	W	W
1971	W	L	L	W	L	W	W	L	W	L	W	W	W	W	L	W
1972	W	A	W	W	L	W	W	L	L	W	L	L	L	W	W	L
1973	W	L	W	W	L	W	W	L	W	W	A	A	L	A	A	W
1974	L	W	W	W	L	L	L	T	L	L	L	W	W	L	A	L
1975																

LEICESTERSHIRE

Results 1969–74	Played 96 Won 54 Lost 32 Tied 1 No result 9	
Highest Total	262–6 *v* Somerset at Frome	1970
Lowest Total	36 *v* Sussex at Leicester	1973
Highest Score	109* B. Dudleston *v* Gloucestershire at Gloucester	1974
Best Bowling	6–17 K. Higgs *v* Glamorgan at Leicester	1973

Playing Record against each County

Season	DERBYSHIRE	ESSEX	GLAMORGAN	GLOUCESTERSHIRE	HAMPSHIRE	KENT	LANCASHIRE	MIDDLESEX	NORTHAMPTONSHIRE	NOTTINGHAMSHIRE	SOMERSET	SURREY	SUSSEX	WARWICKSHIRE	WORCESTERSHIRE	YORKSHIRE
1969	W	L	L	L	L	L	L	A	A	W	W	L	W	A	W	W
1970	W	L	W	A	L	W	L	W	L	L	W	W	A	W	L	L
1971	W	W	L	W	W	L	L	W	L	W	W	W	W	L	W	L
1972	L	W	W	W	L	L	L	W	W	W	W	W	W	W	L	L
1973	W	W	W	W	W	L	L	L	A	W	A	L	L	W	W	L
1974	W	A	W	W	W	L	W	W	W	W	A	W	T	W	W	W
1975																

MIDDLESEX

Results 1969–74 Played 96   Won 41   Lost 45   Tied 1   No result 9
Highest Total   241–6   *v* Worcestershire at Lord's   1970
Lowest Total   23   *v* Yorkshire at Leeds   1974
Highest Score   133*   C. T. Radley *v* Glamorgan at Lord's   1969
Best Bowling   6–6   R. W. Hooker *v* Surrey at Lord's   1969
Playing Record against each County

Season	DERBYSHIRE	ESSEX	GLAMORGAN	GLOUCESTERSHIRE	HAMPSHIRE	KENT	LANCASHIRE	LEICESTERSHIRE	NORTHAMPTONSHIRE	NOTTINGHAMSHIRE	SOMERSET	SURREY	SUSSEX	WARWICKSHIRE	WORCESTERSHIRE	YORKSHIRE
1969	L	L	W	W	L	L	L	A	W	A	W	W	L	W	L	W
1970	L	L	A	W	W	L	L	L	W	L	W	W	L	W	A	
1971	L	L	W	W	L	L	W	L	L	W	L	W	L	L	L	W
1972	A	W	W	W	A	W	W	L	W	L	W	L	L	L	W	L
1973	L	L	L	L	L	A	W	W	W	W	W	A	W	L	W	L
1974	W	W	W	W	L	A	T	L	W	W	L	L	W	L	L	L
1975																

NORTHAMPTONSHIRE

Results 1969–74 Played 96   Won 36   Lost 52   Tied 1   No result 7
Highest Total   239–3   *v* Kent at Dover   1970
Lowest Total   41   *v* Middlesex at Northampton   1972
Highest Score   115*   H. M. Ackerman *v* Kent at Dover   1970
Best Bowling   6–22   R. R. Bailey *v* Hampshire at Portsmouth   1972
Playing Record against each County

Season	DERBYSHIRE	ESSEX	GLAMORGAN	GLOUCESTERSHIRE	HAMPSHIRE	KENT	LANCASHIRE	LEICESTERSHIRE	MIDDLESEX	NOTTINGHAMSHIRE	SOMERSET	SURREY	SUSSEX	WARWICKSHIRE	WORCESTERSHIRE	YORKSHIRE
1969	W	A	L	W	L	L	L	A	L	L	W	L	W	L	W	L
1970	W	L	L	L	W	L	L	W	W	L	L	L	L	W	W	L
1971	L	L	W	L	W	L	W	W	W	L	L	L	L	W	L	
1972	L	L	W	T	W	L	W	L	L	W	W	A	A	L	L	L
1973	A	L	L	W	L	L	L	A	L	L	A	W	L	W	W	L
1974	W	W	L	W	W	W	W	L	L	W	L	W	L	W	W	L
1975																

1975 GUIDE TO THE JOHN PLAYER LEAGUE 217

NOTTINGHAMSHIRE

Results 1969–74	Played 96 Won 32 Lost 59 Tied 1 No result 4	
Highest Total	252–5 v Warwickshire at Birmingham	1971
Lowest Total	66 v Yorkshire at Bradford	1969
Highest Score	116* G. St A. Sobers v Worcestershire at Newark	1971
Best Bowling	5–23 C. Forbes v Gloucestershire at Bristol	1969

Playing Record against each County

Season	DERBYSHIRE	ESSEX	GLAMORGAN	GLOUCESTERSHIRE	HAMPSHIRE	KENT	LANCASHIRE	LEICESTERSHIRE	MIDDLESEX	NORTHAMPTONSHIRE	SOMERSET	SURREY	SUSSEX	WARWICKSHIRE	WORCESTERSHIRE	YORKSHIRE
1969	W	L	L	W	L	T	L	L	A	W	L	W	W	L	L	L
1970	L	L	L	W	W	L	L	W	L	W	W	L	W	L	L	W
1971	L	L	L	A	L	W	W	L	L	L	W	L	L	W	W	W
1972	L	L	W	L	L	W	L	L	W	L	W	L	W	W	L	L
1973	L	A	W	L	L	L	L	L	L	W	A	W	W	L	W	L
1974	L	L	L	L	L	L	W	L	L	L	L	W	L	W	L	L
1975																

SOMERSET

Results 1969–74	Played 96 Won 44 Lost 40 No result 12	
Highest Total	262–3 v Gloucestershire at Bristol	1974
Lowest Total	61 v Hampshire at Bath	1973
Highest Score	131 D. B. Close v Yorkshire at Bath	1974
Best Bowling	6–25 G. I. Burgess v Glamorgan at Glastonbury	1972

Playing Record against each County

Season	DERBYSHIRE	ESSEX	GLAMORGAN	GLOUCESTERSHIRE	HAMPSHIRE	KENT	LANCASHIRE	LEICESTERSHIRE	MIDDLESEX	NORTHAMPTONSHIRE	NOTTINGHAMSHIRE	SURREY	SUSSEX	WARWICKSHIRE	WORCESTERSHIRE	YORKSHIRE
1969	L	W	L	L	L	L	L	L	L	L	W	W	W	L	A	W
1970	W	A	L	L	W	L	L	L	W	W	L	L	L	W	L	A
1971	W	W	A	W	W	L	L	L	W	W	L	W	W	W	L	A
1972	W	W	W	W	W	W	W	L	L	L	L	A	W	L	L	L
1973	W	L	W	L	L	L	A	A	L	A	A	L	L	W	W	W
1974	W	W	W	W	A	L	W	A	W	W	W	W	L	W	W	W
1975																

SURREY

Results 1969–74 Played 96 Won 44 Lost 42 Tied 1 No result 9
Highest Total 231–3 *v* Leicestershire at Leicester 1973
Lowest Total 82 *v* Lancashire at Manchester 1971
Highest Score 120* G. R. J. Roope *v* Worcestershire at Byfleet 1973
Best Bowling 6–25 Intikhab Alam *v* Derbyshire at The Oval 1974
Playing Record against each County

Season	DERBYSHIRE	ESSEX	GLAMORGAN	GLOUCESTERSHIRE	HAMPSHIRE	KENT	LANCASHIRE	LEICESTERSHIRE	MIDDLESEX	NORTHAMPTONSHIRE	NOTTINGHAMSHIRE	SOMERSET	SUSSEX	WARWICKSHIRE	WORCESTERSHIRE	YORKSHIRE
1969	W	W	W	L	L	W	L	W	L	W	L	L	A	W	W	W
1970	L	A	W	L	L	L	W	L	L	W	W	W	W	L	A	W
1971	L	L	W	W	W	W	L	L	L	W	W	L	L	W	L	W
1972	W	L	W	W	L	L	W	L	W	A	W	A	L	L	W	L
1973	L	W	W	A	W	L	A	W	A	L	L	W	L	W	T	L
1974	W	W	W	A	W	W	L	L	W	L	L	L	L	W	L	L
1975																

SUSSEX

Results 1969–74 Played 96 Won 34 Lost 50 Tied 1 No result 11
Highest Total 288–6 *v* Middlesex at Hove 1969
Lowest Total 63 *v* Derbyshire at Hove 1969
Highest Score 121 M. A. Buss *v* Nottinghamshire at Worksop 1971
Best Bowling 6–14 M. A. Buss *v* Lancashire at Hove 1973
Playing Record against each County

Season	DERBYSHIRE	ESSEX	GLAMORGAN	GLOUCESTERSHIRE	HAMPSHIRE	KENT	LANCASHIRE	LEICESTERSHIRE	MIDDLESEX	NORTHAMPTONSHIRE	NOTTINGHAMSHIRE	SOMERSET	SURREY	WARWICKSHIRE	WORCESTERSHIRE	YORKSHIRE
1969	L	L	W	L	L	L	L	L	W	L	L	L	A	W	A	L
1970	L	A	A	L	W	L	L	A	L	W	L	W	L	L	L	L
1971	L	W	W	W	L	L	L	L	W	W	W	L	W	W	L	L
1972	W	L	A	L	W	L	W	L	W	A	L	L	W	L	L	A
1973	W	L	L	L	L	A	W	W	L	W	L	W	W	A	W	L
1974	W	L	A	W	L	L	L	T	L	W	W	W	W	L	W	W
1975																

WARWICKSHIRE

Results 1969–74 Played 96   Won 37   Lost 47   No result 12
Highest Total   249–6 v Worcestershire at Birmingham   1972
Lowest Total   85   v { Glamorgan at Swansea   1972
                            { Gloucestershire at Cheltenham   1973
Highest Score   123* J. A. Jameson v Nottinghamshire at Nottingham   1973
Best Bowling   5–13 D. J. Brown v Worcestershire at Birmingham   1970
Playing Record against each County

Season	DERBYSHIRE	ESSEX	GLAMORGAN	GLOUCESTERSHIRE	HAMPSHIRE	KENT	LANCASHIRE	LEICESTERSHIRE	MIDDLESEX	NORTHAMPTONSHIRE	NOTTINGHAMSHIRE	SOMERSET	SURREY	SUSSEX	WORCESTERSHIRE	YORKSHIRE
1969	A	W	L	W	W	L	L	A	L	W	W	W	L	L	A	A
1970	L	W	W	A	L	L	A	L	W	L	W	L	W	W	W	W
1971	W	L	L	L	L	W	L	W	W	W	L	L	L	L	L	L
1972	L	L	L	A	L	L	L	L	W	W	L	W	W	W	W	W
1973	A	L	A	L	W	L	A	L	W	L	W	L	L	A	W	L
1974	W	L	W	W	L	L	W	L	W	L	L	L	L	W	W	A
1975																

WORCESTERSHIRE

Results 1969–74 Played 96   Won 43   Lost 43   Tied 1   No result 9
Highest Total   258–4   v Sussex at Dudley   1972
Lowest Total   86   v Yorkshire at Leeds   1969
Highest Score   129* G. M. Turner v Glamorgan at Worcester   1973
Best Bowling   6–33 V. A. Holder v Middlesex at Lord's   1972
Playing Record against each County

Season	DERBYSHIRE	ESSEX	GLAMORGAN	GLOUCESTERSHIRE	HAMPSHIRE	KENT	LANCASHIRE	LEICESTERSHIRE	MIDDLESEX	NORTHAMPTONSHIRE	NOTTINGHAMSHIRE	SOMERSET	SURREY	SUSSEX	WARWICKSHIRE	YORKSHIRE
1969	L	W	W	L	L	W	W	L	W	L	W	A	L	A	A	L
1970	L	L	W	W	W	L	L	W	L	L	W	W	A	W	L	W
1971	W	W	L	W	W	W	W	L	W	L	L	W	W	W	W	L
1972	A	L	W	W	L	L	L	L	L	W	W	W	L	W	L	W
1973	W	W	W	A	L	L	A	L	L	L	L	L	T	L	L	W
1974	W	W	L	A	L	W	A	L	W	L	W	L	W	L	L	W
1975																

YORKSHIRE

Results 1969–74   Played 96   Won 46   Lost 41   No result 9
Highest Total   235–6   v Nottinghamshire at Sheffield   1970
Lowest Total   74   v Warwickshire at Birmingham   1972
Highest Score   119   J. H. Hampshire v Leicestershire at Hull   1971
Best Bowling   7–15 R. A. Hutton v Worcestershire at Leeds   1969

Playing Record against each County

Season	DERBYSHIRE	ESSEX	GLAMORGAN	GLOUCESTERSHIRE	HAMPSHIRE	KENT	LANCASHIRE	LEICESTERSHIRE	MIDDLESEX	NORTHAMPTONSHIRE	NOTTINGHAMSHIRE	SOMERSET	SURREY	SUSSEX	WARWICKSHIRE	WORCESTERSHIRE
1969	W	L	W	L	L	W	A	L	L	W	W	L	L	W	A	W
1970	L	W	L	L	L	W	L	W	A	W	L	A	L	W	L	L
1971	L	L	L	A	L	L	L	W	L	W	L	A	L	W	W	W
1972	W	L	W	W	L	L	W	W	W	W	W	W	W	A	L	L
1973	W	W	W	L	W	L	L	W	W	W	W	L	W	W	W	L
1974	W	W	L	A	L	W	W	L	W	W	W	L	W	L	A	L
1975																

PART III – MISCELLANEOUS

Record attendances at John Player League matches

   35,000   Lancashire v Glamorgan at Manchester. Receipts £5000   12 Sep 1971
   32,000   Lancashire v Yorkshire at Manchester. Receipts £3,727   30 Aug 1970

Scoring and wicket-taking rates 1969–74

Season	Runs	Overs	Wickets	Runs/over	Runs/wkt
1969	35,826	9009.3	1883	3.96	19.02
1970	40,506	9269.4	1849	4.36	21.90
1971	40,893	9311.5	1899	4.39	21.53
1972	36,391	8669.5	1750	4.19	20.79
1973	36,580	8544	1660	4.28	22.03
1974	39,502	9137.4	1800	4.32	21.94
Totals	229,698	53,942.3	10,841	4.25	21.18

Playing Record of the Counties 1969-74

	P	W	L	T	NR	Run-Rate	6s	4w	Highest Total	Lowest Total	HS	BB
Derbyshire	96	39	49	—	8	4·14	112	17	260-6	70	94	6-7
Essex	96	51	38	—	7	4·27	146	23	265-6	69	107	8-26
Glamorgan	96	31	56	—	9	3·88	172	19	234-6	65	90	6-36
Gloucestershire	96	34	48	2	12	4·12	126	19	251-9	82	127*	5-10
Hampshire	96	52	35	1	8	4·51	163	19	251	43	155*	5-13
Kent	96	62	28	1	5	4·47	179	26	261-5	84	142	5-19
Lancashire	96	56	31	1	8	4·42	143	25	255-5	76	134*	5-13
Leicestershire	96	54	32	1	9	4·34	110	19	262-6	36	109*	6-17
Middlesex	96	41	45	1	9	4·34	121	25	241-6	23	133*	6-6
Northamptonshire	96	36	52	1	7	4·07	121	23	239-3	41	115*	6-22
Nottinghamshire	96	32	59	1	4	4·14	115	23	252-5	66	116*	5-23
Somerset	96	44	40	—	12	4·25	153	15	262-3	61	131	6-25
Surrey	96	44	42	1	9	4·16	130	12	231-3	82	120*	6-25
Sussex	96	34	50	1	11	4·27	123	24	288-6	63	121	6-14
Warwickshire	96	37	47	—	12	4·41	151	21	249-6	85	123*	5-13
Worcestershire	96	43	43	1	9	4·45	116	22	258-4	86	129*	6-33
Yorkshire	96	46	41	—	9	4·18	167	24	235-6	74	119	7-15

Ball-by-ball Record of Play (SHEET 1)

v. at on

DAY TIME	BOWLERS				BATSMEN						NOTES	INNINGS					
^	END		END		Left of scoreboard			Right of scoreboard			^	TOTALS at END of OVER					
^	NAME	Over	NAME	Over	NAME	balls recd	6s/4s	NAME	balls recd	6s/4s	^	Over	RUNS	W.	L BAT	R BAT	EXTRAS

Innings Scorecard (SHEET 2)

IN at	OUT at	MINS. BATTED	No.	BATSMAN	HOW OUT	BOWLER	RUNS	W	TOTAL	6s	4s	BALLS	N O T E S
			1										
			2										
			3										
			4										
			5										
			6										
			7										
			8										
			9										
			10										
			11										

EXTRAS (b . , lb . , nb . , w .)

TOTAL _____

OFF _____ OVERS _____ IN _____ MINUTES

Hr.	Overs	Runs
1		
2		
3		
4		
5		
6		
7		
8		
9		
10		

Runs	Mins	Overs	Last 50
50			
100			
150			
200			
250			
300			
350			
400			
450			
500			

BOWLER	O.	M.	R.	W.

OVERS/HR.
RUNS/OVER
RUNS/100 BALLS

Wkt	Partnership Between	Runs	Mins
1st			
2nd			
3rd			
4th			
5th			
6th			
7th			
8th			
9th			
10th			

Cumulative Record of Bowling Analyses and Extras (SHEET 3)

O.	M.	R.	W.	4b		O.	M.	R.	W.	4b		O.	M.	R.	W.	4b		O.	M.	R.	W.	4b		O.	M.	R.	W.	EXTRAS B.	LB.	W.	NB.	TOTAL